D0948800

THE
NATIONAL TRUST
FOR SCOTLAND
GUIDE

THE NATIONAL TRUST FOR SCOTLAND GUIDE

REVISED EDITION

compiled and edited by
ROBIN PRENTICE

JONATHAN CAPE
THIRTY BEDFORD SQUARE LONDON

First published 1976
Second edition 1978
Third edition 1981

© 1976, 1978, 1981 by The National Trust for Scotland
Jonathan Cape Ltd, 30 Bedford Square, London WC1

British Library Cataloguing in Publication Data

National Trust for Scotland
   The National Trust for Scotland guide. – 3rd ed.
   1. National Trust for Scotland
   2. Historic Buildings – Scotland
   3. Scotland – Description and travel – Guidebooks
   I. Title   II. Prentice, Robin John
   914.11′04′857   DA870

ISBN 0 224 01903 1

Printed in Great Britain by
Fakenham Press Ltd, Fakenham, Norfolk

Contents

How to Use this Book

The Guide is a complete gazetteer to the properties of the National Trust for Scotland. These are classified according to type. Each chapter begins with an introductory essay. The notes on individual properties which follow are prefaced in every instance by an indication of location.

Properties not described in detail are listed at the back of the book. With the exception of the Palace in Culross, Scotstarvit Tower and Rough Castle and the Antonine Wall, all but incidental reference to those under the guardianship of the Scottish Development Department (Ancient Monuments) is restricted to that section. Properties under Conservation Agreements are not included.

The Guide deals at length with the Little Houses Improvement Scheme. The creation and use of the Revolving Fund to finance the scheme inspired the creation of the Architectural Heritage Fund which is administered by the Civic Trust over Britain as a whole. But it is to be noted that the essence of the scheme is restoration and re-equipment of buildings for private occupation. The Little Houses are not open to visitors. A study of their external appearance and their relationship to their environment will be rewarding, nevertheless.

The distribution of properties is shown in maps on pp. 322–3. The reader is advised to use the Guide in conjunction with the list of properties contained in *The National Trust for Scotland Year Book* and guidebooks to individual properties. Opening times vary from property to property and are subject to change.

General Introduction

by Magnus Magnusson

A many years ago, when I was young at least, I came upon a remarkable and simple fact about Scotland: nowhere in Scotland can you be more than 66 miles away from the sea. Since then I have never ceased to be enthralled by this deceptively obvious but astounding geographical statistic.

Nowhere in Scotland can you be more than 66 miles away from the sea! What – in a country as large as Scotland? For that is how it feels: very large indeed, and at the same time very compact. Yet within this compactness there is a marvellous diversity and range, a whole universe of contrasts, a world containing all the large dramas and the little lyrics of landscape. And this, to my mind, is largely due to that factor of 66. This is the key to the whole Scottish experience. This is what helps to make Scotland for me the most superbly visual country in Europe. It gives the country a roundedness, a balance, for here always is the constant interplay of the prime natural elements – mountain, water and sky: mountains brawling or placid, waters serene or turbulent, skies bright or blustering.

Hugh MacDiarmid, that giant of modern Scottish poetry, made us all aware of this universality in the Scottish microcosm. More than thirty years ago he expressed it brilliantly in his autobiography, *Lucky Poet*:

Scotland small? Our multiform, our infinite Scotland
  small?
Only as a patch of hillside may be a cliché corner
To a fool who cries 'Nothing but heather!' where in
  September another
Sitting there and resting and gazing round
Sees not only the heather but blaeberries
With bright green leaves and leaves already turned
  scarlet,
Hiding ripe blue berries; and amongst the sage-green
  leaves
Of the bog-myrtle the golden flowers of the tormentil
  shining;
And on the small bare places, where the little Blackface
  sheep
Found grazing, milkworts blue as summer skies;
And down in neglected peat-hags, not worked

Within living memory, sphagnum moss in pastel shades
Of yellow, green and pink; sundew and butterwort
Waiting with wide-open sticky leaves for their tiny winged
    prey;
And nodding harebells vying in their colour
With the blue butterflies that poise themselves delicately
    upon them,
And stunted rowan with harsh dry leaves of glorious
    colour.
'Nothing but heather!' – How marvellously descriptive!
    And incomplete!

Scotland, it has been said often enough, is a country of contrasts. Some would go further, and say a country of contradictions. Some of these contradictions are apparent within the Scottish psyche itself, if there is such a thing: a concurrent capacity for fierce pride and abject servility, for patriotic fervour and destructive self-criticism, for grandeur and squalor, for radicalism and reaction, for toughness and sentimentality, for realism and romanticism. Any attempt to describe Scotland as one country is bound to be misleading; Scotland, as Hugh MacDiarmid says, is multiform, and it is this that helps to explain its compelling allure. It takes a very remarkable country to hold so many hearts in thrall – Scottish exiles are notoriously vociferous in their nostalgia for their homeland, notoriously clannish in their affection for the land they or even their forefathers left but never forgot, whatever the social or economic factors that caused them to emigrate in the first place.

The same is true in reverse: in my experience, outsiders who come to Scotland for a short visit, or to take up residence here, rapidly become perfervid in their love for the country – and much more vocal about their admiration than the home-bred Scot, who tends to conceal his feelings under a cloak of diffidence except on certain celebratory occasions, like Saturday nights. As an incomer myself (I have lived in Scotland only since the early 1930s) I have every cause to be intensely grateful to Scotland and the Scots; and since the fact of living in someone else's homeland argues a degree of choice, or at least awareness, I am constantly intrigued and teased by the phenomenon of Scotland. Just why *is* it such an admirable place?

Physically, Scotland is enchanting. There can be no other word for it. Geologically, it is very old and very fascinating.

Proto-Scotland – the original Scotland when the world was being formed into its present shape – was actually part of North America once, when North America and Europe were still very close together. The oldest known rocks in Britain, in the north-west of Scotland (near Scourie, and on the island of Lewis), are American rock, some 2,700 million years old. (Meanwhile, proto-England was a knob on the edge of Europe!) Scotland and England were separated by an ocean then, but came together in violent union some 450 million years ago when North America and Europe collided – a forced marriage if ever there was one. The impact formed the great Caledonian mountains of central Scotland and Norway. Immense upheavals were still to come, when Africa barged into Europe, for instance, about 280 million years ago (Scotland was situated on the equator then), and when North America broke away from Europe 60 million years ago. As Britain cruised northwards, the landscape-formation begun by continental drift and collision was continued by the great ice ages that began some 2 million years ago and ended only 10,000 years ago. What makes Scotland so fascinating to the geologist, to anyone interested in the history of Mother Earth, is that one can still see plainly the evidence of ancient cataclysms – a desert sand-dune in Ayrshire, formed when Britain lay in the tropics; the great basaltic columns of the Inner Hebrides, that marked the departure of Greenland from Europe; the fault along the Great Glen, reminding us of the time, 350 million years ago, when northern and central Scotland slotted alongside each other; the frayed mountain chains pointing seawards like the ends of a broken rope which snapped when North America broke away; the magnificent corries and gullies gouged out by retreating glaciers. Every mountain, every valley, every loch and every river has a story to tell that illuminates the origins of the earth: a true microcosm of macrocosmic events long ago.

Lower Glen Nevis

These gross upheavals of land that shaped Scotland down the millennia and gave the country its marvellous diversity have in different places shaped the people differently, too: there are the tough men of the rolling Border hills, the frontiersmen of Scotland; the people of the windswept uplands of the north, who are honed and chiselled as the mountains themselves; the Gaels and Norsemen alike, whose culture was moulded by the sheer physical exhilaration of the lilting islands; the people formed by the dour fertility of the north-east, jutting its shoulder to the wind and sea, the Aberdonians. And the people, in their varying ways, have helped to reshape the landscapes that are the setting for the long and vivid history of this land.

Man has been present in Scotland for fewer than 10,000 years. By the time the first hunter-gatherers began to infiltrate northwards (from England, probably), Jericho had been a fortified city for more than a thousand years. The first actual farmers – not nomads in search of game and fruit and fish, but people who cleared land for agriculture and formed settled communities – arrived in Scotland some 6,000 years ago: say, 4,000 B.C., heralding the start of the Neolithic Age. For the next 4,000 years of prehistory, Scotland's population was increased and cross-fertilized by immigrants from many places – from Ireland, England and the Continent – each bringing with them new skills, new ways of life; and each leaving behind them imposing prehistoric monuments as well as the more casual debris of their way of life. The fascinating and unique underground village of Skara Brae in Orkney; the brooding circles of standing stones, like the magnificent stones of Callanish, in the island of Lewis (the 'Stonehenge of the North', as it has been called); the mega-lithic chamber tombs (there are more than 360 in Scotland), whose outstanding example is Maes Howe in Orkney; the hill-forts and vitrified forts (forts whose stonework was fused when the building was set on fire) associated with the Celts who began to populate Scotland during the first millennium B.C. as the Bronze Age was superseded by the Iron Age: all these monuments of the ancient past, and the artefacts associated with them that are now on display in museums up and down Scotland, are constant and awesome reminders of the busy, creative and often turbulent centuries of Scotland's ethnic origins before the dawn of history proper – written history – with the Roman invasions.

The Romans left their mark on Scotland, as elsewhere, notably with the short-lived Antonine Wall that straddled the waist of land between Forth and Clyde; its remains, less imposing than those of Hadrian's Wall because it was built of turf not stone, can be clearly seen in distinct stretches guarded by the Scottish Development Department. But the Romans did not find Scotland an easy land to subdue, and settled for occasional punitive expeditions into the menacing mountainlands of the north, though they won in the battle of Mons Graupius between Agricola and the Caledonians somewhere in the north-east – possibly not far from the site of another Scottish defeat, Culloden Moor.

North of the line of the Antonine Wall, and south of it too as the Romans withdrew, history flowed and ebbed and flowed again as new peoples, new ideas, new skills were born and developed. The tower-like brochs of the northern coast-lines, of which the most impressively preserved is that on the tiny island of Mousa, in Shetland, mark the centuries im-mediately after the Roman incursion. The Picts left behind them a series of symbol stones incised or carved in relief with animal and human figures and inscriptions in the language called Ogam, until they were overwhelmed by the Scots in the ninth century. The Norsemen (my own ancestors) colonized the north and west of Scotland with ploughshare and sword, and gave Shetland and Orkney a vigorous era of dynamic adventuring that was crowned by the building of the handsome St Magnus Cathedral in Kirkwall – most imposing of the Norse achievements from the Viking age. From then on, our awareness of history gradually focuses on the epic attempts to assert from all the diverse strands of Scottish population a national identity expressed in national sovereignty, culminating in the wars of independence waged by King Robert the Bruce in the early fourteenth century and the victory over England's might at Bannockburn in 1314.

Bannockburn has had a powerful and profound effect on the Scottish consciousness ever since. It marks the time from which it became possible to speak of a Scottish nation, a nation of Scots, as more than an abstract idea. It became a symbol of resistance and unity, a rallying-call, a romantic banner to flap and furl down the years as medieval moved to modern times.

I had not intended this brief introduction to be a potted history of Scotland, or a collection of superficial historical highlights. But to me a sense of history is essential to a proper appreciation, intellectual and emotional, of the present. And where can one be made aware of this history? To the prehistorian, it is in archaeological sites and excavations; to the geologist, it is in the topography of the land; to the layman, it is literally everywhere – in the growth and development of towns and cities, in the buildings of the past, in literature. My point is that even in an era of rapid, indeed headlong, change one can still find in Scotland a deeply satisfying communion between present and past, between town and country.

Falkland Palace: the Gatehouse

So I get as much pleasure from the handsomely preserved Falkland Palace in Fife (a sixteenth-century hunting palace of the Stuart kings) as I do from the eighteenth-century weavers' cottages in the burgh itself, for Scotland's history is the story of peasants just as much as of princes. A preserved Black House in Lewis evokes a way of life, still redolent of peat smoke and determined domesticity, that has changed only in its material form and is still enshrined in the continuing hearth-culture of the Gaels; to me, it is complementary to, and not contradictory of, Adam's late eighteenth-century extravaganza of Culzean Castle in Ayrshire.

In this book, you will find a continuing tapestry of life in Scotland carved in stone, or sculpted in landscape or reflected in flowers. The themes of this tapestry are largely limited to the areas in which the National Trust for Scotland has exerted its growing influence in the years since 1931. But that does not mean that it is a limited book; for the reader will, I believe, be pleasantly surprised to discover how comprehensive a view the National Trust for Scotland takes of its responsibilities to Scotland – a much broader view, I dare to assert, than the National Trust itself, with its much larger stock of meritorious architecture on the far side of the Border. So this is not a restricted 'house-book', a catalogue of properties to visit and places to admire; it is to my mind, in a very real sense, the story of Scotland.

And that story – let me return to my original theme – is inextricably involved with that matter of '66 miles from the sea'. It is this that has made Scotland a visual and accessible paradise (no matter how deeply remote) for people weary of the suffocation of urban life. Curiously enough, the Scots themselves are probably the last people on earth to realize this, because they have always been able to take it for granted. In Scotland, everywhere the countryside is virtually on your doorstep. The rest of Britain, and Europe too, has awoken to this fact, and that in Scotland we have the last relatively unspoilt reaches of Nature for man to enjoy – and to exploit (that's always the ugly obverse).

I am not against exploitation as such. In fact, I am in favour of it. The whole of history – the kind of history I enjoy – is the story of exploitation of human and natural resources. (If ever there were exploiters in recent history, it was the Vikings, and do you think I'm going to say a word against them?) It is only in recent times that the word 'exploitation' has become a dirty one; but not because the nature of exploitation has changed, only its scale and therefore the scale of its effects.

People have always exploited the country. The act of building towns and cities, even of building villages, was an 'exploitation' of the resources of the countryside and the people who worked it, in that the agricultural surplus of the peasants went towards the creation of an urban civilization. The Border towns on the southern threshold of Scotland are fine, living examples of this harmonious exploitation, in which the town provides services and amenities for the surrounding countryside in exchange for its fruits.

Edinburgh, too, is the outcome of exploitation, as any capital city must be. But what a happy outcome! This is the centre of the nation, dominating the history and imagination of Scotland: both profoundly Scottish and cheerfully cosmopolitan, both ancient and modern. Here, the nation's history was given formal shape: castle and palace, New Town and Old, gardens and galleries, the eternal home of poets and princes and painters and scientists.

To anyone brought up in Edinburgh, as I was, it will always remain the epitome of Scottish cities in the regalities of its stance. A city with a great chunk of geological history enclosed within its boundaries – Arthur's Seat, your friendly neighbourhood volcano; a city that grew from the ground on which it stands, fledging the ridge between castle and palace with teeming tenements and then striding gracefully down the surrounding slopes as the eighteenth century burgeoned.

But Edinburgh has no monopoly of these qualities: take St Andrews, for instance, queen of its own realm of Fife, home of the oldest university in Scotland (junior only to Oxford and Cambridge). Fife, the little kingdom, is Scotland in microcosm: a thousand years ago, Dunfermline was the capital of Scotland; Robert the Bruce lies buried there, and Andrew Carnegie was born and brought up there before emigrating to build another kind of kingdom in America.

Or take Perth. The Fair City, they call it, and with reason. This is the fulcrum of Scotland, where river and mountain meet, where all roads meet. From earliest times it has always been the key to the heart of Scotland, in more ways than one. It straddles one of the finest salmon rivers in the world, the River Tay, comfortably nestled in a bowl of wooded mountains in the foothills of the Highlands proper. Perth is the key city that every invader tries to capture – only to end up by being captured by it.

Or Aberdeen? Cathedral city, university city, fishing port – and now oil metropolis: the Silver City, built almost entirely of granite which gives it that distinctively clean and sparkling look. I have always had a particularly soft spot for that dourly built city, ever since I was told that there actually was a joke factory in Aberdeen churning out Aberdonian jokes for Christmas crackers – surely the acme of exploitation of natural resources! And Inverness, the market-place and meeting-hall of the North, with Loch Ness and the Great Glen on its doorstep, Speyside to the south, and to the west and north the enchantments of that Scotland that slotted into place 350 million years ago. Inverness has a special ambience, of Highlands and Islands, and Lowlands alike; and its hospitality is legendary even in a country where hospitality is not a luxury but a commonplace and cheerful obligation of tradition.

And Glasgow. I have left Glasgow to the last because like all great cities it is the most complex. 'The dear green place' is the translation of its original Gaelic name 'glas', green, 'ghu', beloved; 'The beautifullest little city I have seen in this country,' said John Mackay. But John Mackay was writing in 1723, and the Gaelic name was bestowed when Glasgow was little more than a ford across the Clyde. Today no one would call it green, or the beautifullest; but it has an extraordinary vitality that is immensely infectious. I always associate Glasgow with sparrows: it is garrulous, gregarious, vigorous, roguish, lascivious, with a pavement humour entirely its own and a heart of gold.

Cynics say that the best thing about Glasgow is how easy it is to get out of it, and Glaswegians repeat the joke with zest. But there is another view of Glasgow:

> A few weeks ago upon the Campsie Fells I gazed down at Glasgow. From a mass of dark cloud the sun, himself obscured from where I stood, sloped his golden ladders into that rain-washed city, which lay with all her spires and chimneys, with all her towers and tenements and sparkling roofs, like a vision of heavenly habitations. I have looked down over Athens. I have looked down over Rome. With beauty unparagoned the glory and the grandeur of the past have been spread before my eyes; but in that sight of Glasgow something was added which neither Rome nor Athens could give – the glory and the grandeur of the future, and the beating heart of a nation.

That was said by the late Sir Compton Mackenzie when he was installed as Rector of Glasgow University in 1932. The grandiloquence should not be dismissed as the paying of lip-service to the occasion; this is the view I get of Glasgow every morning from my bedroom window in the foothills of the Campsies. It is a view worthy of Blake; to me the strength and power inherent in Glasgow is a reflection of the agonizing metropolitan experience, the longing for Jerusalem among dark Satanic mills. Today, Glasgow is in the throes of social change; the slum buildings are coming down, the new housing estates have not yet, for the most part, gelled into communities. But the superb Victorian architecture is there for all to see, the enduring monuments of that period of dynamic expansion that went hand in hand with appalling poverty and squalor. Glasgow bears scars that would surely have killed any organism less resilient; but the tide is on the turn, and from my bedroom window every morning, I fancy I can even see it turning before my very eyes.

To a much greater extent than Edinburgh, Glasgow has been the ethnic crucible of Scotland. It is said there are more Highlanders in Glasgow than in the Highlands, and certainly the west of Scotland has had more than its share of racial fertilization. It may be easy to get out of Glasgow – but it has always been easy to get into it, too. And the ease with which you can get out of it should not be seen as a sneer, but as a compliment; because London and other cities must envy Glasgow's surroundings. It's less than an hour to Loch Lomond and the Trossachs, to the Firth of Clyde with its timeless lochs and holiday islands.

Loch Lomond

I said I thought the tide was on the turn for Glasgow. Indeed, I see a tide on the flow for Scotland as a whole. There is in Scotland today a remarkable resurgence of national pride and self-confidence that makes the air tingle, a new optimism about the future. This is not entirely due to the economic boost that the discovery of North Sea oil has given to certain sectors and areas of the economy, although that has undoubtedly helped. There are many intangible factors involved. What is even more important is how that new confidence is expressed. To me, the hallmark of a civilized community is the ability to reconcile material prosperity with a due concern for the things of the spirit; and I would cite the growing awareness within Scotland of the true wealth of our heritage as a facet of that civilization. The fact that the National Trust for Scotland threw itself into the battle to prevent wholesale oil developments in an area of Wester Ross where the long-term disadvantages far outweighed any short-term material advantages is a case in point. When a nation can achieve that sort of balance – and it is only to be achieved by vigilance and self-denial in the face of easy temptation – then it is a nation indeed.

A nation has to be able to carry its past with it into its future. That is what we are learning to do. Scotland is by no means perfect – like good malt whisky, it is the impurities that give it a distinctive flavour and raise it above the tasteless mass-production of mere alcohol. But it's pretty good. In fact, if I weren't an Icelander, I'd say it was the best.

The National Trust for Scotland

by The Earl of Wemyss and March, K.T.

Two of the enduring characteristics of the National Trust for Scotland are audacity and perseverance. (The Scots word for an alliance of these qualities, which is comparatively rare, is *smeddum*.) A third characteristic is universality. The Scottish Trust was founded in 1931 to serve the purposes of Scotland. But part of the inspiration came from a process of lease–lend, in ideas and experience, which began many years before and prospers today. The start may be dated to 1865. There was formed then in London the Commons Preservation Society. One of the main objects of this exclusively English agency was to defend the public's right of access to open spaces for recreation. Robert Hunter became solicitor to the society. Octavia Hill joined the committee early in the 1870s. While they went about their business a young American, Charles Eliot, was making his own study of current attempts at environmental management in London, Paris, Stockholm and Venice. No doubt he had brought to his notice, as has happened to me, the City of London's siege of Epping Forest and its Lords of Manor, and the procedure by which the freedom of 6,000 acres of waste and wildwood was given to the inhabitants of the East End for all time. Charles Eliot, the son of Charles William Eliot, president of Harvard University from 1869 to 1909, was a disciple of the doyen of America's landscape architects, Frederick Law Olmsted. He detected in Europe the gradual acceptance of a new ethos and discovered at home a massive indifference to the preservation of public open space and natural landscape in and around Boston. Eliot's passionate concern led in 1891 to the incorporation of the Trustees of Public Reservations in Massachusetts. Chapter 352 of the Acts approved by the Great and General Court of the State described as a principal purpose of the new corporation: 'acquiring, holding, arranging, maintaining, and opening to the public, under suitable regulations, beautiful and historic tracts of land within this Commonwealth'.

In England Robert Hunter and Octavia Hill were finding that, as their concept broadened, the Commons Preservation Society was an increasingly imperfect instrument. Hunter proposed the creation of a statutory body with wide powers to acquire land and buildings and to hold and manage them in trust for the enjoyment of the public. In this he had the wholehearted co-operation of Miss Hill. What they created in 1895, with the vociferous and indispensable support of

Canon Hardwicke Rawnsley, was the National Trust for Places of Historic Interest or Natural Beauty. With the consent of the Trustees of Public Reservations a great part of the Massachusetts constitution was adapted and applied in the articles of the infant English Trust. In due time the founders of the Scottish Trust borrowed just as freely from London. There are only minor differences in the National Trust for Scotland Act which received Parliamentary approval in 1935, but from the beginning there was a subtle difference in interpretation. The Council and Executive Committee, the elected bodies by which the Scottish Trust is governed and administered, took the view that their main obligation was to promote the preservation of landscape, wildlife, buildings and their appurtenances, gardens, historic sites, islands and coastline, together (so far as possible) with public enjoyment of all of these. We have in our properties an irreplaceable portion of Scotland's patrimony. We treat each of them with intimate and particular care, and get credit for it. What we are never allowed to forget is that the properties are not the Scottish Trust's sole *raison d'être*. In keeping a hold on the past and an eye to the future we must have regard continually for what is happening, or may happen, beyond the policy dyke of the Royal Palace of Falkland in Fife and the less clearly marked boundaries of Glencoe, Kintail or Torridon in the Western Highlands.

Torridon hills

This was the reason why the original sponsors of an Taisce (i.e. the Treasury), the National Trust for Eire, sought counsel from us in 1947 and 1948, and why the constitution of Heritage Canada is based to a substantial degree on that of the National Trust for Scotland and why we are in frequent communication with the National Trust for Historic Preservation in the United States. There are few independent voluntary agencies which fulfil one set of duties as public trustee and another as advocate of right management of the whole environment. We benefit from the cross-flow of personnel and ideas which is now normal and international. The contribution that we make is by no means negligible. The founders were conscious of the context – historical, geographical, political – in which the instrument they were creating would have to operate. They were also acutely aware that in the nature of things there must always, or nearly always, be a chronic shortage of money by comparison with the volume of work to be done. That context and the merits and penalties of independence are seldom out of mind.

Universality, a word which I have used deliberately in reference to the Scottish Trust, implies an outlook which is wide ranging, which is not narrowly insular or local. Such an attitude of mind is natural to a significant proportion of Scots people. It does not follow that readiness to examine new concepts makes them less wary of received opinions. A healthy scepticism, where it exists, has deep roots. Historically, this is one of the smaller and poorer countries of Europe – not the smallest, nevertheless. Scotland is the rough and rugged upper part of Britain, twice as large as Denmark, three times larger than Belgium. Its 30,000 square miles consist of a deeply indented mainland and a fringe of islands (the Hebrides, Orkney and Shetland) and are scattered on a wide expanse of sea. For centuries the inhabitants of the constituent parts were harried and bludgeoned by more powerful neighbours, native and foreign; it would have been small consolation, had it occurred to any of them, that Scotland has never been completely conquered by a foreign power.

The visible proofs of European influence are very variable in form and substance. Of Roman works, the largest remaining above ground are the Trust's three sections of the Antonine Wall. An early connection with Scandinavia has one surprising and magnificent monument in Kirkwall in Orkney: St Magnus Cathedral, founded by a Norse earl in 1137. Whereas Holyrood, Melrose, Jedburgh, Arbroath – great abbeys established in the same century by Scottish kings – are roofless ruins, St Magnus still stands to the glory of God. In Lowland Scotland the links formed in the Middle Ages had two main bases. Overseas trade was largely a two-way traffic with the Low Countries, Scandinavia and the Baltic. Monarchical politics produced the Auld Alliance with France, a royal power-game which was intended to contain the territorial and dynastic ambitions of English sovereigns. The splendour of the Renaissance shows forth at Falkland and in the palace range of Stirling Castle. More modest architectural notions acquired from other parts of western Europe were put to use in tolbooths and in domestic architecture, notably on the east coast. Taste in plenishings and internal decor was naturally affected in turn. I shall leave others to speak of this, of later and heavier assaults on Scottish (as on English) sensibility, and of the extent to which the union of the Scottish and English parliaments in 1707 opened new windows on the world. The flow of overseas settlement which followed shortly on that event is more relevant to my theme.

Many different factors – a restless foot, sheer economic necessity, implication in Jacobite plots or risings, natural ambition – moved the emigrants. Some put down their roots in America before the Revolutionary War and a multitude after it. In Canada they outfaced the French and the Americans in turn and opened the way to the Pacific. That was not all, or nearly all, as I shall be reminded by friends in the Southern hemisphere. We know something of the pioneers from the history books, much more from their upstanding descendants. In the latter the get-up-and-go instinct is not incompatible with a genuine regard for inherited 'mercies' which survive in our respective countries. By a cheerful and convenient convention, far-out kinsmen from foreign parts are cousins and so become members of the family. They do much to enliven the thinking of the old folks at home. The coincidental benefits appear in odd places and unexpected ways. The home Scot on his travels soon notices how often a friend's friend materializes to effect an introduction, roll out the red carpet or resolve some little local difficulty.

Little local difficulties, as may be inferred, are part of our day-to-day business. In a space of months rather than years the Trust emerged as the main element in the 'third force' in Scotland. By this I mean the indispensable voluntary movement. Without it official agencies would find it difficult, if not impossible, to exercise all of their powers, to gain popular acceptance of new legislation, or to accelerate its application; the individual and the community would lack a credible line of defence against insentient commercial exploitation or what, for want of a better word, I shall call the Establishment itself. In Trust philosophy, which may differ sharply on occasion from that of the hard-line preservationist, mediation stands far ahead of agitation or litigation. This does not make any less effective opposition to demolition of a building, or the threat of intrusion on landscape or an area in which the social or ecological balance is delicately poised. On the contrary, it is more likely to ensure that all relative values are given due weight before a final decision is taken by a planning authority or central government. There are instances in which objections have to be pressed to the limit, at great cost in money and energy, by a prescribed legal process. There have been very many, I may add, in which the Trust's 'good offices' sufficed. My own participation in such diplomacy, and other areas of activity to which I shall come presently, spans approximately two-thirds of the history of the Trust. It began in 1946 with an invitation to allow my name to go forward for election to the Council. I was elected chairman of Council and Executive Committee in 1948. Few new entrants to a great enterprise can have had so much cause to praise famous men and the fathers that begat us.

The beginnings of the Scottish Trust were deceptively modest. The initiative came from the Association for the Preservation of Rural Scotland. The Association was inhibited, like the Commons Preservation Society in London at an earlier date, by lack of powers to hold land or buildings. The Chairman, Sir Iain Colquhoun of Luss, Bt., was determined to repair the situation. He had in Arthur W. Russell, w.s. a supporter with the requisite legal expertise and a comparable affection and concern for the Scottish scene. The upshot was the incorporation on May 1st, 1931, of the National Trust for Scotland for Places of Historic Interest or Natural Beauty – a Trust with power to hold land, buildings and chattels 'for the benefit of the nation', independent of government but so constituted as to be capable of working in concert with statutory authorities. At the first ordinary general meeting the founding fathers numbered eleven (equivalent to about one-eighth of the present combined strength of the Council and the Executive Committee, exactly one-fifth of the number of men who gathered in Philadelphia in 1787 to draft the Constitution of the United States). The meeting was held on July 21st, 1931, in the City Chambers, Edinburgh, by invitation of the Lord Provost, Sir Thomas Whitson. It elected the Duke of Atholl, the great Bardie, eighth Duke, to be President and Sir Iain Colquhoun to be Chairman of the Council – the Executive Committee was set up at a later date. The first Vice-Presidents were the twenty-sixth Earl of Crawford and Sir John Stirling Maxwell of Pollok, Bt., who inspired Sir Iain in the first instance.

The passing of the National Trust for Scotland Act of 1935 made the Trust a statutory body. The Act gave the Council power to declare Trust lands and buildings inalienable – that is, to declare them to be subjects which the Trust holds in perpetuity and which can be taken from it only by prescribed Parliamentary procedure. But the Trust was gathering possessions before that point was reached.

Culross: the Palace,
c. 1938

With the advantage of hindsight one can see that there were times when the divinity that shapes our ends pursued an erratic course. Yet there is a rough logic, a dogged consistency, in the choice and above all in the pursuit of priorities. The courage, authority and flair of the founders are matters of record. It is not difficult to trace a direct line from the work done in the 1930s to the present structure and status of the Trust. The first Parliamentary Bill about which the Council was consulted received the royal assent as the Town and Country Planning (Scotland) Act of 1932. Two propositions concerning properties came in at once. One involved the most prestigious house in the royal burgh of Culross in Fife. This was the Palace, built between 1597 and 1611 for Sir George Bruce, coalmaster, port authority and industrial entrepreneur in one person. The history of architecture in Scotland is a history of building in stone. The Palace was characteristic of its period. It had, and has, also such evocative ingredients as pantiles for the roofs, Baltic boards for floors and walls and ceilings, and tempera paintings to astonish and delight the great man's guests. It was, because of economic circumstance, the worst of times to cry 'Haud up' when a structure which could no longer serve a utilitarian purpose seemed to be at risk. It turned out to be the right time to embark on a joint operation, the first of many which bring us into partnership with 'arms of government'. H.M. Office of Works (the guardian at that stage of such historic structures) was as eager as the Trust to attempt a rescue operation. A simple accommodation was proposed. If the Trust would buy, the Office of Works would take the building into guardianship. The whole expense of repairs and rehabilitation, inside and out, and the cost of future maintenance would then be met from government funds. But the asking price was £700. This amounted to nearly half of the free funds of the Trust at that time – a legacy of £1,500 had just been received. The Council made the purchase. The guardianship agreement was concluded. In the second case a national committee led by the tenth Earl of Elgin and Kincardine invited the Trust to accept 'on behalf of the Scottish Nation' the Borestone section of the battlefield of Bannockburn and, with it, a liability of £1,000 to meet the balance of the purchase price. Again the Council took the bold step, on the premise that the safe keeping of a historic site could not await a guarantee of financial help from external sources.

The carefree entry into Culross had memorable consequences. Looking beyond the Palace, the Council discovered that many lesser houses of similar date, admirable examples of Scottish vernacular architecture, were falling into dereliction. Further exploration identified 'one of the oldest backgrounds of Scottish burgh life' – buildings, street plan, cobbled causeways, dykes and stairs which somehow had survived intact since the sixteenth or seventeenth century together with a tolbooth and a mercat cross as symbols of burghal authority. There was no choice but to set about restoration and adaptation to contemporary uses at Trust expense. The practice, now invariable, of making a reconnaissance in depth before a decision is taken on any subject stems from that daunting and, in retrospect, exhilarating venture. The restoration of 'Little Houses', an on-going project, started almost fortuitously in Culross. How it has expanded and gained ever-increasing support and international repute, in that order, is related by other contributors to the Guide. They too take the point that only a fraction of the accomplishment would have been feasible had the Trust not won the confidence of the town council of a small burgh in the first instance and of larger authorities and the Scottish Office, in addition to the Pilgrim Trust, as the work proceeded.

A venture made with as little apparent premeditation as the decision to buy the Palace was to bring the Trust ultimately into the mainstream of national and international action to ensure conservation and scrupulous management of wild landscape. In 1935 it was resolved to add, by purchase, to some relatively small holdings in Glencoe. This was done. The immediate object was to prevent indiscriminate development in the lower, historic part of the glen where an old military way had been replaced by a trunk road (A82). It was noted that the new boundary extended to the summit of Bidean nam Bian. The Bidean was a peak which climbers of the time held in reverence and awe – and which the present generation, with all their mechanical aids, would do well to treat with more respect. No one bargained for the excitement caused some months later by an intimation that the adjoining estate of Dalness was to be offered for sale. With Dalness there went the whole southern massif from the Bidean to Buachaille Etive. This brought P. J. H. Unna, president of the Scottish Mountaineering Club, into the orbit of the Trust. An appeal which he inspired was directed to members of the Alpine Club, the Scottish Mountaineering Club and all other climbing clubs in Britain. An appeal sponsored by the Council seized the imagination of other members of the community by reference to Dalness as a 'national park' with unrestricted access. Dalness came to the Trust in 1937. To this first 'Unna property' others have been added. The Unna monies continue to provide for purchase and maintenance of mountainous country territory. Behind the munificence of this remarkable man there was a simple motive. He appreciated, as few others did in the 1930s, that we have in the Highlands of Scotland one of the last large reserves of wild and semi-wild land in Europe. He apprehended a threat which is now a stark reality – intolerable pressure on areas which are easy of access to a motorized population – and determined that so far as his resources and the wit of the Trust could provide for protection and temperate use, the high places would remain for the pleasure and refreshment of the man on foot. The 'Unna rules' which he formulated some time before his death in 1950 have a spartan simplicity. I pray that we shall be able to abide by them.

My own involvement with the Trust began very near to the point at which great and historic houses began to come into our care. The record from then on is characteristic of a country which relies very heavily on voluntary organizations to sustain cultural values and the quality of the environment. The salvation of much of the national heritage, in stone and lime, plenishings and pictures, gardens and landscape planting, might never have come about but for prevision. There was reason before the Second World War to fear for the future of large country houses. The English Trust was first off the mark and introduced its Country House Scheme in 1937. The Scottish Trust evolved and canvassed a similar scheme in 1942. The Country House Scheme makes it possible for the owner of a house of architectural or historic importance to transfer it to the Trust, together with its contents and an endowment to provide for upkeep. The property is then declared inalienable and its protection is thus assured for all time. On certain conditions he and his heirs may continue to live on it, having regard to the fact that 'for the benefit of the nation' is the operative clause in our constitution and so makes mandatory optimum access for the public. Of necessity, both Trusts apply rigorous criteria in considering every proposition that is put before them. Neither is, or has ever been, acquisitive or afflicted by thoughts of empire-building. Yet by 1946 a situation had arisen in which nothing but action by the Trusts, in concert with central government, could prevent the demolition or abandonment of many a house and the dispersal of its contents.

The good intent of Parliament became apparent in the same year. At the instigation of Dr Hugh Dalton, as Chancellor of the Exchequer, it was decided to exercise the government's powers to accept houses and land in payment or part payment of death duties, so that in appropriate cases houses and land could be conveyed to either Trust for permanent preservation. Of more immediate benefit to the Scottish Trust was the adoption of many, unfortunately not all, of the recommendations of the Gowers Committee. The Ancient Monuments and Historic Buildings Act, 1953, gave authority for the establishment of the Historic Buildings Council for Scotland and introduced a grant system in order to help meet the capital cost of repairs and renewal and, for the Trusts only, the costs of annual maintenance. I acknowledge with gratitude the sympathy and understanding of the Historic Buildings Council and of successive Secretaries of State for Scotland to whom they have tendered advice. Governmental grants, for capital or revenue purposes, are only one element in Trust finance, but they are an indispensable supplement. Their scope could be extended with advantage. The Historic Buildings Act brought in much needed grant-aid for the upkeep of gardens attached to our great houses. It did nothing for gardens *per se*, so neither Inverewe nor Branklyn comes within its ambit. In addition, important gardens in private ownership are manifestly at risk, and the sad fact is that whereas, given the money, one can take remedial action in a building long infected by dry rot, woodworm or other agents of destruction, in a garden the work of a lifetime or of generations of devoted owners and skilled staff can be dissipated in the space of two or three years. However the effect of Dr Dalton's inspiration, formalized in the National Land Fund procedures, was to add dramatically to our range of inalienable properties – Brodick Castle and its superb contents in 1958, Nos 5, 6 and 7 Charlotte Square, Edinburgh, in 1966, Torridon in 1967, Kellie Castle in 1970, Haddo House in 1979 and Brodie Castle in 1980. But for each of them we had to look elsewhere for an endowment, a capital sum to supply the revenue with which to meet the inevitable shortfall of annual income as against annual outgoings.

Brodick: Goatfell

At this date finance is a clamouring cause for concern. The Trust is ill-equipped to grapple with inflation. We rely on membership subscriptions, donations and legacies for the sustenance of the General Fund, our one free fund. It is disconcerting to see the gap widen, apparently inexorably, between outgoings on properties and revenue from the specific funds with which they are endowed. The benefit that may flow to Scotland from exploitation of off-shore oil and gas is impossible to quantify. In any event it will take time to permeate the economy. Ironically, the first phase of related on-shore development consumed part of our substance: it was necessary to resist, through a public local inquiry lasting forty-five days, proposals by two civil engineering companies to expropriate a site on the Balmacara estate in Wester Ross, an inalienable property in a region in which the threat to social balance and indigenous culture exceeded that to the integrity of the natural environment, superlative as that happens to be. Very early in Trust history the Duke of Atholl gave the Council and the Executive Committee credit for ability to cut their coat according to their cloth. The necessity for thrift and discretion has never been more plain. But crises pass.

The Scottish Trust is nothing if not empirical and venturesome. To what extent such characteristics can be related to an increase in membership from 1,300 in 1939 to 14,000 in 1960 and the present strength of over 100,000 I cannot say. That they have been potent elements in widening the circle of allies and associates committed to conservation in its many aspects, in Britain and overseas, I am quite certain. I have cited the curious case of the Little Houses (advisedly without reference to the genesis of the statutory building lists, with which another author has dealt in the introduction to the relevant

Culzean Castle

section). I have indicated how an isolated decision in 1935 about an acquisition in Glencoe set the Trust on a new course. That led, *inter alia*, to my attendance in 1972 at the Second World Conference on National Parks. The experience was the more informative and rewarding for the Trust delegation because of a close relationship with the U.S. National Park Service, the management agency for Yellowstone where the conference opened and Grand Teton to which it adjourned for the plenary sessions. The American connection by direct association through the properties had an odd beginning, but is none the worse for that. In 1792 Captain Archibald Kennedy, R.N., lately of New York, succeeded a cousin as eleventh Earl of Cassillis and inherited Culzean Castle. Up to the American War of Independence (before and during which he had a low opinion of British policy and some regard for the 'rebels') he was a substantial landowner in and around New York. One of his town houses was No. 1 Broadway. In the end he found it prudent to move to London. It is not recorded whether entry into his castle, lately finished by Robert Adam, reconciled him completely to the need for flight and the loss of his American estates. There is no question of the affection in which the next American resident held the place. In 1945 the fifth Marquess of Ailsa and the Kennedy family presented Culzean to the Trust. In a matter of months the Council created, on the top floor of the castle, Scotland's National Guest House and gave to General Dwight D. Eisenhower, Supreme Commander of Allied Forces in Europe in the Second World War, exclusive use of it for his lifetime. General Eisenhower inspired, in his own metaphor, a bridge-building exercise. The effort devoted to it by the Trust and by American agencies and institutions has been continuous. The Scottish Heritage (U.S.A.) Inc., a foundation with analogous aims, based on the City of New York, helped us to perpetuate the general's memory at Culzean. Taking up his faith in inter-communication as the way to international friendship and understanding, the chairman, president and directors have established 'exchange' programmes on strictly practical lines. The first, run since 1967 in association with the Trustees and Director of Longwood Gardens, Pennsylvania, was and is for gardeners. Similar projects have provided for personnel in other disciplines since 1970.

Culzean Castle came to the Trust without endowment. A public appeal, endorsed by General Eisenhower, made that good in 1968. The Council's original act of faith, by which the whole estate was declared inalienable, received full justification in 1969. By agreement between the Trust and the then local planning authorities (Ayr County Council and the town councils of Ayr and Kilmarnock) Culzean's 560 acres of woodlands, fields, gardens, cliff and seashore became Scotland's first country park under the Countryside (Scotland) Act, 1967. In this matrix the Countryside Commission for Scotland, the Scottish Development Department, the Joint Committee for the park and the Trust immediately set in motion a very great experiment. Ostensibly it has the object of providing for public enjoyment. The deeper purpose is to teach visitors of all ages, especially children, how to use and get pleasure and profit from the countryside without abusing it, and the project is being pressed forward in concert with the district councils of Kyle and Carrick, Cunninghame, Cumnock and Doon Valley, and Strathclyde Regional Council.

The readiness of the Trust to work in partnership with statutory authorities, first demonstrated in Culross, is constant. The capacity to take up part of the load is growing. It grew as the list of properties extended. A working partnership with the Nature Conservancy Council, as in St Kilda and on Ben Lawers, led steadily to a 'partnership' relationship in other parts of Scotland. A similar experience with local government at its various levels has been, I hope, of mutual benefit. The authorities have the power, and access to funds, to do formally over a wide field many of the things which we did informally within our territorial limits, as in protecting sensitive areas in public or private ownership by establishing points of attraction and absorption in close proximity, and it is to be noted that for part of the year a deer forest is as much a sensitive area as a National Nature Reserve or Site of Special Scientific Interest. We set out deliberately to fill resident posts with staff capable of being guides and counsellors, and continue to do so pending the creation of what must be ultimately a countrywide ranger service. Help from two sources put muscle into what was *faute de mieux* an elementary guidance and security system. In 1970, with the guarantee of generous grants from the MacRobert Trust, we set up a series of ranger training-courses. This was, by general agreement, a bridging exercise, the means of filling a void until the Countryside Commission for Scotland could establish a national training centre, which they did in 1974. By that time the Commission and the Scottish Development Department had approved grant-aid sufficient to permit the posting of Trust rangers, on a year-round or seasonal basis, on all the mountainous properties and on other locations.

I would not wish to suggest that 'partnership' between voluntary and statutory agencies over so broad a field of conservation is necessarily a Scottish invention. It is certainly not a Scottish monopoly. Time and circumstance gave the Scottish Trust a head start. In a small country communication is easy. It is also an advantage that over the years many of the relevant powers have been put in the hands of the Secretary of State for Scotland. But the growth of the Trust movement world-wide and the effects of economic recession on voluntary societies and governmental activities gives enormous potential to the concept of 'combined operations'. By 1977 the possibility of establishing a systematic interchange of experience and information seemed to be an idea which was worth testing.

In 1978 the Scottish Trust and Scottish Heritage (U.S.A.) Inc. convened the first international conference of National Trusts. It was held in Scotland, based first at Ayr, then at the headquarters of the Countryside Commission for Scotland, at Battleby, Redgorton, Perthshire. The primary purpose was to consider, largely by reference to work in progress in the countryside and in urban areas, to what greater extent 'partnership' arrangements could secure optimum use of the resources available to Trusts and to statutory bodies. Eight Trusts and eight statutory agencies or authorities were represented. Attention was given to two major initiatives by UNESCO – the World Heritage Convention and the Warsaw Convention on area conservation and restoration. At the end of seven days we had a continuing conference on our hands. It was agreed that it be reconvened in the United States in 1980. This was done by Trust and Heritage in association with the National Trust for Historic Preservation, the Trustees of Reservations in Massachusetts and the Adirondack Park Agency.

While such ventures prosper, and I write these additional notes for a third edition of the Guide, we are preparing to celebrate the jubilee. Reflecting on the Trust's first half-century one can rejoice in endeavour and attainment. And let us not gloss over the occasional error or disappointment. To recall precisely where one has come from is to know the more clearly how to lay a course for the future.

From the beginning the Trust has been sustained by what one observer, old enough to have seen it founded, calls 'trust with a small t' – reliance on its candour, integrity and capability; confidence that if or when it fails to deliver, it will not be for want of thought and effort. Faith of this kind is both a private and a public matter. It determines to a large degree the strength of membership, the very foundation of the whole edifice. It may have so magnified the status of the Trust as public trustee as to divert attention from other aspects of the work we do. Yet faith and works are indivisible.

As to 'trust with a small t', I met it very early. Of Threave, in the Stewartry of Kirkcudbright, others tell how the house and the former policy parkland are put to use by the School of Practical Gardening and how the margin by the river Dee became a wildfowl reserve. Back in the 1940s what was remarkable was that the owner should choose the Trust as a vehicle for an enterprise which was fundamentally humane. Threave, an estate of 1,390 acres, had been put together in the 1860s by the grandfather of the laird, Major Alan Francis Lindsay Gordon. Major Gordon wished the property to be maintained as an entity, partly from family sentiment no doubt but also to ensure security for his household and estate staff and the tenants of four farms. He offered an endowment sufficient to meet both obligations. Initially the proposition was received with somewhat modified rapture. The house could not conceivably be said to come within the ambit of the Country House Scheme. Apart from Threave Castle, an adventitious appendage to one of the grandfather's purchases (which was put under the guardianship of H.M. Office of Works as early as 1913), there was nothing of national or historic interest. Nevertheless, the Council resolved on acceptance in 1948, persuaded that one day Threave would serve a useful purpose. It does. What remains to be recorded here is that the major's staff – he died in 1957 – have lived out their lives usefully and happily on Threave, and on the farms the tenant families are all in the third generation. The date of entry in one instance was 1883, the latest 1910.

By contrast, it was a joint initiative by the Secretary of State for Scotland and the Hugh Fraser Foundation which put Iona in the care of the Trust in order to secure in perpetuity a seemly environment for the abbey church and other sacred buildings and sites which the Iona Cathedral Trust has administered since 1899.

This is primarily, essentially, a book about the National Trust for Scotland on its home ground. If I have digressed it is with good reason. We are considering a complex and galvanic organism. One has to begin by looking at what it holds 'for the benefit of the nation'. There could scarcely be a more extraordinary inventory – castles in a Scottish mode of building that reached its apogee in Craigievar, a royal palace, doocots, a water-mill, waterfalls, mountains, islands, scenes of ancient war, the elegance and the urbanity of Charlotte Square. But for the Trust houses and land are not the full sum of its parts, nor would be even if one added the areas for which public-spirited owners have given a permanent guarantee of integrity by entering into Conservation Agreements. Concern for people informs every aspect of Trust policy –

Kintail

concern for neighbours, for our tenants in, say, Fair Isle or Kintail, and for the people who come among them. Our members make the Trust a great fraternity – dedicated, outward-looking, informed and opinionated. The footloose Scots broadened the background from which it draws its inspiration; their children supply part of the spirit which animates it. It is for governments to put under discipline the kind of technological advance by which city streets are made to serve as channels for noxious fluids, clean water and clean air become scarce commodities, and noise pursues one even in the wilderness. May God guide them and give them gumption. The Scottish Trust will continue to concern itself with every matter that affects the environment and the quality of life. From habit and belief it will accentuate the positive. I commend you to the properties and the good people who care for them on your behalf and ours.

I · CASTLES AND COUNTRY HOUSES

with an introduction by Schomberg Scott

Introduction

Whatever may be its reputation as 'the land of the mountain and the flood', even the most fervent and chauvinistic Scot would hardly claim that his native land could compete against the palazzos of Italy, the châteaux of France or the country houses of England in the Great House Stakes. It follows that the care of such places forms a less predominant part of the work of the National Trust for Scotland than it does with its companions in other countries. Furthermore, since the offer or availability of country houses for Trust ownership is bound to be somewhat fortuitous, they cannot be selected and acquired in the same way that a connoisseur of pictures or postage-stamps will build up his collection. Consequently, there is no way of ensuring that a strictly limited number of examples will be fully representative of each stage in their development. The Trust is all the more fortunate therefore in that, if it cannot tell the whole story, it has at least got in its care a sufficient number of houses which are crucial to the telling and which include representatives of the culminating achievements both of Scotland's highly individual indigenous style and of the country's contribution to the wider field of European 'great houses'.

Except for a brief period in the late eighteenth and the nineteenth centuries, neither the history nor the resources of Scotland provided the necessary conditions for building in the grand manner. Some might argue that such an activity is fundamentally alien to the Scottish character and, indeed, that where it occurs it always has about it something of an exotic air, so that one looks around for foreign influences.

In a remarkably precise way, this question of foreign influence in Scotland seems to hinge around the second half of the seventeenth century. One can almost date its arrival to the year 1660. Before that date it was minimal and confined almost entirely to applied, or sometimes misapplied, detail. After that date it is paramount, at any rate as far as the larger country houses were concerned. Some inherently Scottish characteristics persisted, but these become increasingly difficult to identify until they were eclectically reintroduced, along with many a braw new Victorian tartan. In the smaller houses and the burgh architecture, the vernacular traditions were less susceptible to the pressures of fashion and the change was naturally much more gradual. In the case of the landowners, building for themselves on their estates, the indigenous castellated style, unique to Scotland, held complete sway right up to the outbreak of the Civil War. Within ten years of the Restoration, fully integrated classical houses had been built.

The National Trust for Scotland now owns four houses which between them display the full maturity of the country's indigenous architectural achievement: Crathes Castle, almost the last major house to be built, equipped and decorated without regard to what was afoot elsewhere; Castle Fraser, the largest of the four, its grandeur emphasized by the surviving wings of service buildings which throw into relief the height and majesty of the main block, providing a contrast in scale which has unfortunately been lost at the others; Kellie Castle in Fife where one can discern the first hesitant steps away from a strictly national inheritance; and Craigievar Castle in central Aberdeenshire, the apotheosis of the style and a major work of art by any standards, national or international. One day, perhaps, other buildings which mark the stages in the evolution of the Scots style may come to the Trust; and it is to be hoped that they will, for it is a fascinating story which, even if only because it culminates in the creation of a Craigievar, deserves the telling.

It is often said that the earlier Scottish houses and castles show strong French influence, and the political alliance between these two countries is postulated as evidence for and the source of this influence. This is unquestionably so in the case of the royal palaces, as can be seen at Falkland Palace. But Falkland, in so far as French influence is concerned, is completely exotic to the Scottish scene in general. Indeed, containing as it does the very first true Renaissance façade to be built in Britain (1537–39), it stands as the harbinger of that same invasion which was to overwhelm the Scottish style more than a hundred years later.

Crathes, Castle Fraser, Craigievar and Kellie, in spite of points of resemblance to Falkland, come of different stock. With a little imagination their origins can be traced back to those strange circular towers of the north and west, the brochs, constructed around the time of Christ. Though it is fanciful to try to claim a direct line of descent, they at least have two characteristics which remained inherent through all changes to the end; they are buildings which are essentially and uncompromisingly of stone construction and they maintain a persistent emphasis on height. Both these characteristics can be accounted for by the nature of the country and the materials available. That Scotland is a country of stone is so obvious that one blushes to make the observation. What is not so obvious now, and indeed comes to many as something of a shock, is that because of the destruction of natural forest, much of Scotland was until the middle of the eighteenth

Craigievar Castle

century or even later a land devoid of trees of a kind which were of any use as building timber. Right down to the time of Dr Johnson, one journalist and traveller after another finds the bleak, open countryside remarkable. The *First Statistical Account*, published just before the end of the century, has reference after reference to the need for or benefits derived from new plantations on the estates. Dr Johnson himself remarked of the country between Montrose and Aberdeen, in 1773, 'There is no tree for either shelter or timber. The oak and the thorn is equally a stranger, and the whole country is extended equally in nakedness. A tree might be a show in Scotland as a horse in Venice.' As he was prone to do, the Doctor overstates the case a little, for Scotland grew a small amount of oak, but not more or in larger sizes than would make a good stout door and some of the better pieces of furniture (and some of the wood for that purpose came from Sweden). From this it follows that the Scots builders had to contrive the maximum amount of accommodation under the minimum area of roof, using vaulting wherever the resulting thrust could be contained by the strength of the outer walls and, where it could not, by putting one small room on top of another to make the same limited amount of timber serve as both ceiling and floor.

Except for this vertical arrangement, the domestic organization of such a house was by the sixteenth century very little different from its English counterpart. Above a set of vaulted service rooms on the ground floor (emphatically not byres of refuge for cattle in times of strife) was the common living-room, the great hall in England, the high hall in Scotland, with the main entry, through the screens, at one end and the high table at the other, with separate access to a suite of private rooms for the owner and his family nearby. In a Scots tower house, these rooms were usually on the floor or floors above. Right at the top of the house, where the arching roof-timbers left a modicum of open space, lay the gallery, lit by dormer windows and through the corner turrets which are so typical a feature of the external appearance. Both Crathes and Craigievar, in addition to their intrinsic architectural merit, exemplify this vertical way of life extremely well. That the inherent condition of climbing or descending a narrow twisted stair at every movement from room to room was tolerated rather than preferred, is shown at the later houses such as Kellie, where one of the incoming changes is in the expansion of the plan on a horizontal level as soon as the timber shortage was eased by increased trade and larger ships to bring it in from Scandinavia and the Baltic. 'Memel pine' and 'Suadin Burd' (Sweden Board) both figure in Scots building accounts

Crathes Castle

of the period. That there was other less tangible commerce along these same routes is something that becomes evident in considering the decoration of places like Crathes.

The practical difficulties of the building contractor, however, were not the only reason for the development of the Scots tower house. It had other origins, in the nature of the inhabitants and their social and political history. It can be claimed, perhaps, that the Scots have as one of their characteristics a certain independence of outlook which at its best produces a sturdy self-reliant self-sufficiency, and at its worst an inhibiting parochialism. It was the latter which provided Edward I and Edward II of England with many an opening in their attempted takeover of the country, and made almost impossible the establishment of any strong central government under the Stuarts. It was the former which supplied in its place some sort of order through the establishment of each family or clan chief as the local government on his own lands, lands which more often than not were held directly of the Crown without any intervening feudal superior. In making these grants of land and confirming the authority that went with them by the right to hold and administer heritable jurisdictions, sometimes including power over life and death, the Crown was clearly relying on the self-interest of these deputies to keep order within their own bounds on the principle of employing the best poachers as gamekeepers. Since very early times the seat of local authority had been the local stronghold, and during the period of the fragmentation of government the earlier tower houses had required a certain defensive potentiality. Gradually, however, as time went by, the need for actual physical strength declined and it was the symbolism of authority that was desired. As late as 1632 Sir Robert Kerr was writing from London to his son, the Earl of Lothian, 'By any means do not take away the battlement, as some gave me counsel to do, for that is the grace of the house and makes it look like a castle and so noblest.' Sir Robert was no backwoodsman living a generation or more behind the times, but the friend of Charles I and of the poet John Donne, and one of the most enlightened art connoisseurs of his day, the first, it is thought, to have brought a painting by Rembrandt into this country. There is nothing quite like height for lending an air of authority.

In Scotland such seventeenth-century houses as these are almost always styled castles. In so far as this implies a military stronghold or a garrison it must be strictly regarded as a courtesy title. Functionally they are first and foremost complete and sophisticated dwellings. Within there was always that comfort and elegance which has enabled them to maintain their

Kellie Castle

original purpose down to the present time almost without change. Their very compactness has been to their advantage, and now so readily adaptable are they to twentieth-century life that the last few years have seen many of the type restored to use as family homes. By the second half of the sixteenth century the external accoutrements of war of earlier times have all been modified and adapted to serve the ends of architectural design, but their military ancestry remains clear and conveys to the spectator the unequivocal message: 'Here is the seat of authority. *Nemo me impune lacessit.*'

It is thus a style of architecture which grew entirely out of its native soil and in it are fused the character of the inhabitants, their historical background and social organization, the disciplines imposed by the available materials and, not least, the inherited skills of the master masons working in the traditions of their military forebears. Where all these are so blended, sooner or later a work of art is almost inevitable.

The simpler tower houses which illustrate the process of evolution do not yet feature prominently among the Trust's possessions, but an idea of their general character may be derived from the ruined Threave, near Castle Douglas, the enchanting little tower of Scotstarvit in Fife and the old tower which still forms a nucleus at Drum Castle, near Aberdeen. Scotstarvit, which is owned by the Trust and held in guardianship by the Scottish Development Department (Ancient Monuments), is particularly interesting in this context. The date of its construction is uncertain and it may well be that it is really no older than Crathes, but built in a manner which was by then already somewhat archaic. (The Scotsman is nothing if not conservative, in the non-political meaning of the word.) Be that as it may, it does have the almost austere simplicity of the earlier prototypes, saved from being uncouth by the high quality of the masonry.

Whatever the date of Scotstarvit, it is certainly not earlier than Falkland Palace, which is no more than eight miles away and must therefore have been perfectly familiar to the builders. Nothing could illustrate more vividly the gap between the lairds following their inherited traditions and the innovations of the court.

Everything at Falkland is at variance with the lairds' tower houses, and this in spite of a fairly prolonged building programme covering more than one change in style. The great twin-towered gatehouse has other Scottish parallels, all of them derived from the military strongholds of the thirteenth century, of which Dirleton, Caerlaverock and Tantallon are the best-known examples. But this gesture of authoritative strength once made, and again it is more of a gesture than a reality, the rest of the palace is spread wide open round a courtyard, nowhere more than two floors high above the vaulted cellars and with external façades of galleries and large windows, in marked contrast with the almost organic integrity of the shaft of the traditional Scots tower. Of the surviving parts of the palace, in general terms, the structure and the external façade of the south range can be dated to the time of James IV (1488–1513) and the embellishment of the courtyard façades to his son James V (1513–42). The former are still predominantly Gothic in character; the latter is wholly in the new fashion, complete with columns, pilasters and classical mouldings. Here was the first incursion of new ideas from 'furth of Scotland' and to all intents and purposes its influence was precisely nil.

In matters of internal decoration, the case was rather different. Although the accession of James VI to the throne of England in 1603 did little to open the closed frontier of ideas between the two countries, there had been much coming and going for some time across the North Sea with Scandinavia and the Low Countries. The political ties with France may have been strong in earlier days, but when it came to commerce and cultural relationships, these were Scotland's partners. One of the most interesting manifestations of the ties with Scandinavia is to be found in the painted designs with which the rooms were decorated, spread over the ceilings, whether of timber or vaulted, as well as many of the wall surfaces. Crathes Castle contains some of the finest and could once show far more, but it should not be regarded as in any way exceptional. The type of decoration preserved there demonstrates the way in which Scots houses were resplendent with brightly coloured designs, sometimes figurative, sometimes abstract, wherever the surface was of a nature to take them and allow them to endure. Such comparison as has been made with similar decoration in places like Gripsholm and Vadstena show remarkable affinities. This is not to say that the painters in Scotland were Swedes or Danes – the evidence is all in favour of their having been Scotsmen – but there must certainly have been traffic in both design and technique.

Another potent source of influence from abroad was the import of pattern-books and wood-cut illustrations produced by the printing presses of the Low Countries. It has been suggested that the ceilings at Crathes must have been the work of foreign, probably German, craftsmen on the evidence of the styles of armour and costume worn by the figures. It does not necessarily follow. On the analogy of other similar examples, where the original publications have been identified and in view of the literary concept of the themes employed (the Nine Nobles, the Muses, the Seven Virtues), imported books seem to provide much the most likely source of inspiration.

This is perhaps the right place to digress for a moment to record the way in which the care and maintenance of such places as Crathes can and has unexpectedly led the Trust into undertakings which spread far outside the confines of the properties themselves. When Crathes first came to the Trust very little was known about this particular type of painted work; there had been very little research into the history and techniques of its production and the whole question of its proper treatment and care had hardly been studied. Nor was it realized how large a number of examples had survived throughout the country. The one thing that was becoming apparent was that the conservation methods used hitherto were not standing up to the test of time. It fell to the Trust, therefore, to initiate, with the help of Mrs Eve Baker from London and Professor Wildenstam from Stockholm, a survey of the most important examples known at that time. Subsequently, with financial backing from a generous grant from the Gulbenkian Foundation, a research and training programme was initiated, leading in turn to the establishment of a conservation centre, initially for the preservation of these sixteenth- and seventeenth-century decorative paintings, which, once interest was aroused, were coming to light in increasing numbers. In no time at all the services of the conservation centre were spread far beyond the confines of Trust properties and in very little time after that they could no longer be limited to paintings on ceilings and walls. By 1969 the centre had grown to a point, both in scope and techniques, where it could no longer be regarded or managed as a legitimate Trust activity and it was taken over by the Department of the Environment to handle all conservation problems from sculptured stones to easel paintings.

To return to the early years of the seventeenth century, a new form of internal decoration began to make its way up from the south at this time. This was moulded and enriched plaster-work. Craigievar is among the earliest and finest exponents of this new fashion, and there is very similar work to be seen at The Binns. Both of them, as far as the plaster goes, can be dated to the year of the accession of Charles I. By the time the plaster-work was being installed at Kellie thirty-five years later, the Jacobean style had gone a long way along the road of transition to the Caroline. The real *tour de force* in this new fashion is to be found in the far north at Brodie and dates from about the year 1670. The quality of the

Craigievar Castle: the High Hall ceiling (detail)

plaster decoration on the dining-room ceiling there would be remarkable in any setting; in that time and place it is absolutely astonishing.

During this early period, of course, there were no architects as such. It has been said that Craigievar seems to grow out of the ground and it is as easy to imagine the design for an oak tree being set out in two dimensions on a piece of paper. Records of names are scant. In Aberdeenshire the names of two families of master-masons are recorded, one Leiper and the other Bel. One or more of these may have been concerned with both Crathes and Craigievar. At Castle Fraser both families were employed at different times and I. Bel signed his name on the great armorial achievement set high on the north façade. The accounts for the royal work at Falkland are better documented and it is from these that it is known that at least two Frenchmen of the names of Moyse Martin and Nicholas Roy were employed there.

There is no record now of master of works or master-mason at Kellie, but the house features in the contract drawn up for another house nearby. Sir Philip Anstruther stipulated in this that his new house at Dreel was to be 76 feet by 24 feet within the walls; the windows of the Hall were to be 'as large and compleit as those of the Hall at Kellie'; the gate was to 'conform to the principal gate at Balcarres' and there was to be a doocot 'of the quantitie of Sir James Lumsdaine his doocot'. After that, working with materials supplied to him by the master of works, it was up to the master-mason to do the best he could in the light of his own skills and inspiration. It seems to have been no bad way to achieve 'firmness, commoditie and delight'.

Inevitably the Civil War and the state of near bankruptcy in which Scotland emerged from it caused an interruption in any major building projects. Somewhat paradoxically, this conflict, since loyalties had cut completely across national frontiers, did more to bring the two kingdoms together than anything else since the union of the crowns.

In 1671 Charles II commissioned the rebuilding of his palace at Holyroodhouse. True to the precedents set up by his family, reinforced by his English upbringing and foreign travels, there was no question of carrying on from the point where Scots traditions had left off. What was wanted and what Sir William Bruce as Surveyor of the Royal Works provided was a completely classical building 'in pillar work conforme to and with the Dorick and Ionic orders', to which Sir William added the Corinthian order and a carved pediment for good measure. This time, in sharp contrast to the earlier occasions, the royal example was universally accepted. Under the leadership first of Sir William Bruce and later of William Adam, the new form of a simple rectangular block with a break in the centre of the front elevation to carry a pediment became the standard for every type of house, from a great palace like Hopetoun to modest farm houses. This basic unit was sometimes set off with low wings on each side connecting the central block with flanking pavilions and, in the grander examples, embellished with classical pilasters, cornices and architraves. Among the houses in the Trust's care Haddo House in Aberdeenshire, designed by William Adam in 1731, perfectly exemplifies the prototype.

As the eighteenth century wore on there was more and more opportunity for such houses to be built. The revolution in agricultural methods which took place at that time and extensive new road construction encouraged the change in the social and domestic way of life and also provided the prosperity needed to finance it, so that today the descendants of Haddo form an almost commonplace but none the less delightful feature of the Scottish countryside.

Leith Hall: west front (c. 1868)

Leith Hall, also in Aberdeenshire, gives us an example of the process at work. It is not a prestige mansion or carefully designed masterpiece. Rather is it a very modest and vernacular interpretation of the ideals current at the time. There was an old house on the site, one of the few to be built during the time of the Civil War and one of the last in the traditional Scots way: tall, narrow and turreted, with a walled enclosure of service buildings on the south side. Some comparatively minor improvements were carried out in 1756 but agricultural reform and prosperity were slow to reach the valleys of the upper Garioch and it was not till 1797 that a major attempt was made to bring the house up to date. Even then it was all very modest. The old house was retained almost unaltered but relegated to a subsidiary role, while a new block was constructed straight in front of it across the courtyard to the south. It is a plain rectangle harled white, with stone margins round the windows and without cornices or moulded architraves. Neither the hard Aberdeenshire granite nor financial restraint would permit such things, but the spirit of the times could still be given expression in a charming oval drawing-room on the first floor and three-light windows, the centre one arched, with over them the visual effect of a pediment marked by flat stone bands brought through to the face of the harling. All the language of Vitruvius could say no more.

For the first half-century Scotland trod the Palladian measure step by step with England. But there was one nobleman who was not altogether keeping time and this was Archibald, third Duke of Argyll. He had inherited at Inveraray a fairly typical old Scots baronial tower, dominating the small burgh which clustered under its walls. In 1745 he commissioned Roger Morris to prepare drawings for a completely new house to replace the old. Although Gothic as an elegant style for a gentleman's residence was still in the future (this was two years before Horace Walpole bought a small house at Twickenham called Strawberry Hill), the idea of battlements and arched openings was obviously so much in keeping with the Duke's position as chief of a great clan and with the rugged scenery of Loch Fyne that it won acceptance over any neoclassic alternative. It was not altogether a new inspiration. Some years before, Sir John Vanbrugh had made a sketch for the same project which, with his eye for the dramatic, had more the character of an operatic prison than a nobleman's seat. Roger Morris's variation on the same theme was much more urbane, but it still bore no relationship whatever to anything seen in those parts before. The round corner towers at each end of flat façades, the battlements and the pointed windows were all as much an exotic importation as columns, pilasters and pediments had ever been. None the less, it was a style which seemed entirely appropriate to the Scottish scene.

William Adam became involved at Inveraray as Roger Morris's man in Scotland in the last years of his life, and his young son Robert worked there with him. At Mellerstain, in Berwickshire, his first major Scottish commission after ten years of success as a classicist in England following his return from Italy, the latter turned back again to the Gothic manner, at any rate as far as a parapet of battlements and square hood mouldings over the windows made it Gothic. In spite of its impeccable proportions, somehow the exterior fails to carry conviction. Culzean Castle, overlooking the Firth of Clyde, put that right nearly ten years later.

Just as at Crathes and Craigievar the Trust holds the culmination of the Scottish native style, so at Culzean it has in its care the house in which Robert Adam came as near as possible to the perfect synthesis of eighteenth century classical urbanity with the romantic outline which Scotland seemed to demand. Certainly the site did all it could for romance: an old Scots tower on a cliff-top looking across a wide expanse of sea to the peaks of Arran and the low profile of Kintyre on the far horizon, with a deep cleft running almost parallel with the coast to protect the house from the mainland.

Since the building of Mellerstain, Robert Adam had come to reject the use of Gothic detail as an element in his designs; and everything at Culzean, inside and out, is strictly classical, with the exception of a few small windows shaped like crosses and the corbelled and battlemented parapets. Externally there is very little ornament of any kind. Culzean was created in two stages. The first was the complete modernization of the old tower, amounting to a virtual rebuilding, and its enclosure between two wings to achieve a classical symmetry; the second, the addition of a magnificent suite of rooms centred on a great drum tower on the very edge of the cliff. Again there was an interval of nine years between these two stages, an interval during which Adam had gone even further towards the elimination of applied decoration externally, relying entirely on form and the relationship of the various masses. There was still an empty space between the two parts of the house, which Adam finally filled in with his great oval staircase, surely one of the most inspired of his achievements, which by its interplay of light and dark, space and enclosure, would alone give Adam his architectural standing and finally quash the idea that he was only a stylish decorator. Even as one admires it, one is struck again by the total absence of any conflict between this wholly classical composition and the battlements without; those battlements which, seen from a distance, give Culzean perfect harmony with its setting of cliff, sea, mountain and woods. Mr John Fleming has suggested that in thus rejecting any specific reference to medieval design, Adam was thinking back to the fortifications of imperial Rome. Certainly, the absence of any incongruity between outward military form and classical content at Culzean supports this thesis.

Royal Scots Dragoon Guards at The Binns

Only after Robert Adam's death did country-house building really get under way in Scotland, clothed in whichever of the accepted costumes the client and his architect agreed to adopt. To represent this early nineteenth-century phase as far as external appearance goes, there is The Binns, between South Queensferry and Linlithgow. Here again there is an extended building history: the old house was constructed in the first years of the seventeenth century; more elegant and spacious rooms were added at about 1750; then, in 1810, William Burn gave it the battlements supported on minuscule machicolations, and the drip mouldings over the windows which, in the Napoleonic period, met the need for the romantic without surrendering to the uncouth or to the uncomfortable. One cannot but regret the loss of the original seventeenth-century work which, to judge by five dormer windows that have survived and the interior, must have been of considerable interest and high quality. Luckily the plaster-work on the ceilings was not disturbed and the Binns holds very fine examples of Scots work in this medium during the short interval between its arrival north of the Border and the outbreak of the Civil War.

It was James Gillespie Graham, another of the great names among Scottish country house architects, who gave Brodick Castle on Arran its present appearance. Here, in his work, it is possible to discern almost for the first time influences derived from the native Scots style of 250 years before. Brodick is, in fact, the oldest habitable house owned by the Trust, in part going back to the fourteenth century though with little visible earlier than the sixteenth and seventeenth centuries. Brodick belonged to the great family of Hamilton for most of its history and it was for the tenth Duke that Gillespie Graham almost doubled the size of the house with a new wing added at the west end in 1844. This was towards the end of his career and most of his work had been in a much more orthodox Gothic idiom. One can discern at Brodick the birth of that style which was to prove so acceptable in those areas to which the red deer and the grouse at last brought prosperity of a sort, which the agricultural improvements of the previous century had been unable to effect.

Hill of Tarvit

There remains the last stage of the country house, represented among Trust properties by Hill of Tarvit, designed by Sir Robert Lorimer in 1906. Much of his work was concerned with the rehabilitation and restoration of old Scots vernacular towers in his own somewhat individual manner; and in his new houses, such as Rowallan and Ardkinglas, he shows a truer appreciation of their essential quality than most of his predecessors in the previous century. But Hill of Tarvit is different. It is one of those houses which the early twentieth century produced in quantity, traditional in that they break no new ground, yet deriving design almost wholly from the architect's personal assessment of how to provide the required accommodation in a pleasing and harmonious form, without specific reference to any antecedents. It is possible to regard architecture such as this as the fallow ground in which the seeds of the modern movement were sown.

So far this survey of the castles and houses in the care of the National Trust for Scotland has concentrated on their place in the history of Scottish domestic architecture with hardly any reference to the role they have played in national history. This may seem perverse, particularly with reference to Scotland which is generally thought of as a country with far too much history for happiness. The Trust holds a number of properties specifically on account of their place in the nation's story, but, in the main, the castles and houses are not among them. Not one is an essential entry in the index of the history books nor have any been the scene of events which have affected the country's destiny.

Brodick Castle has its place in the life of Robert the Bruce, who waited there for a time until conditions were ripe for him to start his campaign to win the country to himself. Some time later it was attacked and sacked by the English, a hazard which altered nothing one way or the other and which might happen almost anywhere.

Falkland is unquestionably the principal 'historic' house, on account of its long association with the Stuart dynasty. But even there, there are few historical occasions to recount other than the death of James V in 1542, when his infant daughter Mary succeeded to the throne, and, just over a hundred years later, the visit of Charles II on his way to defeat at Worcester. Only once was the present palace the scene of strife and that was the almost farcical occasion on June 28th, 1592, when Francis Stuart, fifth Earl of Bothwell, in one of his not infrequent moments of mental aberration, attacked it in an attempt to kidnap his cousin, James VI.

There is, however, one historical detail which is not only commemorated but perpetuated down to the present day at Falkland, and this is related to the fact that it is not a Trust property at all. It remains a royal palace in the hands of the Sovereign. The Trust holds the position of Deputy to the hereditary Constable, Captain and Keeper, an office which has been held in the past by many families and which goes back to the year 1371, when the association of the Stuart family with Falkland first began.

Certainly, it does not require great events or forceful personalities to give a house historical significance. Great events can pass and leave no mark at all on the places where they happened so that the association is at the mercy of imagination. But that same house has taken its very form from the philosophical ideas, political climate and social organization current at the time of its construction and, in any modifications, since. It is inevitable that it must reflect the way the national genius has reacted to changing circumstances and tell us directly and intimately of those whose customs, traditions and ways of thought make up our own.

'Society is a partnership between those who are living, those who are dead and those who are yet to be born.' So said Edmund Burke. Our historic houses, even if their history is no more than the trivia of daily domestic life, are among the capital assets of that partnership, assets which though limited in quantity, include some which are masterworks beyond time and circumstance.

The Scottish Interior

by Sir Steven Runciman

Scotland has always been a poor country; and, until the later
years of the eighteenth century, the poverty was nowhere
more apparent than in the primitive simplicity of Scottish
domestic life. To travellers from the richer kingdom in the
south Scottish living conditions seemed appalling. An English
traveller in 1704 quoted feelingly the words of his compatriot,
the poet Cleveland:

> Had Cain been Scot, God had ne'er changed his doom,
> Nor made him wander, but confined him home.

It is likely that the ill-success of Ben Jonson's visit to Drum-
mond of Hawthornden in 1618 was due less to the cantanker-
ousness of the two poets than to the discomforts of the
Scottish mansion; and, a century and a half later, all Boswell's
patriotism could not wholly disguise Dr Johnson's disapproval of the crudity of life north of the Border.

In the earlier Middle Ages a Scotsman in search of comfort
would have to retire to a monastery, where at least there were
stone walls to protect him. When stone castles began to be
built in the fourteenth century and stone towers for the lesser
lairds from the fifteenth century onwards, the furnishings
were still very primitive. In a tower house in the crude form
of the peel tower there would usually be a ground-floor room
into which the favourite rams, the favourite bull and the
favourite servants could be crowded during a raid. Over it
was the laird's living-room, entered from outside up a ladder;
and a ladder inside went up to a trap-door through which the
bedroom was reached. The narrow windows were unglazed.
Wooden shutters kept out the cold and also the light. There
would be a large open fireplace, without a grate. Cupboards
were dug out of the thickness of the walls, the salt cupboard
being next to the fire. There were rushes on the floor; and in
the richer houses simple tapestries hung on the bare stone
walls. The furniture consisted of crude benches and tables
made by the estate carpenter, with perhaps a special chair for
the laird and one for his lady. There were beds everywhere,
some of them boxed in recesses in the walls, but most of
them in the middle of the room. These were simple four-
posters, with hangings all round, so as to make a snug, stuffy
chamber within, large enough often to take three or four
sleepers. Complete strangers might be put to lie together, so
weighed down by sheepskins that chastity was guaranteed.

Not only had the laird's family to be housed, but there were visitors to be entertained, especially in winter, when the short daylight and the muddiness of the tracks made travel slow, and inns were very few.

It was a grim life in the tower houses, and in the castles too. Enemy raids were more frequent in summer; but the winters must have been harder to bear, with the family shivering in the wan light of tallow candles and living on an interminable diet of oatmeal, kale and turnip, and an occasional pigeon from the laird's doocot. Food was, however, fairly plentiful. In 1433 James I legislated against over-eating, in particular the eating of bake-meats, (pastries), 'dishes neuer before this mans daies seen in Scotland', so William Harrison tells us, writing a century later. No one under the degree of gentleman was to eat them, and then only on 'high and festiuall daies'.

Life in the towns was scarcely more comfortable, though the town walls provided a certain security. The houses were mainly of wood, and there was a perpetual risk of fire; while the sanitation was even more unhygienic than in the countryside. But there were craftsmen in the towns, masons, carpenters and weavers; and there were therefore better appurtenances than in the countryside.

Standards everywhere began to improve in the later sixteenth century, when a marked increase in trade brought new wealth into the whole country. In particular, new amenities appeared in the tower houses. Storeys were added to old houses and new tall houses were built, with enclosed spiral staircases and glazed windows, though the glass was often rather coarse. Sanitation was provided, with ducts cut in the walls of the upstairs closets dropping down to a main drain, large enough for a boy to enter to clean it, along which the filth could be flushed into a pit or a nearby stream. Many of the 'secret passages' of which proprietors of ancient houses like to boast are in fact the drains.

The painted ceilings with which many of these new houses were adorned (see pp. 38–9) gave a new cheerfulness to the rooms, together with finer matting or carpets on the floors and better tapestries on the walls. Furniture was now more plentiful and usually made by professional craftsmen. There were heavily carved oak chests and cupboards. Beds were more elaborate; and, though humbler folk still had to sit on stools, the laird and his lady now had magnificent chairs, becoming more imposing as the seventeenth century advanced. Amongst the finest examples are the chairs made for Alexander Burnett of Leys and Katherine Gordon, his wife, in 1697, which are still in their proper place at Crathes.

By the beginning of the seventeenth century wood, which

had become scarce in Scotland after centuries of deforestation, was being imported from Scandinavia and the Baltic. It was now fashionable to panel rooms, especially with 'Memel pine'. The panelling meant that tapestry was no longer needed. Instead, family portraits began to appear on the walls. These were for the most part primitive works, produced by some itinerant painter, who would not only make rough likenesses of the laird and his family but also, if required, provide him with a number of pictured ancestors. The first distinguished Scottish artist was George Jamesone, born in Aberdeen in 1587 and trained in Flanders under Rubens. Examples of his work can be seen at Crathes. But throughout the seventeenth century the nobility tended to have their portraits painted when they were visiting London. The one fashionable portrait-painter in Scotland was a Spaniard, John Medina, who settled in Edinburgh in 1688 and was eventually knighted by the Lord High Commissioner.

There was a similar increase in comfort in town houses. Rich burghers, or noble families who wanted to spend the worst of the winter in the town, liked to have large houses, comparable with Gladstone's Land in Edinburgh or Lamb's House in Leith; and there, under painted ceilings, you would find furniture made by superior craftsmen or imported from abroad. But shortage of space in the cities meant that most citizens lived in high tenement buildings, men and women of all classes and professions sharing the same building. The humbler folk lived on the lower floors, while the gentry preferred to be fairly high up. It was a wearisome climb up the dark and usually filthy communal stairway, which was often so narrow that ladies could not keep their voluminous skirts clean on them, and the manoeuvring of coffins down them was always a problem. But there was fresher air and better light in the upper floors. A Scottish gentleman who visited London in the early eighteenth century was shocked to be told that rooms at the top of a house were cheap and despised. He angrily replied that 'he kenned very weel what gentility was, and when he had lived a' his life in a sixth storey he wasna come to London to live on the grund'.

Inside the flats of the gentry, in spite of the squalid approach, you would find elegant furniture and hangings, well-carved mantelshelves and, by the end of the seventeenth century, plastered ceilings. Few servants could be kept, for lack of accommodation. It was not unusual for a maid to have to sleep in a drawer in the kitchen, while the children of the family occupied beds that had to be tidied away during the daytime. A higher rent could be charged for an apartment guaranteed to be free of bugs.

In the smaller burghs and the villages, where ground space was less restricted, houses were seldom more than two storeys in height; and the cottages of humbler folk contained little more than the but and the ben. They would have a box-bed and built-in presses and the necessary tables and stools, and little else.

Meanwhile the revolution in the architecture of larger houses, outside the confines of the city streets, a revolution begun by William Bruce and carried on by the great Scots architects of the eighteenth century, involved a revolution in house decoration. With what might be termed the change from vertical to horizontal architecture, rooms became larger, and they could open out of each other. There was more floor space and more wall space. More furniture was required, and there was room for more pictures. Windows were larger and had to be curtained. The old painted ceilings were no longer appropriate. The new taste was for plaster-work, often very elaborate. In the more remote country districts the old vernacular styles of furniture lingered on; but in the great houses of southern Scotland there was a growing tendency to follow English fashions. Wealthier nobles and ambitious adventurers spent more and more time in London, to keep in touch with the court and inevitably wished to keep up with their English rivals. In the later seventeenth century, in Scotland as in England, the very rich liked to acquire pieces of French furniture. The wars at the end of the century restricted its import; but the Scots, moved, no doubt, by a sentimental regard for the Auld Alliance, continued to follow French models far longer than the English. There were cabinet-makers in Edinburgh throughout the eighteenth century who specialized in French designs.

It was above all Robert Adam who brought English and Scottish taste together. Much of his best work was done in England, but he frequently returned to his native Scotland; and his influence on house-decoration and on furniture was paramount in both countries. After the middle of the eighteenth century few gentlemen's houses in Scotland were not decorated in Adam's neo-classical manner. Plaster-work was moulded and woodwork carved in Grecian designs and furniture had classical lines and proportions. By the end of the century, when the New Town of Edinburgh was being built, the interiors of its houses, as well as the exteriors, all were consonant with the claim of the city to be 'the Athens of the North'. The influence of Chippendale was not greatly felt in Scotland; but the later, more classical designs of Hepplewhite and Sheraton were studiously reproduced by the cabinet-makers of Edinburgh.

Culzean Castle:
ceiling of the Round
Drawing-room (detail)

49

Scottish houses perhaps contained fewer amenities than their English equivalents. Scottish silver was fairly abundant; but porcelain was rare. There were no Scottish factories, though good pottery was produced in various places, the best coming from the Delftfield works at Glasgow, founded in the 1740s. Pewter was still in use as table-ware till towards the end of the eighteenth century, when china dinner-services began to be imported in large quantities from the Far East. Scottish textiles had a good reputation in the eighteenth century; and curtains and carpets would be of high quality. There were few pictures as yet, apart from the family portraits and an occasional rather primitive landscape let into a panel over the mantelshelf. There were by the middle of the eighteenth century a number of Scottish painters; but there were few families who were as enlightened as the Clerks of Penicuik and showed them patronage. By the later decades of the century scions of the nobility who went on the Grand Tour were coming back with Italian or Flemish old master works, and perhaps with their own portraits painted by Battoni; and Scottish visitors to London, as we have seen, if they could afford it had their likenesses painted by their compatriot, Allan Ramsay, or by Gainsborough or other of the fashionable artists of the English capital. Scottish libraries, on the other hand, were often well stocked. Dr Johnson, who was not easily impressed, was pleased by the books that he found in Scottish houses, even in the remoter Highlands.

Life in the great houses of the eighteenth century – and in many smaller houses that followed their lead – and in the elegant terraces of the New Town in Edinburgh, copied on a smaller scale in Glasgow, which was rapidly developing, in the old town of Perth and in unyielding granite in Aberdeen, well reflected the age of the Scottish Enlightenment, with its international outlook. The nineteenth century saw a return to what was believed to be the Scottish idiom. For this Sir Walter Scott was largely responsible: though it must be said that his Abbotsford owes more to eighteenth-century English Gothic than to the tower-house tradition of his native land. Victorian Gothic was even more of an unhistoric fantasy. The castles might have thick walls and steep gables and high towers ornamented by pepper-pot turrets; but a laird of older times who entered them would have felt utterly bewildered by their vast, high-ceilinged halls and great staircases, all elaborately decorated, their pretentious, over-carved pieces of furniture, their heavy plush curtains and tartan covers and cushions, and stags' heads hanging on the walls (made of wood if the real thing was not available), together with Highland scenes painted by Sir Edwin Landseer and his followers. The old laird would have felt more at home in the low warren-like rooms of the vast basements or in the poky attics where the domestic staff was expected to live, surrounded by furniture rejected as being out-of-date by the owners. But 'Scottish Baronial' represents a definite style of its own, and at its best it had a certain picturesque exuberance. The furniture was always well made, and the pictures well painted; and many of the lesser ornaments, the china, the glass and the silver, often show a quaintness and a fantasy that still have their charm. And many of the greater buildings that have lost their roofs and are falling into decay, make, at least at a distance, very romantic ruins.

In the world of today with its mass-media and its easy communications, local characteristics are quickly dying out. Inside the high-rise blocks and the housing estates that now disfigure so many Scottish burghs there is a drab uniformity in the furnishing; and, indeed, the interior of the crofter's cottage now looks much the same as the interior of a small villa in the London suburbs. But there are still houses in Scotland which are essentially in the Scottish idiom; and many of them contain carefully preserved heirlooms or pieces of old furniture, lovingly collected to fit the atmosphere. There are, too, houses and cottages which the National Trust for Scotland and other bodies have taken over and restored, to show us how life was led in them in the past. In such places we can be aware of the continuing Scottish tradition; and let us hope that a better knowledge of the homes of Scotland will bring a better appreciation of that great tradition. We may be coming to the end of an old story; but we have not yet reached the last page.

Castles and Country Houses

15 miles west of Edinburgh, off A904 between South Queens-ferry and Linlithgow

The House of the Binns, Lothian

It is a happy coincidence that the alphabet should place The Binns first in this section for it was the first house which the National Trust for Scotland took into its care under the Country House Scheme. This was on November 9th, 1944, with all the established ritual of signed charter and symbolic gifts. The name, although perhaps seeming a curious one, is no more than a variation of the familiar Scots word 'Ben', meaning a hill.

The form of the house, basically of the early seventeenth century, has become something of an amalgam of different periods and styles; its history on the other hand is dominated by the single figure of Sir Thomas Dalyell, who lived from about 1615 until 1685. His father was one of those who, having no assured future at home, was free to make the most of the opportunities offered by the accession of James VI to the throne of England. It did not take him long and in 1612 he returned to Scotland and, having bought the estate of Binns, so enlarged the old house thereon as to constitute a virtual rebuilding.

By the time his son was grown up and had returned from the customary Continental tour, the country was sharply divided between those who were for the king and those who *The Binns*

were against him. The sentiments of most of his neighbours notwithstanding, young Thomas, or Tam as he is still popularly known, took up a military career on the royalist side. His single-minded and often vividly expressed adherence to that cause provides the keynote for all the stories and legends that grew up around his subsequent career. The first of these concerns his oath on hearing of the execution of Charles I: never to cut a hair of his head again until the monarchy was restored. In fact he seems to have retained his long beard for some time after 1660, for Jonathan Swift reports that it was a matter of comment, even some embarrassment, at the court of Charles II. He fought and was taken prisoner at the battle of Worcester, but escaped and, after further adventures, travelled to Russia where he reached high rank in the imperial armies of Tsar Alexis Michaelovitch. He returned to this country in 1665 where, as Commander-in-Chief in Scotland, he stood out as a protagonist of royal policy in the religious controversies of the late seventeenth century. It was then that his single-minded vehemence and his Russian reputation earned him the nicknames of 'Bluidy Tam' and the 'Bluidy Muscovite'.

His most enduring memorial is the regiment that he raised at Binns in 1681, which was to achieve lasting renown as the Scots Greys. Many relics of him are preserved in the house: his Bible, his Russian sword, his riding-boots and spurs, his sealskin trunk and the comb for his beard.

The house which Thomas Dalyell, father of the general, built on his return from London still forms the nucleus of the present building, although there is now little of it to be seen externally, no more than the steep pitched roof and the wall-head broken by a row of dormer windows overlooking the south courtyard. These are very much of their time, the old Scots tradition modified to incorporate the broken pediments and the little obelisks of the new Italianate fashion. Also, within the house, the rich decoration that has survived from this period shows that all was of high quality and in the latest taste, with elaborately moulded plaster ceilings and cornices bearing coats of arms, heraldic motifs and medallions depicting the heroes of old.

Just after the Jacobite rising of 1745, the first major alteration was made by the addition, along the south side, of a saloon and ante-room, over the top of which appear the older dormer windows. Sixty years later the house underwent considerable alteration and was almost completely re-faced externally by the architect William Burn to give it the appearance it has today of a country mansion of the Regency period in the Gothick manner: symmetry was contrived by balancing

The High Hall

round towers to divide the main façade into three bays; the windows were much enlarged and given the rectangular hood moulds which since the days of Robert Adam at Mellerstain had been the hall-mark of the Gothick style; and all the walls were crested with battlements. No doubt the result is not one of particular architectural distinction; but at Binns there is to be seen a record of changing taste, with a value and interest independent of aesthetic achievement.

1½ miles north from Brodick Pier

Were some 'quiz-master' to ask for the link between Robert the Bruce and William Beckford, builder of Fonthill Abbey and author of *Vathek*, between a mountain nearly 3,000 feet high and a treasure-house of pictures, porcelain and silver, the contestant might well suspect that someone had got his references mixed up. The connection is, of course, Brodick Castle. It is one of those rare places where, within a setting wholly 'stern and wild', lie the fragile and the exquisite; and the impact of each is enhanced by its association with the other.

Dominating all, Goatfell (2,866 ft) has the grandeur of isolation which, with views stretching from Ben Lomond and Jura to the coast of Ireland, more than compensates for its comparatively modest and attainable height. And there is more to it than a relatively gentle uphill stroll; the cliffs and corries that ring the summit are as dramatic as any to be found in the Western Highlands.

A direct association of Robert the Bruce with the castle itself cannot be substantiated. At almost the lowest ebb of his fortunes, in 1306, he was driven to take refuge in Rathlin Island off the coast of Ireland. Boredom and frustration soon led his companions, Sir James Douglas and Sir Robert Boyd, to try a landing on Arran and an attack on Brodick Castle, at that time garrisoned by the English. They were strong enough to keep the English shut up within the castle, but lacked the means to drive them out. Before long, Bruce joined them in their camp in a nearby glen. It was from there, when the time seemed ripe, that he returned to the mainland at the start of seven years of campaigning that ended at Bannockburn.

Brodick, as it now stands, is almost completely the creation of the Hamilton family. In 1503 it was granted to James, second Lord Hamilton, with the title of Earl of Arran, by his cousin James IV (his mother had been the Princess Mary, daughter of James II). Today the castle is a long narrow

Goatfell from the String road

Brodick: the south front from the Formal Garden

block, lying east and west, of which the tower at the east end is the oldest part, built about 1558. This was in the time of the second Earl of Arran, Duke of Chatelherault in the peerage of France and heir presumptive to the throne of Scotland. He had been guardian to the infant Mary Queen of Scots and also regent of Scotland until 1554. Brodick was too remote to be the centre of great affairs of state, rather was it a retreat for hunting or when a spell out of the limelight seemed prudent. The family's somewhat wayward political career brought about such spells, though it also brought its rewards, a marquessate in 1599 and a dukedom in 1648. The first duke died on the scaffold six weeks after Charles I; his brother, the second duke, was wounded and captured at the battle of Worcester, and died nine days later. Thereafter, Brodick was taken over by a garrison of Cromwell's forces who, presumably because of its strategic position on the Clyde, strengthened it with a new battery at the east end and an extension of the tower to the west. Only the discerning eye will notice the difference between this addition, put up in 1652, and the older tower built just one hundred years before, so persistent were the traditions of Scots tower architecture.

The eighteenth century saw the Brodick estates undergo

the transformation of an agricultural revolution, in common with the rest of Scotland, but the castle remained unaltered and almost unvisited. Then in the nineteenth century two marriages, each in its own way, made truly remarkable contributions to the house as it is today. The first took place on April 26th, 1810, when Alexander, tenth Duke of Hamilton, married Susan Euphemia, younger daughter and co-heir of William Beckford of Fonthill. Now, after two great sales of his possessions in 1822 and of his library in 1882, and the even greater sale of the contents of Hamilton Palace in 1862, Brodick holds all that remains of William Beckford's once amazing collection of works of art.

The second marriage, on February 23rd, 1843, was between William, son of the tenth Duke and Susan Beckford, and Princess Mary of Baden, daughter of the Grand Duke. She was also a great-niece of the Empress Josephine, for her mother had been a de Beauharnais. It was a period of great prosperity for Scottish estates, coinciding with the Victorian romantic rediscovery of the Highlands. In the year after their marriage the young couple commissioned James Gillespie Graham to design another extension to the west of the old house which more than doubled the accommodation, terminating in the great west tower.

James Gillespie Graham, who had a large practice throughout Scotland in the middle of the nineteenth century, was the architect of the period who, perhaps above all, appreciated the essential character of the indigenous Scots baronial style as distinct from the eclecticism of the Gothic revival, and his work at Brodick is an excellent example of this. Built of red sandstone, both the sixteenth- and seventeenth-century blocks

The top of the staircase

to the east were as austere externally as they could well be, even the pattern of corbels under the battlemented parapet being simplified into three continuous courses of projecting masonry. This austerity Gillespie Graham carried on into his extension to the west. There is a little softening of the severity in the arched heads over the windows of the great saloon on the first floor, but, as on his models, it is only round the head of the massive tower at the south-west angle that he allowed himself the richness of corbelling and corner turrets. It is a building such as only Scotland can show, making its effect, like its seventeenth-century prototypes, by height and the almost stark simplicity which at first belies and then enhances the richness within.

Brodick remained in the possession of the Hamilton family for only one more generation. The direct line died out in 1895 and Brodick passed to the twelfth duke's daughter, who became Duchess of Montrose.

Of the contents, those pictures and objects which derive from William Beckford must always have a fascination all their own, but he was not the only connoisseur in the family and nothing could provide a greater contrast to his taste than the Hamilton collection of sporting pictures. The treasures of the house, the exotic flowers of the garden, in their setting of mountain and sea, are not inappropriate to the tale of *Vathek* itself.

The drawing-room, furnished with Italian marquetry and French gilt and ormulu pieces, a Chinese screen and Venetian mirrors

Brodie Castle, Grampian

4 miles west of Forres, 6 miles east of Nairn, off A96

Brodie is one of those places which have been so long in the hands of one family that, since the records began, that family has never acquired any other name than that of the lands they occupied. The Brodies are first recorded here in the reign of Malcolm IV, a time when the Earldom of Moray, vested in the Crown, had to be put under the direct control of men loyal to it. There is further mention of them in a charter from the reign of Alexander III referring to Malcolm Brodie as Thane and confirming his tenure of the lands of Brodie and Dyke. Unfortunately, all the family records and charters for the next four hundred years were lost when the house was 'byrnt and plunderit' by Lord Lewis Gordon, acting under instructions from the Marquess of Montrose during the Civil War. It is thus impossible to reconstruct the earlier family history except for a few flashes of information from outside sources. One of these flashes reveals how Alexander Brodie, the twelfth laird, was at feud with his neighbour Alexander Cumming of Altyre, and that he with 126 companions waylaid Alexander Cumming and a party of his servants outside Forres and, after inflicting wounds and considerable damage, put them to flight. Alexander and his friends then defied the summons to stand trial for this offence. They were therefore declared rebels and 'put to the horn', that is, outlawed. This was in November 1550.

This twelfth laird is none the less the first of the Brodie family who comes into the story of the house as it stands today. High on the gable of the south-west tower is a carved stone bearing the date 1567. His brush with the law does not seem to have inhibited him in any way from building himself a handsome new house.

It is now impossible to say what sort of a house stood on the site before this time or how much of it, if any, is incorporated in the present structure. The house that resulted from this sixteenth-century work shows all the signs of having been a very typical house of the period, a central block with square towers at diagonally opposite corners, one to the south-west and one to the north-east. The main entrance, now lost, would most probably have been at the base of the north-east tower, giving direct access to the service rooms and kitchens occupying the whole of the ground floor and leading on up a broad stair to the east or screens end of the high hall which filled the whole of the first floor of the central block. The laird's high table, placed across the west end of the hall in front of the great fireplace, had, just behind it, a door leading through into a charming small room with vaulted ceiling. From there a little corbelled turret stair in the angle went on up to more rooms above, the south-west tower thus containing the laird's private suite.

Thirty years after the date on the house, the estate of Brodie was erected into a barony. This was in the time of Alexander's son David, the thirteenth laird. Then again the darkness descends except for the record that the fourteenth laird, another David, who succeeded his father in 1626 and died six years later, married a niece of the Admirable Crichton.

With the birth of their son Alexander in 1617 a steadier light begins to shine, for he grew up into a very remarkable man, much occupied with public affairs, who kept a copious diary. He seems to have had something of his great-uncle's qualities; he was a man of great learning and ability to which he added extraordinary piety. Unfortunately for later generations, his diaries are more concerned with religious experience and argu-

Brodie Castle

ment than daily events, but none the less they give some insight into his life and times. At the age of ten he was sent into England for his education, but his father died only four years later and he succeeded to the estates. In 1640 he took part in a raid on Elgin Cathedral, presumably to drive out the Roman Catholics who were still using parts of the ruins for religious purposes. At the age of twenty-six he was representing the County of Elgin in the Scots Parliament and in 1649 he was one of the party that went to Holland to treat with Charles II for his return to Scotland, on the expedition which would end disastrously at Worcester in 1651. A staunch upholder of the National Covenant all through the Commonwealth, he took an active part in the government of Scotland but he remained, in his own words, 'resolved and determined in the strength of the Lord, to eschew and avoid employment under Cromwell'. Exactly three months to the day after Cromwell's death he took his seat on the bench as a Senator of the College of Justice, becoming known as Lord Brodie.

Meanwhile the first addition had been made to the original house, possibly as part of its restoration after the damage inflicted by Lord Lewis Gordon in 1645. This was the rectangular block, very plain externally, fitted into the angle behind the south-west tower and backing on to the high table end of the main hall. The original laird's room in the tower is quite small and this new addition provided a much more spacious 'Chamber of Dais' where the laird could entertain visitors and clients in some privacy and far greater splendour away from the noise and confusion of the common room. Whatever the external simplicity, this new room was indeed 'all glorious within', for it was embellished with a richly moulded plaster ceiling which would be a *tour de force* anywhere and which, in these rather austere surroundings, is quite astounding.

Where the laird of Brodie got his inspiration to order a work of this kind or the craftsmen to carry it out, so far remains a mystery. It is certainly according to the fashion of the time, in line with the work done for Charles II at Holyrood and for the Duke of Lauderdale at Thirlestane, and Brodie's involvement with the government and the great men of his day would have made him familiar with both of these examples. But his ceiling goes quite a long way beyond these in richness and the degree of figure sculpture. Some of the motifs seem to point to Dutch or Danish origins and one is tempted to look back to the visit to Breda in 1649 for the germination of the idea. There is much to be seen at Brodie of art and craftsmanship, but only at Brodie is there such a ceiling as this.

Alexander was succeeded by his son James, a man of similar tastes and again a diarist but who took far less interest in public affairs. As he left no son, only nine daughters, he was succeeded by a cousin who had married one of them.

Next after him came another Alexander, a strong supporter of the Hanoverian side in 1745 and holding the office of Lord Lyon King at Arms. He was laird of Brodie for thirty-eight years from 1716 to 1754, and his activities on the estate seem to have been more concerned with the grounds than the house. Or rather perhaps one should say his wife's activities. She, Mary Sleigh by name, gets a special footnote to herself in Sir John Sinclair's *First Statistical Account* of 1793 for the benefits she wrought in the garden, on the estate and, indeed, to the whole countryside around her. In spite of these improvements, or perhaps because of them, her husband, the Lord Lyon, died heavily in debt.

And so the story goes on through the eighteenth century and into the nineteenth, the burden of debt always seeming to outweigh the benefits from estate improvement. In 1759 there was again no direct male heir and James Brodie of Spynie, a cousin, took over. In 1767 he eloped with Lady Margaret Duff, daughter of the Earl of Fife, but so forgiving was the earl that, when debts became so pressing in 1774 that the estate had to be put up to auction, he undertook to outbid all other offers so that it could be handed back to his son-in-law. Alas, in 1786 tragedy struck. For the second time Brodie went up in flames, and Lady Margaret died of suffocation. That the upper parts of the south-west tower seem to belong to an earlier age than the wall-head and roof of the central block may well be the outcome of reconstruction after one or both of these fires.

The Drawing Room at Brodie Castle

James Brodie and Lady Margaret were not a lucky pair. Their only son James was drowned at Madras, where he had gone to build up the family fortunes, and the next laird was their grandson William.

In spite of pressing debts and a regime of rigid economy, William immediately carried on with a scheme, perhaps initiated before his grandfather's death in 1824, for extensive additions to the house. For these William Burn was the architect and the eastern end is all his work. For it he adopted the somewhat formalized 'Gothick' style of the period, one which owes nothing to Scottish ancestry but provides for the spacious, airy and well-lit rooms which the Regency period demanded. So well lit was the new wing that there were fears that the panes of glass would prove too large to withstand the northern gales.

And so Brodie stands today, not as an architectural masterpiece, but as the home of a family of exceptional antiquity which reflects each era of the history that has passed over it, while still containing, in spite of all the troubles and difficulties, a very fine collection of the furnishings and belongings which illustrate and give vitality to that history.

Castle Fraser, Grampian

18 miles west of Aberdeen, off the A96 on to B994 and through Kemnay or north off A944 at Dunecht

Castle Fraser belongs to the same great period of native architectural achievement as Crathes and Craigievar and it is the largest and grandest example of this indigenous style owned by the Trust.

The building history of Castle Fraser is a complicated one which has been the subject of much archaeological conjecture ever since the time when Sir Walter Scott had his attention drawn to a small secret chamber, discovered not long before, over the vault of the high hall and was inspired thereby to contrive such another in the Tower of London by means of which *The Fortunes of Nigel* could be happily resolved.

However, the problems and doubts of constructional chronology do not much matter. The important thing here is the outcome which exemplifies, almost better than anywhere else, the grandeur of which the native castellated style, without any departure from inherited traditions and techniques, was capable.

It was about the year 1575 that Michael Fraser decided to build a great new house on the family's 'up-country' estates, then known as Muchalls-in-Mar. Before then, ever since the family came to Aberdeenshire in the time of James II, their

Castle Fraser

principal residence had been at Stoneywood, just outside Aberdeen. The reason for the move is not clear, except that the second half of the sixteenth century was a period of great building activity among Scottish lairds as the older towers, with their emphasis on defence, began to seem increasingly cramped and uncouth in an age of expansion. Moreover the Muchalls lands were extremely fertile.

Internal evidence within the existing house suggests that before 1575 there was already a plain rectangular tower-house on the site, probably not unlike the old tower at Drum Castle with a parapet walk behind battlements round the top and the main entrance at first-floor level reached by an outside stair. The fireplace in the high hall and the break in the masonry of the vault over it indicate the position and extent of the original hall of the old tower. Michael Fraser started his new house by adding a square tower, known to this day as the Michael Tower, at the north-west corner of this old block. This contained a new main entrance and a grand staircase leading up to the high hall. The space above was occupied with a series of small rooms, one on top of the other. It is possible that he planned and started to build the great drum tower at the

The Victorian Room, Castle Fraser

south-east corner. But in 1588 Michael Fraser died, his work far from complete, to be succeeded by his son, then still a minor. There was thus quite a hiatus in the work of rebuilding and it seems that the young man, when he in turn took up his father's project, had rather grander ideas, for by the time he had finished the whole castle was both larger on plan and taller than seems to have been originally envisaged. It is this later work which today makes the castle stand out among its fellows as a 'great house' in the grand manner. The corner turrets carried up through two floors instead of the more usual one, the traditional elaboration of blind machicolation, cable mouldings, batteries of stone cannon, all contribute to an ensemble of more than usual splendour and at the same time afford a wonderful example of the skill of the Aberdeenshire craftsmen in imparting an effect of great richness to such an intractable material as granite without for a moment detracting from its inherent quality of unyielding permanence. The external decoration reaches its climax in the great heraldic frontispiece high on the north side, part of Michael Fraser's earlier work. In size and intricacy of design, this great blazon at Castle Fraser is rivalled only by the sculptured assertion of power and authority over the entrance to Huntly Castle, put up by the Marquess of Huntly some twenty-five years later.

By 1621 the internal finishings were being installed – a contract was made with James Leiper for stone paving to be laid in the high hall. Even so, the roof was still not complete, for in 1631 young Andrew Fraser had to get permission to export ten chalders (approximately 7,600 gallons) of meal to Norway in exchange for the timber he still needed. In 1636 the building as it stands today was completed with the construction of the two low wings flanking the entrance courtyard and containing those service quarters which in earlier days would have been a much less formalized group around the inner face of the barmkin wall, but which are here given an architectural sophistication worthy of the main part of the house. In contrast to most places where they have been swept away, the survival of these 'laigh biggins' at Castle Fraser helps us to appreciate how much they contributed to the scale and magnificence of the towers rising far above them. Bel and Leiper are two of the great names among the northern master-masons of the sixteenth and seventeenth centuries and both families were at different times involved in all this fine work.

The building was scarcely complete before it became involved in the troubles of the Civil War. The lands around were harried by Lord Aboyne on the Royalist side in 1639 and again by Montrose five years later, but the castle itself escaped un scathed. In spite of this, later generations remained staunchly Jacobite after the Revolution of 1688 and one of the Frasers died by falling over a cliff near Banff while in hiding after taking part in the rebellion of 1715. For services to his cause James III and VIII in exile rewarded the dead man's son with a peerage in 1723. Meanwhile the castle and lands round it had passed into the hands of another branch of the family who in 1695 changed the name from Muchalls to Castle Fraser.

After the years of famine in rural Scotland there followed the agricultural reforms which brought wealth to such estates as this. The good fortune which had brought the castle unscathed through the ravages of the Civil War also preserved it, unlike many another, from the 'improvements' of peace and prosperity. It is true that Miss Eliza Fraser, a lady of redoubtable character who held the estates from 1792 to 1814, could not entirely resist a temptation to change things with the times, but she must be forgiven. Her architectural solecisms, a new entrance on the south front and the shifting around of some coats of arms, are details of very small account on so splendid a whole and moreover weigh very light in the balance set against the rise in the standard of living on the estate which she helped to foster by her encouragement of new farming methods.

In 1921 the castle was bought by Viscount Cowdray and it remained with his family until 1975 when his granddaughter, Mrs Michael Smiley, made it over to the Trust. During this period, although it was not lived in as a family home, much careful preservation and restoration work was carried out so that, to add to its external splendours, Castle Fraser now provides an unusually vivid insight into the domestic arrangements within a Scottish great house in the pre-classical era.

The Worked Room,
Castle Fraser

26 miles west of Aberdeen, entry on the west side of A980 **Craigievar Castle,**
2 miles north of the crossroads with A974 **Grampian**

Where should a masterpiece be set? In the heart of things, where its presence will be constantly felt and its inspiration a continual experience? Or set apart in isolation, where its impact is never diminished by familiarity and distracting incongruities and where its surroundings can remain inviolate? The setting of Craigievar is certainly of the latter kind and the traveller comes upon the tower set among trees in a world of its own like some fabled treasure. With its simple stem rising in the subtlest entasis to the elaboration of the turreted skyline, he can hardly escape the impression that this castle, like the trees, has grown up of itself out of the ground.

It was, in fact, built between 1600 and 1626, its builder being one William Forbes, a merchant of Aberdeen and brother to the bishop of that city. In common with many another at that time on the east coast of Scotland, he traded largely with the Baltic ports, excelling his rivals at least to the extent of earning the nickname of 'Danzig Willie'. Trade also brought him the wealth needed to buy up the lands of the Mortimers in upper Aberdeenshire and the unfinished walls of the castle they had recently started to build. Like the great prodigy houses of Elizabethan England, Craigievar is thus the creation, not of an old landed family, but of the new plutocracy. It coincided with a time when the skill of the master masons, in this case almost certainly a family called Bel, working within the stern disciplines imposed by their material, Aberdeen granite, had reached its peak, and when the traditional native architecture, evolved through three hundred years from military origins, was free from the limitations of war to express the ideals and aspirations of the new lairds. Of this indigenous architectural style, Craigievar is undoubtedly the apotheosis. In nothing is this more manifest than in its form of almost organic integrity, to which we have already referred.

Craigievar Castle

The Blue Bedroom

If Craigievar is the culmination of native tradition in its structure, the internal finishings belong to the new generation. William Forbes, his Baltic affiliations notwithstanding, would have none of the old-fashioned painted decoration such as the Burnetts had recently completed at Crathes, or Provost Skene of Aberdeen, another Danzig merchant, was to commission for his town house just at the time that Craigievar was almost complete. Instead he would have the elaborately moulded plasterwork which had begun to take its place. The technique might be new to Scotland, but the motifs and inspiration remained much the same; running floral patterns interspersed on the vault of the high hall with representations of the heroes of antiquity. In the place of honour over the hall fireplace, the royal arms of Scotland proclaim the laird's role as representative of the king's authority within his own lands. There can be few armorial achievements in any medium, let alone plaster, so impressive as this. It seems that no record has survived as to the identity of the craftsmen responsible, but in view of the correspondence of many of the moulds used on these ceilings with others of similar date up and down eastern Scotland, it seems likely that there was a group of craftsmen specializing in this new Renaissance decoration during Scotland's brief sunshine before the storm of the Civil War.

That war passed the castle by, though the owners were active on the Parliamentary side. So, most fortunately, did the combined waves of prosperity and romance which engulfed so many a Scots house in Queen Victoria's reign, leaving behind a detritus of billiard-rooms and servants' quarters. Indeed, some time before, a contrary impulse swept away the original domestic offices and all but a small part of the enclosing barmkin wall. The west side alone remains with the old arched entrance and a small circular bastion at the south-west angle to define where once they stood. Historically this must be regretted. Aesthetically it remains a matter of conflicting opinion as to whether the shaft of the tower would be seen to even greater advantage rising high over the cluster of smaller buildings at its foot or standing isolated and serene as it does today.

Crathes Castle, Grampian

14 miles west of Aberdeen and 2 miles east of Banchory on A93

Crathes Castle was a long, long time a-building, though the reasons for this are not clear. The Burnetts had held lands in and around Banchory, on the north side of the Dee, since the time of Robert the Bruce. The little ivory hunting-horn, symbol of their right of tenure of part of the old royal forest, is still preserved within the castle. When in 1552 Alexander Burnett, now laird also of much that had hitherto belonged to the Abbey of Arbroath, decided to leave his old stronghold on an island in the Loch of Leys, just to the north of Banchory, and build himself an up-to-date house befitting his status as a great landowner, Mary Queen of Scots was a girl of ten at the court of France. Long before the building work was complete her stormy life had ended in tragedy. All was not finally finished and the house occupied until the Elizabethan era itself was passing away. But none of these national events made much impact on conservative Deeside, and the Burnetts continued to prosper. They may have been long about the building, but when everything was done they had achieved one of the great examples of that wholly indigenous and highly sophisticated Scots style of domestic architecture which, evolved from the fortifications of war, is without parallel in Europe and which, within sixty years of the completion of Crathes, was to die out, suddenly and completely.

Impressive as the outside is in this context, the greater, and nearly unique, fascination lies within. Here, more vividly than almost anywhere else, it is possible to look back into the

Crathes Castle

domestic surroundings of a prosperous Scots laird at about the time that James VI was exchanging Holyroodhouse for Whitehall. Nowhere inside the tower have the proportions or arrangement of the rooms been changed. Inevitably, there has been the introduction of new furniture and fittings; but there are still some notable pieces made for the first owners, and there are other details, such as the window frames with fixed leaded glass above and wooden shutters below, which are today as they were at the beginning.

But, above all, the character of the old rooms is retained in the painted decoration on the beams and boards of the ceilings. It is perhaps this for which Crathes is chiefly famed.

The south front – 'evolved from the fortifications of war'

*The Nine Nobles
ceiling showing Judas
Maccabeus (detail)*

These paintings make a brilliant display which shows beyond question that the rooms in which the subjects of James VI and I lived were as colourful and elaborately decorated as the clothes they wore. Too many Scots castles and tower houses give a false impression of bare stone walls and naked beams; Crathes provides the perfect antidote. In these rooms the design is largely allegorical in character, supported by texts and proverbs along the sides of the beams, all this in perfect accord with the amalgam of legend, philosophy and morality which runs through so much sixteenth- and seventeenth-century literature.

Although the present wing to the east of the tower clearly does not belong to the same date, there has always been a building of about this size in this position, originally forming the north range of the barmkin, or forecourt, which enclosed an area to the south and east of the castle itself. All except the north side was probably swept away in the time of Queen Anne when the first steps towards the creation of a garden were taken with the planting of the great yew hedges which have today reached such splendid maturity. Another writer deals with the fascinating garden they now enclose.

The years of the eighteenth and nineteenth centuries passed quietly from generation to generation at Crathes, neither of the Jacobite risings of 1715 or 1745 making more than a passing stir on Deeside, with demands for support politely acknowledged and then ignored, at least in the case of the Burnetts.

The latter part of the nineteenth century brought to the castle the addition of a new Victorian wing overlooking the upper garden. This was built by the eleventh baronet, who had made a modest fortune in America. It did not last very long. It was burned down again in 1966, and it was decided not to rebuild this part of the house, but rather to reduce the east wing back to the original proportions and height of the 'laigh biggins' as these had been revealed when the fire-damaged structure was cleared away. This had the great advantage that it restored something like the original dominance of the great tower over the buildings at its foot.

If Crathes Castle cannot quite compete with Craigievar as an architectural masterpiece, it is only a very short way behind. In the details of craftsmanship there is little if anything to choose between them; and as an historical document it has an importance all its own. Taken in conjunction with one of the finest gardens in the north-east and the surrounding woodlands with their nature trail, Crathes must surely be as 'complete' a property as any the National Trust for Scotland has to offer.

12 miles south of Ayr on A719, 5 miles west of Maybole by B7023

Culzean Castle, Strathclyde

From the twelfth to the early seventeenth century Culzean was but one of a dozen small castles in the hands of the Kennedy family from which they dominated all the land along the Firth of Clyde for thirty miles and more south from the town of Ayr. Although not their principal stronghold during this time, Culzean was particularly well suited for the purpose: an easily held rock plateau atop the sea cliff with a steep little valley and escarpment to give protection from the landward side. A series of caves in the rock beneath contained 'two dainty spring wells'. In the hands of a cadet branch before it became the seat of the head of the family in the middle of the eighteenth century, it remained a comparatively modest and typical Scots tower house. Its outline is known from an old drawing. From this and from the description of Sir William Brereton, who visited the house in 1635, it is safe to assume the usual arrangement of an L-shaped tower with vaulted service quarters on the ground floor, a single great hall occupying the whole of the first floor and a cluster of small private apartments on the floors above.

On May 11th, 1602, Sir Thomas Kennedy of Culzean was murdered on the Sands of Ayr. It was the final shot which brought a merciful end to years of turmoil and feuds, feuds

Culzean Castle

which Sir Thomas had done much to foment. The seventeenth century brought civil and religious strife enough of its own, particularly in south-west Scotland where Covenanting zeal was so strong; but without the bitterness of family rivalry as well there was at last the chance for domestic amenity to replace the restrictions of defence. From 1693 we get a description of the castle 'flanked on the south with very pretty gardens and orchards, adorned with excellent tarrases'. These last are the oldest features which have survived, apart from the caves.

The head of the Kennedy family had been created Earl of Cassillis in the time of James IV and the title remained with his direct descendants until the eighth earl died without children in 1759. It took two and a half years of legal dispute to establish that the rightful successor was a second Sir Thomas Kennedy of Culzean. It was a time for fresh starts. New agricultural techniques were beginning at last to bring prosperity to Scottish fields. The ninth earl was first and foremost one of the 'improving lairds' over the now combined acres of the Cassillis and Culzean estates. He died unmarried in 1775 and was succeeded by his brother David, another bachelor. The new earl lost no time in commissioning Robert Adam to remodel the old house. The latter was already involved in the district, for he had just designed a new parish kirk for Kirkoswald at the request of the late earl. His first work at the castle was to build up the great south front overlooking the 'tarrases' and incorporating some of the masonry of the old tower within the central block. Next came the urgent task of bringing the service quarters up to date – a new kitchen wing to the east and another wing on the west containing the brew-house. There then followed an interval of some years before the great drum tower on the very edge of the cliff was added. Finally, the central well was filled with the great oval staircase. At the same time, Adam's work extended beyond the castle itself and included the stable buildings to enclose the forecourt, the home farm on the next headland up the coast and the mock ruined arch and causeway which now formed the principal approach to the castle. Within the house there were designs for furniture and fittings, tables, mirrors, sconces and carpets.

Culzean: the long drawing room

Culzean must represent one of the most complete examples of Robert Adam's inspiration, not only through the architecture and its carefully controlled approach, but in everything from the colour of the rooms to the whole landscape setting. Alexander Nasmyth gave perfect expression to this inspiration in the two views he painted of the castle, which now hang within the house. It can be said that here Adam brought about as nowhere else the perfect synthesis of the dramatic external form which the site demanded with the disciplined classical elegance to which the eighteenth century aspired.

The tenth earl, who brought all this about, did not long survive its completion. He was succeeded by a cousin, one who had been born and brought up in America and for whom the War of Independence proved wholly disastrous. During the Napoleonic Wars, Culzean again briefly took on a military air with gun emplacements along the cliff top to the west of the house and with the recruitment and drilling of the West Lowland Fencible Regiment, whose weapons now provide a great display of arms around the walls of the entrance hall. This was in the time of the twelfth earl, a close friend of the Duke of Clarence who made him Marquess of Ailsa on his accession to the throne as William IV.

The oval staircase

Culzean had been built for a bachelor. Large as it was, it would not do for a Victorian family of six children and their household staff. In 1879 the house took its final form with the addition of the west wing on the site of Adam's brew-house, to the designs of Messrs Wardrop and Reid.

Since the National Trust for Scotland came to Culzean in 1945, it has always been something more than just another great house open to the public. The gardens, which were already noteworthy in the seventeenth century, have been almost constantly developed ever since so that they now have all the exoticism and fascination that the exceptionally mild west-coast climate makes possible. In 1969 the 'policies', to use the Scots word, became Scotland's first country park for which Robert Adam's home farm buildings now act as central focus. The emphasis here is all on the natural surroundings. Each age has found at Culzean what it sought; first security in times of strife, then a romantic wilderness in which to build a private Elysium, and, in our own age, the shore, the cliffs and the woods give the seclusion needed for the conservation and study of our threatened wildlife.

10 miles west of Aberdeen, off A93

Drum Castle, Grampian

The Irvines came to Drum under precisely the same circumstances as the Burnetts to neighbouring Crathes. Before the thirteenth century the Crown held extensive lands along the north bank of the Dee, principally as a hunting forest, and these two estates were both granted by King Robert the Bruce in return for services rendered during the struggle for independence. William de Irwin of Woodhouse in Dumfriesshire had been the king's armour-bearer and clerk-register and the charter granting him these lands, which still exists, was dated at Berwick-upon-Tweed on February 1st, 1323.

When he came north to take possession he found already there a stronghold built for King Alexander III not more than forty years before. The great square tower dominates the house to this day and provides a typical and very fine example of a tower house of this period, the root-stock from which Scottish domestic architecture was to grow right down to the end of the sixteenth century.

Through eight generations this tower remained the home and stronghold of the lairds of Drum. The family name got changed from Irwin to Irvine, but, one after another, the Christian name remained consistently Alexander, even to the extent that when a younger son called Robert succeeded his elder brother who left no children of his own, he changed his name to Alexander. The elder brother had fallen at the Battle of Harlaw in 1411, fighting most gallantly against the MacLean of Duart, a single combat in which both the contestants were killed and which earned Irvine a verse to himself in the ballad recounting the battle.

Drum being so close to Aberdeen, the family were always involved in the affairs of the city. Robert Irvine, who changed his name to Alexander, was appointed in 1437, consequent upon the murder of King James I, to the post of Captain and Governor of the burgh to oversee its defence and protection. This is a post he held for two years, a unique case for there is no other record of the existence of this office in Aberdeen.

The Irvines too were always staunch upholders of the Crown and, unlike many other families of similar status in Scotland, of law and order. Alexander, the seventh laird, was rewarded by James V for 'good and thankful service done to the king in searching, taking and bringing his rebels to justice'. His son was killed in 1547 at the battle of Pinkie during his father's lifetime.

In spite of the turmoil, the family prospered, particularly during the last decades of the sixteenth century and the early years of the seventeenth. It was a time of expansion throughout Scotland and the country's trade flourished, especially through such east coast ports as Aberdeen. It was the time when William Forbes, 'Danzig Willie', was making the fortune which enabled him to create his masterpiece at Craigievar. The ninth laird, Alexander again, was sufficiently well-to-do to provide quite handsome endowments before he died to Marischal College in Aberdeen and to the Grammar School there and he made a name for himself with other charities. He seems even to have been in a position to lend money to his sovereign, James VI. In 1619 this wealth and prosperity found

expression in a new house at Drum, built alongside the old *Drum Castle*
tower. To compare the design of this new house with Craigievar, almost exactly contemporary with it, and with Crathes,
only four miles away and begun some seventy years before,
makes a fascinating study. Both these are in the old Scots
style of tall towers with rooms one on top of another under the
smallest possible area of roof. For the new house at Drum on
the other hand, although the mason's traditional techniques
and trademarks remain the same, the planning has altered
radically from the vertical to the horizontal. Yet the social and
domestic arrangements which that planning was designed to
serve remain precisely the same as before; vaulted service
quarters at ground-floor level, the great high hall on the first
floor, reached by a wide straight stair opening into the screens
area with a small turnpike service stair from the kitchen below
in the opposite corner, the laird's high table at the far end of
the hall with a door beyond it leading into his private apartments, all this now spaciously spread out. The change in
design must surely have been due to and made possible by
the changed situation with regard to the availability of structural timber. The great increase in trade across the North Sea
provided both the ships to carry it and the money to pay for
it and at Drum, with only ten miles of level ground to reach

75

the port at Aberdeen, there were no transport problems such as still made it inaccessible to places farther up-country. Economy in the use of timber for roof and floors was no longer a governing factor.

The fate which overtook the new house, however, was sadly consistent with others of its kind. The tenth laird had barely succeeded his father in 1629 before the troubles of the great rebellion overwhelmed him. He was staunchly Royalist. Drum Castle was besieged and sacked during his absence and all that was portable carried off. During part of this time his son, who was to succeed him in 1658, had been a prisoner in Edinburgh Castle and under sentence of death for his activities on behalf of the king, but a lucky change in the fortunes of war released him before this could be carried out. By the time these troubles were over, he was so impoverished that when Charles II offered to make him Earl of Aberdeen he felt compelled to decline the offer. The king did, however, handsomely record his gratitude for the family's loyalty and service.

It was this laird who became the second member of his family to feature among the Scottish ballads. He married a daughter of the second Marquess of Huntly but, after her death, he fell deeply in love with a local damsel far below him in social station. The ballad tells how she at first refused him on account of this difference in rank but how he persisted, both with her and her father, till all was agreed and he finally brought her happily home to Drum despite the stern disapproval of all his relations.

Then, once again, growing prosperity during the eighteenth century revived the family fortunes and called for more ordered and formal surroundings than the hugger-mugger of the old baronial high hall. This was then divided into dining room and withdrawing room with a lobby between them and a new door in the centre of the south front reached by a flight of steps.

So the house remained till the middle of the nineteenth century. Then, to the designs of David Bryce, the barmkin courtyard was reconstituted with a new arched entrance to the north, though retaining the original one to the west. A new broad staircase and gallery were formed along the north side of the seventeenth-century house and, as part of these changes, the great vaulted hall of the old tower was brought back into its own. In mediaeval times this had been divided into two levels by a floor across under the vault. Now it became a great library with the intermediate floor taken out and the vault lined with a new heraldically decorated plaster ceiling. The great east window to this room dates from this time, the only significant change to the external appearance of the tower.

Drum therefore is one of those houses which vividly illustrate the changes in fortune, social custom and fashion which have passed over them, from the mediaeval fortress, through the community life of a seventeenth-century Scots barony and the elegance and order of the eighteenth century to the elaboration and romanticism of Victorian times.

The Royal Palace of Falkland, Fife

11 miles north of Kirkcaldy and 11½ miles west of Cupar on A912, 3 miles off A91 at Auchtermuchty and 38 miles from Edinburgh via M9

Falkland is rightly called a royal palace for it remains to this day, as it has been since 1437, the property of the sovereign.

The visible remains, however, go back beyond the time of royal ownership and even of the Stuart dynasty. In the garden, a little way to the north of the present buildings, there breaks through the grass the base of the great round tower of the old castle of Falkland, stronghold of the Macduffs, Earls of Fife. About 1360 it passed by marriage into the Stuart family and so, after an all-too-typical interlude of treason and revenge, starting with the mysterious death of David, Duke of Rothesay in 1402, it came into the hands of the king himself.

As an addition to this castle, James II constructed a new banqueting hall. Like the castle, it too has gone, but its position and outline, the great oriel windows which lit the high table clearly defined, are marked by the paving of the rose garden which encloses the north side of the present courtyard. When James IV came to the throne, he made this great hall, the Lyon Chamber as it had come to be known, the nucleus of his new palace. For all the Stuarts, Falkland

Falkland Palace and the orchard from the north-west

Scots Guards at the Gatehouse; the Palace was the birthplace of the Regiment

was a place of recreation and hunting, and it was in this mood that the buildings were set out round a large court, open to their surroundings on all sides with scarcely a thought for defence.

The east range contained the suite of apartments which royal protocol required. The king's guard hall was at the south end, leading through into the presence chamber; to one side of this, in a separate projecting tower between two galleries, was the king's bedroom; and at the north end of the range, also opening off the presence chamber, lay the privy chamber. On the upper floor lay a similar suite of rooms for the queen. The wing of approximately similar length across the south side of the courtyard was almost completely taken up by the chapel royal. At the south-west corner the great twin-towered gatehouse was designed to contain, as it does today, the private quarters of the Constable, Captain and Keeper, in whose charge lay the security of the whole palace. Of all these buildings only the south range has remained roofed throughout the years, but lack of use as a royal residence, which led to neglect and decay, has also inhibited change so that Falkland remains a remarkably clear example of the way a royal palace was laid out in the late medieval period.

James IV built in the Gothic style and this, interpreted according to the Scots idiom, can be seen on the buttressed south front which faces the High Street of the burgh. The new palace was still incomplete when James IV died at Flodden in 1513. His son, James V, completed what his father had left unfinished. During his reign the political link with France was as strong as it had ever been, and with his second French wife came also new ideas of the Renaissance and the craftsmen to carry them out. Thus it happened that the courtyard façades of the south and east ranges became the earliest essays in full Renaissance architectural design in Britain.

Separated from the palace by the length of the garden, another building of special interest has survived from these times, one unique to Scotland and one of only two in Britain. This is the sixteenth-century royal tennis court. This one at Falkland was built for James V in 1539, eight years after Henry VIII had constructed his at Hampton Court. Now, once again restored and fully equipped, it is from time to time the scene of contests in this royal and most ancient game.

Although James VI promised in 1603 to revisit Scotland every three years, the court was seldom at Falkland thereafter. Charles I stayed there in 1633, and Charles II lodged there in 1650 and 1651 during the attempt to overthrow the Commonwealth which ended at Worcester. The palace was occupied by Cromwell's troops for a time; and it was then that a fire

The King's Bedchamber

did extensive damage, and destroyed the great hall on the north side. After the Restoration it was never again a royal residence, although the Keepers continued to occupy it till the Revolution of 1688. There followed almost exactly two centuries of neglect so that by the beginning of the nineteenth century the buildings were mostly ruinous.

Since only the south range has remained roofed, the chapel, still in use as such, has alone retained anything of its original fittings or decoration. Two items in particular deserve special mention. One is the oak screen of turned balusters over a low panelled dado which separates the chapel itself from the ante-chapel. This is a particularly important example of Scots craftsmanship of the sixteenth century, typical in its direct and economical use of a material constantly in short supply. The other feature is the painted decoration on the ceiling and along the upper part of the wall facing the windows. Basically, this dates from the later years of James V's reign but it was refurbished with new monograms, etc., for the visit of Charles

I in 1633. The hangings which originally covered the walls below the level of the dado have of course gone, but they have recently been replaced by a fine set of Flemish seventeenth-century tapestries depicting scenes from the story of Joseph.

Inevitably here, as throughout the whole palace, there is much restoration work, the greater part of it carried out by the third Marquess of Bute during his time as Keeper from 1887 till his death in 1900. It was a period which is not, perhaps, generally associated with conscientious care in the treatment of old buildings, but the work of the third marquess provides the criterion by which the shortcomings of the others must be judged. There have been few restorers so scrupulous in differentiating the restoration from the original and who, at the same time, have been so successful in harmonizing the one with the other both in design and in spirit.

But Falkland is more than a fine building of royal quality with a place in Scottish history and in the evolution of the country's architecture. It is also an integral part of the burgh which grew up around it to meet the needs of the court, its officials and staff, and which remains a fascinating example of a small Scots town containing much excellent vernacular building. There is another section to tell of the Trust's activities with regard to such houses as these. At Falkland, however, they cannot be altogether separated; so closely linked and so complementary to each other are palace and town that to wander through one and pass by the other is to hear but the song without the accompaniment.

| Haddo House, Grampian | 20 miles north of Aberdeen, off B999, and 10 miles north of Oldmeldrum, off A981 |

With the building of Haddo House, on which he started in 1731, William Adam gave Aberdeenshire its first essay in classical architecture and William Gordon, second Earl of Aberdeen, a residence appropriate to his station and vast possessions. It stands today, amid parks and woods, like a punctuation point marking the beginning of an epoch, a pattern for houses great and small all over the country, copied until it became the new vernacular style.

From the time they received title to their lands in 1496 the Gordons of Methlick and Haddo had need of a defensive house. Their House of Kellie was lost in the time of the 'bishops' wars', when, in 1644, the Covenanting Marquess of

Argyll put it to the torch. George Gordon, the laird who was to mend the family fortunes and set the rural parishes on the road to economic take-off, was then a boy of seven. He lived to be eighty-three. By middle life he was an eminent lawyer and an earl. The new peer fell out of favour with Charles II, but the Revolution Settlement and the Union of the Parliaments produced relatively stable conditions in which he could apply to the improvement of his estates the wealth acquired by his practice at the bar.

The second earl pursued the same course, so prudently and to such purpose that the third, who neglected Haddo, had money enough to buy three great houses in which to install his mistresses. With the succession of George, the fourth earl and the first Haddo Gordon to emerge on the world stage, the balance was redressed. Having taken the house in hand, it was he who ordered the landscape planting which gives it a setting of such ordered beauty. That was not all, or nearly all. The process set in motion early in the nineteenth century, in

Haddo House

abhorrence of a landscape of treeless waste and bog, transformed the Haddo estates – some 60,000 acres, nearly ninety square miles – into productive land, and put the tenant farmers into substantial houses and ample steadings. Diplomat and ultimately Prime Minister (1852–5), Earl George never lost the regard of his sovereign. His influence helped to focus Queen Victoria's attention on Balmoral. He hung on his wall a view of the old castle as it stood when she and Prince Albert bought the property in 1848. The life-size bust, in white marble, of the queen was a personal gift, presented in 1857 after a visit she made to Haddo from the new Balmoral Castle.

Haddo House

To the entrance front, which the 'Premier earl' left unaltered, William Adam gave distinction by thoroughly economical means. If Duff House at Banff (now impeccably restored by the Department of the Environment), only twenty miles away and started the year before Haddo, is anything to go by, Adam, left to himself, would probably have preferred something much more flamboyant; but his client, by all accounts a much more prudent man than William Duff, kept

in the closest touch throughout the building operations with Sir John Clerk of Penicuik who could always be relied upon to restrain his architectural protégé's inborn vitality and exuberance. The great curved wings to the north and south were treated with similar restraint. The whole composition is little changed except for modifications made in 1880. The front door was brought down from first-floor to ground level, and the double curved stairways, originally grouped together in the centre, were moved out to the ends of the balcony now extended across the whole length of the main block.

This work, and much besides, was done to the order of John Campbell Gordon, seventh Earl of Aberdeen and first Marquess of Aberdeen and Temair. Like the 'Premier earl', he took naturally to high office – Viceroy of Ireland in 1886 and again from 1905 to 1915, Governor-General of Canada 1893-8; unlike him, he developed princely habits when he came into his inheritance. (In these he was not discouraged by his Countess, Ishbel, daughter of Sir Dudley Coutts Marjoribanks, later Lord Tweedmouth; late in life, somewhat reduced in circumstances but not in generosity of spirit, they were revered as 'We Twa'.) The new laird was not content with a new front door. That necessitated the construction of a grand staircase. Then the London firm of Wright and Mansfield was called in to convert the decor of much of the interior to 'Adam

The Drawing Room, Haddo House

revival' – in imitation of Robert, William's brilliant son. The whole first floor on the inner side of the north wing was modified and furnished to accommodate the library. The Chapel, which dates from the same period, was the last work of Sir George Street, and in 1890 the Hall was built on an adjacent site as a working man's club for the estate.

The Chapel and the Hall took on new life in 1945 when June, Marchioness of Aberdeen, and David, fourth Marquess and tenth Earl, founded the Haddo House Choral and Operatic Society. That has given Haddo international repute for concerts, opera and drama. In the last year of his life – he died untimely in 1974 – Lord Aberdeen took steps to put the house and its contents, plus endowment funds, into the care of the Trust. With the consent of his trustees and the participation of the Secretary of State for Scotland the conveyance was made under National Land Fund procedures.

Hill of Tarvit, Fife

2½ miles west of Cupar on A916

Hill of Tarvit is just seventy years old, an unfortunate age for houses as for men; not old enough to be interesting antiques but too old to command much attention in a brave new world. Not that the latter was ever the ambition either of Mr F. B. Sharp, who built the house, or of Sir Robert Lorimer, its architect. Mr Sharp was a connoisseur of considerable taste and discernment, albeit orthodox and conservative, who wanted a house where he could live surrounded by his collection of furniture and pictures, each room providing a harmonious setting for the pieces it was to contain.

Hill of Tarvit: the passage to the dining-room

The result is something which perhaps only the heyday of the Edwardian era could have produced and it surely will not be long before it is valued and appreciated as a near-perfect record and illustration of that way of life which now seems so remote from our own. The very high quality of the contents must always command respect in any setting; the combination of the two gives Hill of Tarvit an interest fast becoming unique.

If the client's requirements led Sir Robert to design a house with less individual architectural panache than other examples of his work, it still remains a lesson in urbane good manners. But the real point of Hill of Tarvit lies in those contents and the way they have been set into the house: the central hall panelled in oak as the background for two fine sixteenth-century Flemish tapestries and, in contrast, the drawing-room light and open as befits the French eighteenth-century furniture by J. C. Saunier, Adam Weisweiler and others. English furniture is concentrated in the dining-room.

The pictures are mostly portraits and still life by such artists as Henry Raeburn, Allan Ramsay, Jacob Cuyp and Bogdani, individually of high quality and together eloquent of the taste prevailing among amateur collectors in the early twentieth century.

The garden front

Just having the public rooms open to visitors would leave much of the house unused, and a happy outcome to this problem has been provided by converting part of the building into a number of self-contained flats and leasing them for residential use. Thus every part of the available accommodation is used to the full in a way which allows the careful arrangement of the public rooms and their contents to remain undisturbed.

Hill of Tarvit stands on the site of an earlier house built in 1696 and perhaps designed by Sir William Bruce. Its more ancient predecessor, however, still stands nearby: Scotstarvit Tower is about a mile to the west across the public road. From its appearance one might take it to be a fortalice from the most turbulent years of the fifteenth century, plain and simple to the point of austerity with an open parapet walk round the wall-head. In fact it was not built until the early

years of the seventeenth century, nearly one hundred years after the Renaissance work at nearby Falkland. It clearly shows how little impact the royal example had on the still vigorous traditions of the vernacular style. Only some of the carved ornament internally shows an awareness of Renaissance motifs. Its builder was Sir John Scott (1585–1670) who was granted these lands in 1611. A man of wide learning, he was largely responsible for the earliest topographical survey of Scotland, and was a minor poet and a patron of scholars. It was at Scotstarvit that he wrote the delightfully uninhibited biographical sketches of his countrymen which were later published under the title of *Scott of Scotstarvit's Staggering State of Scots Statesmen.*

The tower, owned by the Trust, is under the guardianship of the Scottish Development Department (Ancient Monuments).

Scotstarvit Tower

The House of Dun, Tayside

3 miles west of Montrose on A935 to Brechin

The House of Dun remains almost, though not quite, complete as a characteristic example of the work of William Adam, more restrained in ornament than some, but still displaying much of his exuberance. He prepared a design for it in 1723 or shortly before. This failed to get acceptance and before the building work was carried out in 1730 some fairly drastic and fundamental changes had been made to the plans.

His client was David Erskine, a lawyer who had spent some of his earlier years studying in Paris and who then rose in his profession to become one of the Lords of Justiciary in 1713 with the title of Lord Dun. This branch of the Erskine family first became lairds of the lands of Dun in 1375.

The most famous member of the family in the intervening generations was Sir John Erskine, born in 1508 and succeeding to his inheritance at the age of five when his father, grandfather, great-uncle and an uncle were all killed at the Battle of Flodden. He was brought up by another uncle and grew to become a man of considerable learning, early converted to the reformed religion and a staunch supporter and patron of John Knox. None the less he retained the respect of all parties amid the divisions of the time and Mary Queen of Scots herself aptly described him as 'a mild and sweet-tempered man and of true honesty and uprightness'. His learning and his character enabled him to exert a considerable influence on the affairs of his time. He died in 1591, aged eighty-two. Lord

86

Dun, who built the present house, was his great-great-grandson.

The site for the new house, a little way away from the old family tower, provided a slope for terraced gardens leading down towards the upper end of the Montrose Basin. To the attractions of the place today therefore is added the wildlife which gathers on and around this tidal lagoon.

William Adam's first drawings seem to retain something of the character of a traditional Scots tower, decked out in classical dress. It consisted of a tall square block of four principal floors, one on top of another, with a half-sunk basement and an attic in addition. A principal feature of this design was a high arched recess over the main entrance, flanked by Ionic pilasters. This, one of the most notable features of the first design, was retained to the end and still seems to sound an echo from the very similar arches high above the doors at Fyvie and Craigston. For the rest, the later and accepted design greatly modified the plan in which all the principal rooms are concentrated on two main floors and gathered round the great saloon in the centre of the south front. It is this saloon, with its rich stucco ornament on the coved ceiling and trophies over the two fireplaces, which marks the house as the work of William Adam. He is often criticized for the over-elaboration of his decorative embellishments but it is hard to resist the enthusiasm and vitality which they display.

Time has removed some of the ornamental features from the outside, such as stone urns and a length of balustrade from the wall-head, but the house stands today as the prototype of much that was to follow over the next hundred years, to the great enhancement of the countryside. The House of Dun is itself comparatively modest in size; all through the lowlands, so richly developed agriculturally during the eighteenth century, stand medium-sized houses such as this, having a simple rectangular façade with the centre bay slightly advanced in front of the sides and carrying a balustrade or shallow pediment. How perfectly they, like the House of Dun, harmonize with their setting.

Kellie Castle, Fife

3 miles north-north-west of Pittenweem and 11 miles south of St Andrews, off A921, between Leven (11 miles) and Crail (8 miles).

Kellie Castle stands at the heart of the East Neuk of Fife, that peninsula with fields sloping gently down to a coast ringed with an almost continuous line of small burghs, each with its harbour, which James VI called the 'golden fringe on a grey cloth mantle' on account of the prosperity brought in by the trade across the North Sea with the Low Countries and the Baltic ports.

The history of Kellie goes back before these days of prosperity. There was a tower or small castle there in the thirteenth century held by the Siward family who had come to Scotland in the time of Macbeth. In the ensuing century it passed from one family to another, but it was not until the second half of the sixteenth century that the house, which had been owned by the Oliphants since 1360, began to expand beyond the simple tower or keep that still stands at the north-west corner. The first extension was made in 1573, by which time the flourishing trade of the nearby coast towns was well established. In fact it was not strictly an extension since the new buildings took the form of a second completely detached tower some fifty feet to the east of the old one. The year 1573 was also the year in which the laird of Kellie, the fourth Lord Oliphant, married Margaret Hay, daughter of the seventh Earl of Errol.

The gap between the two towers did not remain long un- *Kellie Castle*
filled. With the start of the new century work was in hand
to transform the house from the old characteristic verticality
by the construction between the towers of a new great hall
and a withdrawing or privy dining-room opening directly
off it (much more spacious than anything an old tower house
of Scots tradition could have contained), vaulted cellars below
and a suite of bedrooms on the floor above. Although the
master masons still worked with their inherited skills and
techniques of rubble masonry, steep pitched roof and corbelled
turrets, the wider outlook of local commercial prosperity and
the easy proximity of plentiful supplies of Baltic timber
coming into the Fife ports combined to encourage an expansion of the plan under a much larger area of roof, the first
stage in the transition from the old vertical tower house, such
as Crathes and Craigievar, to the mansions of the seventeenth
and eighteenth centuries.

It seems that with the building work complete there was no
money to spare for fitting up the interior of the new rooms.
Whatever the cause, the castle and estates were sold in 1613.
Then the Civil War intervened, during which the family of
Erskine, now owners and Earls of Kellie, were staunch
Royalists. This in turn led to an enforced absence from home
during the Commonwealth. Thus it was not until after the
Restoration that the plaster-work and panelling for the rooms
built sixty or seventy years before were installed. Two of the
ceilings bear the arms of the third earl and his second wife,

whom he married in 1663. These later ceilings are comparable in style, though generally lighter in character, with those carried out for Sir William Bruce at Holyroodhouse and Thirlestane, and altogether different from the strapwork designs in the south-east tower put up in the Jacobean tradition before the Civil War.

The Earls of Kellie remained supporters of the Stuart dynasty till Culloden put an end to their cause. Again there was a sale (in 1769) which this time separated the house from the landed estates around it, and there followed a long period of neglect. About 1875 the forlorn old house came to the attention of Professor James Lorimer, who conceived the idea of making it a summer home away from the smoke of Edinburgh. By then the buildings had reached the last stage of dereliction before actual ruin set in: leaking roofs, broken windows, choked gutters and chimneys. Just in time, Professor Lorimer, as improving tenant, set about the necessary repairs so that, in spite of the years of neglect, remarkably little was lost. Nothing is more susceptible to the ravages of damp than plasterwork and paint; but in spite of all the coats of arms and the elaborate 'vine' ceiling remained intact. So too did the little imaginary landscapes with which the panelling in the privy dining-room had been decorated when it was first installed in the time of Charles II.

Although there have been at least two occasions since its rescue by Professor Lorimer when the future of the castle has been in doubt, the story has generally been one of revival and rehabilitation; 'restoration' is too strong a word, for

The garden front

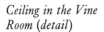

Ceiling in the Vine Room (detail)

hardly any modern replacement of old work has been necessary. The achievement of the Lorimer family at Kellie, first the Professor, and more recently his grandson and granddaughter-in-law in particular, has been that they have brought back vitality to the house and its garden and equipped each with the furnishings and works of art which most happily fit into and complement its setting.

In the year 1663, Sir Philip Anstruther, building a new house at Dreel within a few miles of Kellie, specified that the windows of his hall were to be 'as large and compliet as those of the Hall at Kellie'. From the beginning, Kellie set a pattern to be followed. More recently, through the work of the Professor's youngest son, Sir Robert Lorimer (who was architect of Hill of Tarvit, see p. 84), its influence spread across a much wider range of Scottish buildings. The inspiration of the house where he spent much of his youth can be discerned in many of his designs. It is therefore appropriate that one of the tower rooms should be devoted to a small exhibition of his work and that furniture which he designed is to be found in some of the rooms.

By Kennethmont, 34 miles north-west of Aberdeen and 8 miles south of Huntly on A979, near junction with A97

Leith Hall, Grampian

Accounts by early visitors to Scotland from Froissart to Dr Samuel Johnson are consistently unanimous about one thing, the bleak and barren poverty of the countryside. Yet by the end of the nineteenth century the fame of the expertise and success of Scots agriculture, particularly in Aberdeenshire, was worldwide. The Scots laird was one of the key figures in this change from endemic famine to rural prosperity and the Leiths of Leith Hall were a family of just such lairds. The house which they built and lived in for three centuries, though not particularly distinguished architecturally, vividly evokes the changing patterns and the changing fortunes throughout the years. Starting with a simple rectangular block and courtyard in the vernacular style of seventeenth-century Scotland, each successive addition has filled in another side to a quadrangle in the characteristic taste of its period.

The family of Leith came originally from lands on the eastern outskirts of Edinburgh where their interests lay, at any rate partly, in shipping out of the port from which they took their name. By the middle of the fourteenth century they were established in the same trade with success and considerable influence in the city of Aberdeen. From there,

Leith Hall

The south front

various branches of the family spread north and west, acquiring land as and where they could. Early in the seventeenth century one of them, a certain James Leith of Barns, bought land on the watershed between the valleys of the Deveron and the Don and, in 1649, his son laid thereon the foundations of a new house. It was typical, in a fairly modest way, of many built during the first half of the seventeenth century, a rectangular block of rubble masonry, white harled, nowhere more than one room thick and rising through four floors, with little corbelled turrets at the corners of the roof. It stood on the north side of the enclosing courtyard and today still forms the north wing of the present house.

For a time, apart from the ever-present threat of crop failure and famine, particularly severe in the last decade of the seventeenth century, all went reasonably well. But the eighteenth century was not an easy time for the Leith family, one laird dying as a young man while his heir was yet an infant; that infant in turn murdered at the age of thirty-five and, in the third generation, the laird falling a victim to consumption at the age of nineteen, to be succeeded by his younger brother.

However, the business of the estate went on, largely thanks to two gallant women and the brother of one of them who made over his own lands to help his young nephew, as a result of which his surname of Hay was added to that of Leith. New domestic offices and the first half of a proposed circular stable court were built in 1756. Forty years later a new suite of reception rooms more than doubled the size of the house. By this time the Palladian architecture of the eighteenth century had provided the basis for a new vernacular style and the south front of Leith Hall provides a particularly charming example of this as interpreted in a fairly remote country area. There is the central block with flanking pavilions, still the old simplicity of harled walls with stone dressings round windows and doors, but the importance of the main reception rooms within is now expressed externally by three-light Venetian windows, the pediments of classical tradition above them deprived of all mouldings, but none the less represented by bands of stone set flush with the wall-face.

The still-open west side of the courtyard was filled in in 1868 with a new wing comparable in size with each of the other three but in a manner architecturally somewhat more sophisticated, with an ornamented archway into the hollow centre of the house. But it remains the seventeenth-century north side and the eighteenth-century south elevation which charm the eye and give the house its architectural character.

With the agricultural revolution accomplished by the early part of the nineteenth century, families such as the Leiths, now Leith-Hay, of Leith Hall were free to turn to wider fields: politics, the army and an expanding colonial empire.

The music room

93

They contributed something to each, but it was in the army that they principally distinguished themselves: in particular in the persons of Sir James Leith, Commander of the 5th Division under Wellington in the Peninsular War, and of his great-nephew, Alexander-Sebastian, who stood in the Thin Red Line at Balaclava and who led his regiment, the 93rd Sutherland Highlanders, to the relief of Lucknow.

In the rooms at Leith Hall have been gathered the pictures, the mementoes and the keepsakes from each generation; items connected with Prince Charles Edward Stuart (the Leiths and the Hays were all Jacobites), with the war against the French for the control of North America in the 1750s, with the Peninsular War, the Crimean War and the Indian Mutiny. Along with these are the treasures of glass, porcelain and needlework which tell of the continuing life at home.

It is not a place to seek the striking, the magnificent or the dramatic, but, for that very reason perhaps, it offers the truer representation of family life in a Scottish country house through three centuries when that now almost-forgotten way of life was a vital component in the country's affairs.

II · LESSER HOUSES AND THE URBAN SCENE

with an introduction by Basil Skinner

Introduction

Ordinary house-building in Scotland developed different spectacular qualities at different times. In the eighteenth century there stands out above all else the precise discipline of a classicism that could inform equally the urban street, the church manse or the farming laird's small house. In the century before it was essentially a manner of house arrangement unique to Scotland, a carefully contracted marriage between convenience and security.

Lesser men in seventeenth-century Scotland, whether country lairds or merchant burgesses of the towns, were highly aware of the need for protection. The architectural historians MacGibbon and Ross produced, in *Castellated and Domesticated Architecture of Scotland*, a masterly summation when they wrote of this period, 'Scotland can scarcely be said to have had much experience of the benefits of peace'. In a country that could produce the destruction of the town of Dunkeld in 1689 or the neighbourly fratricide of Glaister of Glack in the Garioch of the 1660s, the minor-estate mansion house was essentially built to withstand casual raids while the town-dweller adopted certain building expedients of his own in order to remain within the overcrowded pale of the town's walls. As this century progressed, however, the dictates of comfortable living tended to overcome the constrictions of defence procedures. James Smith, a leading 'architecteur' of the 1690s, can be found quietly praising one of his own houses (though admittedly he speaks here of a 'great house' rather than a lesser house) with the words, 'There is not a more convenient dwelling-house nor any better built in the whole of North Britain,' and it is this emphasis on *convenience* that distinguishes the best of middle-class building in seventeenth-century Scotland. An earlier owner might have praised his house for its strength, an English contemporary might have looked more for the prestigious expression that would proclaim his rank, but for many Scottish lairds it was the down-to-earth requirement of convenience, 'utility' in a later vocabulary, that mattered.

With a main eye to utilitarian organization certain features of house-building emerged that may strike one today as primarily decorative, or at least appealing through their unexpected quality, but which were in origin functional. The overhanging protrusion of the upper floors of houses as in Provost Ross's house in Aberdeen or the Study at

Culross could produce additional floor space above without exceeding the extent of the feued ground below. The decorative string-course of dressed stone that can meander across the harled face of other buildings, such as Lamb's House in Leith, served the useful, indeed essential, purpose of throwing off from the wall-face down-coursing rainwater from an unguttered roof. Again, windows are thrust through walls at the points and of the sizes functionally required, without any great thought for balance, symmetry or proportion. Almost inadvertently, utility produced attractiveness.

There were, however, certain points in the laird's house where conventionally decoration was lavished for decoration's sake. These included quite obviously the main door-lintel where, as at Stenhouse, the owner could display his initials, sometimes those of his wife, his arms and the date of his building. Urban lintels could also attract improving mottoes of which the Greek inscription at Culross is an unusual translation of the commoner 'Dominus Providebit' often rendered in Scots as 'God's Providence is Our Inheritance'. The gablets of dormer windows at roof-level sustain initials and dates occasionally, as can be seen at Hamilton House, with such finial decorations as thistles, roses, stars or crescents. Also at roof level the skewput, or anchor-stone where the house-gable joins the wall-head, was usually large and solid enough to bear ornamentation, often in the form of rope-work or spiral motifs. In Fife there was clearly a well-founded tradition of placing here house-dates or builder's initials.

Despite these functional considerations, the traditions of an earlier defensive architecture persisted. With the complete acceptance in fifteenth- and sixteenth-century Scotland of the tower house as a highly secure and economical form of dwelling, it was inevitable that the tower should provide the precedent for the lesser laird's seat of later generations. But the tower was never a simple monolith. Delightfully, in the Borders, in Angus and especially in Aberdeenshire, it had wandered in extension into a whole alphabet of ground plans – L-blocks, T-blocks, E- and H-blocks, and above all the splendid terminal ebullience of the Z-block. Of all these possible permutations of the idea of vertical living it was the L-plan that found most general acceptance for its sheer unchallengeable convenience, and this is the model for Stenhouse, Plewlands, Hamilton House – the list could go on. The true and original L-plan house provided its main rooms in the principal block and its more private chambers in the jamb. Occasionally the lesser wing held the stair, but commonly a special stair tower with the main front door was

Hamilton House

placed in the re-entrant angle between the wings. At once protection and surveillance of visitors was easily achieved and a whole range of opportunity for decorative embellishment was opened up. If the stair-tower came to the ground it could be circular or polygonal; if it did not, then it could be supported by a system of corbelling where the full ingenuity of the mason could be lavished. In either case a conical hat could crown this leading feature of the house.

These houses are truly vernacular – though not, of course, the vernacular of the clay-walled, cruck-framed peasantry – in the sense that they were put up without benefit of aesthetic idealism, by local men using local materials and always with a strict eye to the budget. Dressed stone, expensive in labour-cost, was on the whole confined to essential openings and corners; elsewhere rubble was the normal wall material with a protective skin of harling and a decorative wash of colour. Locally made pantiles gave a strong and colourful roof, at least on the east coast, and, inside, room sizes were kept in their floor-beam width to the normal extent of easily obtainable timber. Gladstone's Land carries economy to the extreme in its ingenious re-use in the later stair of timbers from a broken-up ship.

The L-plan of the country laird's house can be found on occasions translated to the burgh scene. Where space allowed – sometimes at the back-end of a burghal lot – a landed family stepping into town or a merchant family of unusual pretension put up an urban echo of the small tower house. More usually, however, the town building was somewhat simpler. Indeed it had to be, for it was necessary to occupy in any Scottish town a very narrow street-frontage and for the house to marry successfully, and physically, with its neighbours. The plain rectangular house was ideal, but even in cases like this the height of the buildings necessitated strong and well-provided access and the inevitable protrusions of stair-towers resulted. By the early seventeenth century, the larger burghs of Scotland, still constricted within their walled perimeters yet expanding in terms of wealth and population, were forced to adopt particular building expedients. Houses, or 'lands', developed upwards in multi-storey blocks and in Edinburgh, where Gladstone's Land stands as a notable example of this, urban towers of seven or eight floors were common, ten or eleven floors possible. What characterizes them is their narrow frontage, their height and the accommodation thus provided for many families in each land. The names of seventeenth-century occupants in Gladstone's Land listed in the relevant entry below goes a certain way to confirming that in at least certain Edinburgh properties the 'democracy of the common stair', the intermixture of different social classes, was a real enough thing.

In their interiors, the lairds' houses and the merchants' houses had much in common. Rooms were small, panelled and dark. Light came from windows, in restoration as seen at Culross, where the glass, expensively obtainable only in small panes, was confined to the fixed upper section while wooden shutters opened in the lower half. Ceilings of the main rooms were painted in strong colours in designs of fruit, flowers or grotesque figures (as at Gladstone's Land) or occasionally and expensively modelled in plaster with Royalist symbols (as at Stenhouse). Walls could be panelled or hung with drapes, although the elaborate tapestries of the great houses were probably beyond the reach of the small lairds, and always paint, painted foliage, painted sculptural arcades, could provide a poor man's alternative to richer hangings or wood-work. The occasional inventories that survive indicate that furniture at this social level was neither plentiful nor elaborate, and indeed remind us of the necessity of reading the seventeenth-century domestic environment against an entirely different convention from our own. In the houses of the lairds or the guildry firm definition of room-use by specialized function could be rare. One wealthy burgess in Edinburgh, dying in the first decade of the eighteenth century, had listed a bed or beds in every room so that around these dominant features he conducted his business, his wife her domestic economy and his eight children their natural lives. Again, as late as the 1740s, an eye-witness recalled of the laird of Castle Dounie that 'his own constant residence and the place where he received company and even dined constantly with them was in just one room only and that the very room where he lodged'. The laird of Frendraught's allocation of rooms in Gladstone's Land was 'a hall, two chambers, a kitchen and a low cellar within the close'.

These points of comparison between the small country houses of the lesser lairds and the grander houses of the burgh merchants are entirely justifiable, for to a great extent the lairdship and the guildry were the same people, and they shared membership too with the echelons of bench and bar. In the seventeenth and eighteenth centuries the same families that peopled the smaller estates had sons at law or sent them to earn a renewed fortune in trade, and mobility of personnel was complete between the landowning, trading and professional groups. A good example may be taken from the family of Hope, with Henry Hope a merchant burgess of Edinburgh in the 1560s, his son Thomas reaching high legal office in the service of James VI, and *his* sons – all judges – establishing the three landowning families of Hope of Craighall, Hope of Kerse and Hope of Hopetoun. The common bond between the three social groups was that of capital. On one side this came from agricultural rents, on another from the perquisites of political or legal office and on the third from the proceeds of brokerage in goods, the 'wild adventures' in foreign trade that were the mainstay of the wealthy merchants.

There was a very marked movement in the late sixteenth and seventeenth centuries from the burghs into the country areas around them. The Ellises at Stenhouse and the Scotts at Malleny were among the middle-class families who appeared as landowners around Edinburgh between 1600 and 1650. Their objectives were probably economic – to diversify their capital investment into agriculture or rural industry; but often over-ambition brought its own catastrophe and a rapid turn-over can be seen in the pattern of late seventeenth-century ownerships. The break-up of the larger estates of the sixteenth century had made these smaller holdings available and provided the new units upon which these families based themselves. This helped to account for the great number of small lairds' houses built at this time, particularly near the major towns. So James Brome, writing of Edinburgh in 1669 in his book *A Historical Account of Three Years' Travel Over England, Scotland and Wales* (1694), says 'Within seven miles round the city there are noble and gentlemans' palaces, castles and strong-builded towers and stone houses, as we are inform'd, above an hundred, and besides the houses of the nobility and gentry within it, here dwell several merchants of great credit and respect.'

Turning now from the individual houses of the smaller lairds to the aspects of the urban scene to which they were accustomed, the obvious and necessary contrast to be drawn is between the vernacular townscape of the seventeenth century and the sophisticated ground plan of the eighteenth. Almost every ancient burgh in Scotland retained and was controlled by its medieval, organic layout – the traditional attributes of high street, market-place, and burghal lots with back-streets developing at their hinder ends. Upon this skeleton individual houses were built, collapsed and reappeared in only lightly controlled array. The virile disorder of the seventeenth-century town is nowhere better seen than in Culross: the line of the street follows one dictated, surely, by habit and repute; the houses march on to it at almost haphazard angles and with many variations in size and arrangement; and the street itself is narrow, cobbled and difficult. For this reason perhaps, the urban quality most admired by the early traveller was not related to the buildings that made up the town but rather to

Cobbles in Culross

the convenience of movement. Thomas Morer, who, in *A Short Account of Scotland* (1715), described a visit to Perth in 1689, speaks of its 'two long spacious streets, besides others of lesser moment, for intercourse, which being well-paved are at all times tolerably clean'. 'The houses,' he goes on later, 'are not stately but after the Scotch way make a good appearance.'

'The Scotch way' as it was to develop is admirably demonstrated on a small scale at Dunkeld. In Cathedral Street order steps in and produces a semblance of a uniform street-frontage really before the classic ideal of uniformity had established its grip upon the sophisticated Scottish mind. The uniformity of Dunkeld is accidental and it is not until the metropolitan developments in Edinburgh, from the 1750s in George Square and from the 1760s in the New Town, that planned controls produce the anonymous restraints that regiment whole blocks and streets. A classical sense of discipline there certainly is, but lurking there also is the dead hand of the monotony of which Ruskin, also in Edinburgh, was much later to complain.

The avoidance of monotony was to depend upon composition – the idea that a block of tidy, ironed-out houses in an urban terrace could be given rhythm by composing the façade as one would the balanced image of a stately home. This is the contribution, the object-lesson, of Robert Adam's north side of Charlotte Square. It is a block of eleven separate houses; its occupants could be assumed to have no common interests beyond the superficial but many separate tastes; yet the autonomy of design is complete and the eleven owners are for ever knit together in a unified, composite whole. Never had this been seen in Scotland before, but its influence was immediate and widespread.

The mechanics of the thing are obvious. The central house has the benefit of strong emphasis in its colonnaded pediment; the wings protrude and have the dignity of garlands and roof-top sphinxes, and the intervening houses just run along in exquisite good taste, pulled together by these dominant features. Yet the whole composition is extremely subtle in its reconciliation between vertical demands and horizontal necessity. Eleven houses built together must imply a strong horizontal. This Adam accepts and allows to speak in the ordered lines of main floor, first floor and second floor windows – all dressed upon their marker from the right. Monotony he avoids by the protrusions and recessions of his emphatic features, rhythmically flowing along the façade. Yet each house itself is a vertical unit, basement and four upper levels of domestic accommodation, and each level is varied in the nature of its stonework and the dignity of its openings according to aesthetic and room-use considerations. So, like a layered confection, the servants' workrooms lie in the sunk basement with rusticated masonry, the ground floor reception rooms are just above pavement level with expensively chanelled ashlar to give pomp and visual weight and with windows recessed to underline their quality; and on the first floor the masonry is smooth-dressed for lightness and the windows are large to allow the master bedrooms a pleasant outlook. On the second floor social differentiation is achieved by the sort of smaller windows that suit night-nurseries and unmarried daughters. This compact between good taste and social gesticulation could only have been achieved in the later eighteenth century.

But what happened to the small lairds in this *settecento* Scotland? Many of them, firmly rooted in their vernacular L-plans, just went on. Some added little classically proportioned wings to their houses like the two Regency rooms at Malleny; others – like Archibald Shiells at Inveresk Manor in 1748 – built classical houses *ab initio*. It is worth remembering that Newliston, designed by Robert Adam, in his very last years, was commissioned by a merchant in Edinburgh, Thomas Hog, and represents just the same middle-class movement into the near-urban countryside that we have been watching in the case of Stenhouse or Hamilton House. Newliston, in the last analysis, is just a small piece of Charlotte Square put down in a West Lothian field.

Charlotte Square, Edinburgh

One nice reprise can be seen in the nineteenth century. For one reason or another, but mostly because Sir Walter Scott inspired the idea, the judges of the 1830s emulated their seventeenth-century predecessors. Lord Jeffrey and Lord Cockburn, like Scott, had ambitions to play the country laird, but the houses they built were not the civilized, classically balanced buildings that might have reflected their enlightened, balanced minds. Instead, they were vernacular towers – Craigcrook, Bonaly, like Abbotsford – that immediately look back to the vernacular of Lord Magdalens or Lord Clerkington. The clock of taste had moved full circle.

Lesser Houses and the Urban Scene

Church Street

One could scarcely find a more typical laird's house of the
sixteenth to seventeenth centuries than Abertarff. Its plan, a
single rectangular house-block with protruded stair-tower,
is almost mandatory for its period; its harled walls, crow-
stepped gables and irregular fenestration all speak of its
origins. Above all, the unexpected expansion of a circular
stair-tower to a square upper storey is a gimmick as Scottish
as it is decorative, even if inspired by the functional necessity
of acquiring more floor-space upstairs. Given a small allow-
ance for individual taste, Abertarff and the Study at Culross
come from the same stable and together are paralleled – to
take but one example from farther south – by Darnick Tower
at Melrose. The style and manner are all-pervasively national –
simply, indeed, the way that ordinary builders built.

The precise date of Abertarff hangs upon one's interpretation of the surviving date-stone – 1593 or 1597. At one period
in its history it belonged to the family of Fraser of Lovat,
notorious in an earlier generation for participating in the
revolution of 1745. The house and garden were presented to
the National Trust for Scotland in 1963 by the National
Commercial Bank and were subsequently restored, gaining a
Civic Trust award. In conformity with its policy elsewhere,
the Trust has let the premises for practical use by An Comunn
Gaidhealach, who could well be described as the British
Council of Gaeldom and who organize from here the annual
National Mod; and it is open to the public.

*Abertarff House,
Inverness*

The three houses which form the centre part of the north side of Charlotte Square have been in full ownership of the National Trust for Scotland since 1966, although No. 5 has been its headquarters since 1949. They were restored to their original external appearance in the 1920s through the interest of the fourth Marquess of Bute, and they passed to the Trust upon the death of the fifth Marquess. Together they constitute the main emphatic feature of what has been with justice described as the most triumphant of Robert Adam's urban designs.

Charlotte Square closes the west end of James Craig's Georgian New Town, planned in 1767 but not built until the years from 1792 to 1820. Robert Adam undertook the commission to design the square in 1791, the year before his death, and it was completed under the supervision of Robert Reid and others. In practice, it was left to individual builders or prospective owners to erect houses along the square according to their own initiatives but strictly conforming to the master plan and the overall elevation laid down for each side. Even for those days, the cost of building cannot have been low.

A characteristic provision comprised a parlour, dining-room and library on the ground floor, a drawing-room and two bedrooms on the first floor, and four other bedrooms on

*Charlotte Square:
the north block*

the second floor. An attic gave lesser bedrooms and a basement provided kitchen, store-rooms and domestic offices, the whole totalling about eighteen rooms. There is a considerable advance here in social planning compared with the days of the first New Town houses where domestic offices were frequently provided in a detached block at the end of the garden, as at Adam's No. 8 Queen Street. In Charlotte Square there are no attendant buildings, not even coach houses or stables – a curious anomaly considering the status of the occupiers. The average family in the square consisted of three to seven members, and a normal complement of servants seems to have been eight or nine, although Alexander Campbell of Cammo, living in No. 6 from 1844 to 1889, had only four.

No. 5 Charlotte Square, the headquarters of the Trust, has one or two fine rooms, notably the first-floor drawing-room which has a splendidly enriched ceiling. The house was put up by a builder, Thomas Russell, in 1796 and sold immediately to the Grants of Rothiemurchus. It has the distinction, therefore, of being the birthplace in the following year of that Elizabeth Grant who wrote so delightfully *The Memoirs of a Highland Lady*. After the Grants' time, that is from 1802, the house passed through the hands of a number of landed families – the Abercrombys of Tullibody, the Ladies Erskine, the Fergussons of Kilkerran, serving each as a town house and eventually in 1903 coming into possession of the fourth Marquess of Bute.

No. 6, next door, is the official residence of the Secretary of State for Scotland and is not open to the public. It is the centre point of the north side – one might say, indeed, of the whole square – and its interiors are among the finest. The house was erected by 1797 by Orlando and Macduff Hart, members of a family of Edinburgh shoemakers who were here apparently indulging in a speculation in building. For ten years from 1806 it was the home of Sir John Sinclair of Ulbster, the agriculturalist whose portrait by Raeburn in the uniform of the Caithness Fencibles is a notable adornment of the National Gallery of Scotland's collection. Curiously, from 1825 to 1844 No. 6 served as a hotel run by one Charles Oman; he extended also into an 'annex' at No. 4. Later, for twenty-nine years from 1889, it was owned by Sir Mitchell Mitchell-Thomson of Polmood, in his time Lord Provost of Edinburgh.

No. 7 provides in its upper floors a residence for the Moderator of the General Assembly of the Church of Scotland and in the rest of the building the Georgian House rearranged and furnished in 1974–75 by the National Trust for Scotland to provide a complete, and unique, example of a living environ-

The kitchen of the 'Georgian House', No. 7 Charlotte Square

ment of the reign of George III. The builder of No. 7, working in the two years following 1796, was Edward Butterworth, described as a 'writing-master', who had been a speculator in several New Town houses. Members of the family of Farquharson of Invercauld held the property from 1816 to 1845, and from that year until 1889 it was owned by Lord Neaves, a distinguished member of the Scottish bar, and by his trustees. The ground floor of No. 7 has a stone-flagged entrance hall and inner hall with the dining-room of the house (showing a fire-grate of Adam design) to one side; the room to the back has been furnished as a bedroom. Below these apartments in the basement the kitchen has been completely re-equipped, and its range and bread-oven are accompanied by a complete *batterie de cuisine* brought from Forglen House. The main rooms are upon the first floor, with the drawing-room to the front and a library to the back; both rooms have carved chimney-pieces, the former a particularly fine example.

The restoration and opening of No. 7 Charlotte Square is the most significant contribution of the National Trust for Scotland to the architectural understanding of New Town, Edinburgh. It represents a major achievement by the Trust's staff, by a great many private donors and by many others who have lent furniture to the furnishing of this important house.

The Palace, Culross, Fife

12 miles west of Forth Road Bridge off A985

The complex of buildings that makes up the so-called Palace at Culross, standing within a walled court at the Sandhaven and so originally at the sea-edge, is the finest expression of a Scottish laird's town house of the period that one could wish to find. The name 'Palace' was attached to it in the nineteenth century through a misunderstanding of the ancient legal term 'pallatium', best translated into Scots as 'great lodging'; its more ancient and appropriate name was 'the Colonels' Close'.

Of the two free-standing blocks, the larger is the earlier, commenced as the date-stone attests in 1597 by Sir George Bruce of Carnock. Coming of a landed family of long standing in Fife and Clackmannan, George Bruce was the first to show industrial enterprise and was responsible indeed for developing the most extensive coal-mines and salt-pans that existed at that time upon the Forth; one mine ran out under the sea. Bruce died in 1625, and his effigy, with those of his wife and eight of his children, can be seen in the important monument in the abbey church of Culross. During his lifetime Bruce built out upon his original house, adding rooms in E-plan to the south and the separate block with byre and stables to the

north-east in 1611, and a kitchen wing to the north. The whole *The Palace, Culross*
property was occupied by Bruce's grandson and great-grand-
son, the first and second Earls of Kincardine, but about 1700
it passed by judicial sale to Colonel John Erskine of Carnock,
popularly called 'the Black Colonel'. He was an occasionally
philanthropic and normally vitriolic elder of the local church
and seems to have shared his 'great lodging' with another
Colonel John Erskine, differentiated as 'the White'. Hence
the name of 'Colonels' Close'.

The buildings today have many points of great interest.
Externally the ornamented gablets of the dormer windows and
the half-shuttering throughout (as restored) are typical of their
period, as also is the concentration of living quarters upon the
first floors with access by a stairway external to the earlier
building, internal to that of 1611. The former gives access
immediately into the long gallery, the sort of Scottish reflection, as at Craigievar or Pinkie, of one of the main features of a
great house of Tudor England. At the south end of this gallery
a room with painted woodwork may have been a bedroom. At
the other, a business room opens through an iron door into
Bruce's private counting-house – a stone-vaulted, fireproof,

Woodwork and painted wall-decoration for a thrifty laird

burglar-proof strongroom, with additional safes sunk into the walls among shelf-fixtures yet with a good window and a fire-place for comfort. The second floor has one of the most important painted ceilings in Scotland, with allegorical figures, Latin mottoes and improving thoughts in translation, all this again recalling the painted gallery at Pinkie. Thus we can read, 'Mens pleasures fond do promeis only joyes / Bot he that yeldes at lengthe him self destroyes'; the accompanying figure is a Sirene.

Beneath all this the kitchen wing protrudes towards the terraced garden in a separation of function characteristic for the sixteenth and seventeenth centuries. Wine and victuals must certainly be stored beneath the master's rooms and under his direct control, but cooking and baking are detached for security to an outbuilt range. To the great fireplace there was run in a sophisticated arrangement for ducted water.

Finally the 1611 block presents, upstairs, four more rooms in which painted wall-decoration survives. In one, the east wall was covered with a design of the Judgment of Solomon, which must have afforded to Sir George Bruce the same visual pleasure as a tapestry but at a fraction of the cost. In another, the walls are covered with geometric designs and elsewhere one can see where the paintings stopped to allow for hanging-drapes on the lower wall surface. The stable and the byre located immediately below the wooden floors of these rooms must have promoted their overall warmth.

Culross Palace is under the guardianship of the Scottish Development Department (Ancient Monuments).

In the Lawnmarket, Royal Mile

It could hardly be challenged that Gladstone's Land as restored by Sir Frank Mears and Robert Hurd following the Trust's acquisition of the property in 1934 is the most important example of seventeenth-century high-tenement housing to survive in Edinburgh. Facing the Lawnmarket, its site and the extent of the accommodation that it offered clearly mark its prestige in terms of mercantile dignity. At the same time the anciently determined width of the lot upon which the house was built implied the possibility of extension only in depth or upwards.

The Thomas Gladstone who owned the property for about fourteen years and altered it architecturally to such an extent that it bore his name ever after was an ambitious but undistinguished merchant from Kirkcudbright. His move to Edinburgh, with status of burgess from 1610, may have been due to a desire to extend his shipping and trading interests from the Solway to the North Sea. In 1617 he purchased this site in the Lawnmarket from the family of Fisher, whose name survives, incidentally, across the street (but in a later context) at Fisher's Land.

Gladstone's Land

The house that Gladstone bought was set back from the street, possibly by a courtyard, at a distance of some sixteen feet. Inside the present building – for example, at the arcade-painted wall on the first floor – the old street-front can be detected in the centre of the newer house. It was an L-plan building of late sixteenth-century date, with a circular stair at the back and wooden cantilevered balconies at the front, reached through the archways in the music room wall. Gladstone's contribution was to build the entire fore-part of the present building, one room and a staircase deep, carrying it over an open pavement arcade, and probably to heighten the whole edifice. The west main gable bears his initials and those of his wife, Bessie Cunningham. Internally, economy was matched with a display of fashionable taste: on the one hand refurbished curved timbers, possibly from a demolished ship, have been used in the stair framing, while on the other the wooden beam-and-board ceilings of first, second and third floors all show the painted designs of fruit and flowers (and the date 1620) that characterize interior decoration of the period.

The extent of Thomas Gladstone's occupation in the build-ing was, as was common, limited to one floor; and it was unusual in that it was a lower floor. In his time his tenants on other levels were the Rev. William Struthers, another mer-chant called John Riddoch, James Nicolson, gild officer, and Sir James Crichton of Frendraught in Aberdeenshire. Each had an average of two or three good rooms and a cellar, but the minister did best with four. Further subdivision followed in the next three centuries, although the distinction of the eighteenth-century panelled room on the first floor seems to imply that that level at least remained in sophisticated occupa-tion. Under threat of demolition in 1934, Gladstone's Land was saved by Miss Helen Harrison who bought it and con-veyed it to the National Trust for Scotland. On termination of a lease to the Saltire Society, effect was given to a resolution that the building, furnished with re-creations of seventeenth-century shop stalls at the entrance behind the arcade, should serve the same purpose in the Old Town as the 'Georgian House' in Charlotte Square.

Hamilton House, Prestonpans, Lothian

$8\frac{1}{2}$ miles east of Edinburgh off A198

A group of lairds' houses at the west end of Preston village in East Lothian provides an object lesson in change of taste and needs. Preston Tower itself represents the older, fully

fortified ideal, a strong and defensible dwelling with small acknowledgment of the requirements of comfort. Northfield, 300 yards away, is a four-floor house of 1611 which has resulted from a happy marriage between strength and convenience. Hamilton House of 1628, situated between the two, ignores defence; it is a building of only two floors that provides a remarkably extensive ground-plan and an example of a small laird's house on most comfortable standards.

The earlier name of the house and its land was 'Magdalens' and from this its builder Sir John Hamilton, brother of the first Earl of Haddington, took his judicial title, Lord Magdalens. One of his colleagues on the bench wrote of him as 'a good man but void of learning'. He married Katherine Sinclair, a sister-in-law of his neighbour Joseph Marjoribanks of Northfield, and their initials, IH KS, appear on the dormer pediments. On the lintel of an upper window appears the motto 'Praised Be The Lord My Strenth and My Redeimer'.

Hamilton House: Lord Magdalens's front door

The highly ornamental character of the house and the treatment of its detail has provoked the supposition that it may be the work of William Wallace, King's Master Mason. Despite its much smaller scale there are certainly points of comparison between Hamilton House and Pinkie or Winton, Wallace's greater houses in the vicinity, and its builder marched in the same social rank as Wallace's other patrons. Wallace himself lived for a time in Musselburgh.

A curious passage occurred in the later history of the building when in 1814 it did duty as a barracks for coastal defence troops. When the National Trust for Scotland bought it in 1937 it was much run down. It has since been restored for private occupation, and is not open to the public.

Inveresk Lodge, Musselburgh, Lothian

In Inveresk village on A6124, off A1

The village of Inveresk constitutes a very remarkable example of eighteenth-century villa development. At this point, only five miles from Edinburgh and ideally situated on the east bank of the Esk, a group of small residential properties was established which had no other purpose than the provision of pleasant living for their owners. In the case of most of these houses the original builders were professional men or wealthy merchants from Edinburgh, for example, Bailie James Rhynd, who built Halkerston House, and Archibald Shiells, builder of Inveresk Manor House.

Inveresk Lodge

At least seven of these sophisticated villas were built at Inveresk in the eighteenth century, but they were antedated by three older houses – Halkerston, just mentioned, which was put up between 1637 and 1642; Inveresk House, the original mansion of the neighbourhood, built about 1597; and Inveresk Lodge, built between 1683 and 1700. The Lodge is a quiet, unpretentious house of L-plan formation, a later equivalent perhaps of Hamilton House (see p. 98). Its interior decoration is of a slightly later date than its fabric, with plaster-work of about 1704 and panelling of the middle of the eighteenth century. Also at a later time a wing was extended from the original structure.

Its earliest occupant was Sir Richard Colt, solicitor-general in the reign of Charles II. Thereafter it passed through various families, including the Wedderburns of Blackness and the Skirvings from East Lothian; Archibald Skirving, the famous portrait-painter, died here in 1819. The house and garden were presented to the Trust in 1959 by Mrs Helen E. Brunton. The house is leased for private occupation, but the garden is open to visitors.

In Water Street

Lamb's House, Leith, Edinburgh

The nineteenth-century writer who described Lamb's House as constructed with 'every variety of convenient aberration from the perpendicular or the horizontal which the taste or whim of its constructor could devise' identified precisely the source of interest of this building. At root it is a straight-forward rectangular block of four storeys but the inequalities of its chimney-stacks and the unexpected illogicalities of its corbelled stair-tower give it the air of a tower-house of complicated plan and make it a spectacular example of the Scottish vernacular architecture of its time.

Quite what that time is has indeed been questioned. The house has been given stylistically to the early seventeenth century, and it may well have been the house where Andrew Lamb lived and where he died in 1634, having been successively Bishop of Brechin and of Galloway and minister of South Leith. Corroboration may be drawn from the lineal connection between him and the Dr Cheyne and Colonel Cheyne, father and son, who lived here between 1800 and 1822. What is not correct, however, is the tradition that relates the present structure to the 'Andrew Lamb's House' where Mary Queen of Scots 'remainit be the space of ane hour' on August 19th, 1561, having just come ashore at the harbour. This Lamb may have been related to the bishop.

Lamb's House

The house was built as a tenement of flats with a common stair. The best features, internally, are the two ogival-headed 'sinks' set into the wall of this stair for the outpouring of household slops which would spill down an enclosed chute to a drain hole at the foot of the building. This seems to have been a remarkably sophisticated, even unique, expedient for its time. In the eighteenth century the main rooms were remodelled; but the house, and a warehouse which occupied its lower floor, had become ruinous by 1938 when it was purchased by the fourth Marquess of Bute. After renovation it was presented to the Trust by his son, Lord David Stuart, in 1958, and now serves as an old people's day centre.

Malleny House, Lothian

In Balerno, near Edinburgh, off A70 on Balerno Road

The proprietors of Malleny from 1647 to 1882 (that is, through seven generations) were the Scotts – a family of landowners in Ayrshire in the fifteenth and sixteenth centuries who moved into the Edinburgh legal profession in the seventeenth. William Scott, purchaser of Malleny, was the second of his family to practise advocacy in Parliament House and rose to the bench with the title of Lord Clerkington, taken from part of his estates. The family's policy of territorial aggrandizement, which led them to acquire Clerkington, Lymphoy, Currie, Harperrig, Buteland and Malleny lands, all on the rising moorland south-west of Edinburgh and not more than an hour's journey from the law-courts, was a story typical of the seventeenth-century professional class. What was rather more unusual was the length of their successful occupancy, at least of Malleny, standing in contrast to the over-optimistic speculation of many land-purchasers of the period. When the property came to the National Trust for Scotland in 1968, their descendant Mr Wrey Gardner gave to the house, to hang there in perpetuity, a group of portraits of the Scott lairds which includes John Scott by Alexander Nasmyth. This John Scott added on the later, Regency, wing to the house, which comprises two elegantly proportioned reception rooms and a hall, and shows an excellent fireplace.

The original building of Malleny antedates the Scott owner-ship. It is hardly to be supposed that the date-stone, 1589, contained within the house today can refer to much of the present fabric, but it is entirely likely that the plain, rectangular older part, of good lines broken only by a small projecting stair to the rear, was built by Sir Thomas Murray of Kilbaber-ton soon after he acquired the estate from the Hamiltons of Kilbrackmont in 1634. Murray was King's Architect in Scot-land to Charles I and had already put up in 1626 his house at Baberton, Juniper Green, which still survives. The handsome doocot and probably the original garden enclosure also go back   *Malleny House*

to the seventeenth century, although the 'Twelve Apostles' yew trees are now reduced to four. Seasonally the place is enlivened by the presence of children from primary schools in Edinburgh, intent on learning about country things. Guided by staff from the Trust's Gardening Advice Centre, they plant and sow early in the summer term and return in the autumn to harvest the fruits of their labours.

First ventures by young 'Scotch gardeners'

Among the later owners of Malleny were the Earls of Rosebery (possessing the property from 1882 to 1955), Lord Geddes (1955–60) and Commander and Mrs Gore-Browne-Henderson (1960–68). These last gave the house and garden to the Trust. In 1882 and for some years after the actual occupiers of Malleny were Sir Thomas and Lady Gibson-Carmichael, and the wrought-iron garden gate is a relic of their time. Sir Thomas was a keen executant of metal-work of this sort and other examples of his work, formerly at Malleny, can now be seen at the family house in Skirling, Peeblesshire.

The older part of Malleny House is now the home of the curator of the National Trust for Scotland. The newer part has been furnished in keeping with its period and provides a display for visitors.

Shiprow, off Castlegate

The 'Ship Raw' where Provost Ross's House stands is a survival from medieval Aberdeen – one of the winding streets that led up to the Castlegate from the quays. A charter of 1441 uses the name, referring to 'the land lying in the Ship-raw', and it was clearly the sort of situation to attract the houses of the wealthier merchants – one eye to the sea, the other to the landward trade. In October 1669 a major fire destroyed the houses at the top of the street and later urban improvements have caused more recent demolitions, but Provost Ross's House has survived both.

The house was built in or about 1594 for Alexander Farquhar, possibly at the hand of Andrew Jamieson, master mason. Subsequent owners can be identified as members of local families with interest both in trade and in landed estates – Andrew Skene, James Sinclair of Seba, James Nicolson of

Provost Ross's House

119

Tarbrown and others. In 1702 it became the property of John Ross, whose name it has borne ever since. Ross was in succession merchant, provost of the burgh and proprietor of the lands of Arnage, which he bought in the same year that he moved into the Shiprow.

In its interior arrangement the house retains some of its original features. The old kitchen survives on the ground floor and this and the adjoining apartment show beam-and-board ceilings. On the first floor and second floor the fireplaces are ancient but the panelling has been replaced in sympathetic evocation of the original.

Aberdeen does not boast many buildings of this period other than the ecclesiastical, but Provost Ross's House and Provost Skene's House (the property of the city) are the oldest and the best. Provost Ross's House was reopened in its present state in 1954, having been acquired by the National Trust for Scotland and restored with the financial support of the City of Aberdeen. It accommodates the maritime museum of the City of Aberdeen District Council.

Sailor's Walk, Kirkcaldy, Fife

In High Street

The building which is today called Sailor's Walk faces directly across the street to the old harbour of Kirkcaldy. It is a fine seventeenth-century block, once divided into four dwellings – the East House, the High House, the Garret and the Laigh House. In 1771 Robert Oliphant, one of an old Kirkcaldy family, acquired one of these properties and gradually extended his ownership over the whole block – for which reason its name was for a long time 'Oliphant's Land'.

Externally Sailor's Walk presents some of the most attractive features of Scottish vernacular building: total and appealing irregularity of design, dormer windows and a harled wall-surface. A spiral stair, increasingly steep as it rises, gives access to the west end of the building, now restored as offices for the architectural firm that undertook the reconstruction. To the east a bookshop occupies the ground floor and the offices of H.M. Customs and Excise the upper. Within the ground-floor bookshop can be seen a fine old fireplace with plaster panels exhibiting flowers and fleurs-de-lis above it; the ceiling is supported by massive beams clearly supplied by those accustomed to handling ship's timbers.

Upstairs, a small room at the back is finely panelled, perhaps from the date of Robert Oliphant's occupation, but the most important apartment is the public office of the Customs. This room has a beam-and-board ceiling with contemporary

Sailor's Walk

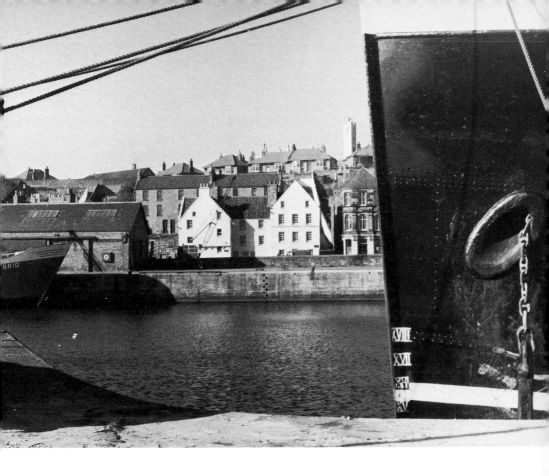

painting of a quality as impressive as the examples at Culross. The boards are treated in the usual pattern of foliage. The beams bear upon each of their sides long and elaborate quotations from the Old Testament providing a whole course of moral instruction. The second beam from the window, overlooking the harbour, has 'They that go down to the sea in ships They do business in great waters' while, with even greater appropriateness for the room's present use, its neighbour reads 'I will pay my dows [dues] unto the Lord now in the presence of all his people'. A third quotation nearer to the door is the prayer 'Deliver my soul, O Lord, from Lying Lips and a Deceitful Tongue'.

This work was revealed beneath a later plaster ceiling, now removed. Traces of its seventeenth-century appearance survive in a small section of frieze and in the notable royal arms of Charles II on the wall. The fireplace lintel bears a late inscription in which the date 1676 and the initials BW, possibly relating to one time occupation by the Whyte family, can be detected.

'They do business in great waters'

The Sailor's Walk was saved by public action in 1935 and restored by the National Trust for Scotland in 1950, gaining a Civic Trust award.

Stenhouse Mansion, Edinburgh

Gorgie Road

'Went out by Gorgie Mills, then by Saughton Hall, then by Bell's Milne to Stanipmilne Eleis.' In these words Lauder of Fountainhall recorded in his journal of 1668 a four-mile expedition west of the Old Town of Edinburgh that brought him to Stenhouse on the Water of Leith. The former name of this building, Stanhopemilne, recalls not only its earlier role as one of the many mill-houses on the river but also the identity of its eponymous owners, the family of Stanhope who in 1511 obtained from the Abbot of Holyrood a 110-year tack of the property. It is clearly to this family's occupancy in the sixteenth century that the older (north) wing of the house goes back, a simple, rectangular, stone-vaulted block rather lower than its present height and with provision at the lowest level, as can be seen today, for hen-boxes and a baking-oven.

Stenhouse Mansion

This block was heightened, extended to the south, and facilitated by a new stair-tower in 1623 by Patrick Ellis soon after he acquired the lands. His initials and arms with the date and the characteristic motto 'Blissit Be God For Al His Giftis' appear over the door. Patrick Ellis, merchant-burgess and treasurer of the town of Edinburgh, was a member of a family who at this time owned other peripheral estates at Elliston, Plewlands, Mortonhall and Southside, and himself entertained sufficient dynastic ambitions to marry in succession into the Inglis of Cramond and Seton of Parbroath families. In other words, Stenhouse as a home represents the ideal of a seventeenth-century merchant-laird on the ladder of self-advancement.

The building remained with the Ellis family through three generations until 1684. It was therefore their taste or sense of political expediency that produced the plaster ceiling decorated with post-Restoration Royalist symbols which forms one of a series identifiable in various other houses besides Stenhouse round Edinburgh.

A much-damaged Stenhouse came to the Trust in 1937, and repairs began. The war years brought renewed deterioration, but by 1965 the building had been totally refurbished to serve its present purpose as a restoration centre for painted ceilings, paintings generally and ornamental stonework — mostly the decorative artefacts of the period to which the building itself belongs. Operated initially by the Trust, the restoration centre is leased to the Scottish Development Department (Ancient Monuments) (see p. 39).

Treatment of tempera painting in the Restoration Centre

III · GARDENS

with an introduction by J. F. A. Gibson

Introduction

It is probable that a bigger range of plants from the temperate zones can be grown in Great Britain, particularly on the west coast, than anywhere else in the world. This may seem surprising when one considers that the country covers the same sort of latitudinal bracket as Labrador. The explanation is the encouraging effect of the Atlantic Drift, which keeps the west mild and damp and only on rare occasions brings with it the tail-ends of Caribbean hurricanes. However, despite the fact that we are thus spared the extremes of Continental conditions, climates in Scotland differ widely.

The middle country – the Clyde, Forth and Tay basins and Strathmore, the great central valley running from south-west to north-east parallel with the Grampians – does not share the beneficent Atlantic influence. Neither does it suffer to the same degree the withering south-east winds that afflict the eastern coastal levels. But weatherwise all is not loss for gardeners in any of these regions. Many of the smaller high altitude plants, such as the gentians, the temperamental primulas, paraquilegias, cassiopes and meconopses, do better at Keillour and Ascreavie and even as far to the east as Branklyn than they do in west coast gardens. They are plants which in the wild are under snow for many months, and they like a definite winter rather than relentless wet.

In the west, with its high rainfall and relatively mild winters, one expects, and finds, ideal conditions for growing a very diverse range of trees and shrubs from what may be loosely called the Himalayan area (which includes much of Burma and south-western China as well as Sikkim, Bhutan, Nepal and the non-arid parts of Tibet) and from New Zealand and Chile. Gardeners owe a great deal to the French missionaries of the nineteenth century and to individuals such as Wilson, Forrest, Rock, Kingdon-Ward, Farrer, Ludlow and Sherriff, who explored the difficult Himalayan countries and introduced many hundreds of plants from them. Perhaps they owe most to the younger Hooker, who showed by his journeys in Sikkim in the late 1840s that it could be done. Some of the original plants from seed collected by him survive in west coast gardens, though apparently not in any of the Trust gardens. Probably rhododendron species are the predominant plants, but there are many other good things. There are notable collections, for example, at Logan and Lochinch in Wigtownshire, at Crarae, Ardkinglas, Stonefield (which has the biggest group of Hooker originals, including some enormous

The main avenue,
Achamore House,
Gigha

plants of *Rhododendron arboreum*) and Arduaine in mainland Argyll, on the Argyllshire islands of Gigha and Colonsay, and at Glenarn in Dunbartonshire.

The Trust first took to gardening as a contingent obligation, a necessary part of the management of a great estate, when it accepted Culzean Castle in 1945. Three more large gardens came as a component part of a larger property – Crathes Castle in 1951, the Royal Palace of Falkland in 1952 and Brodick Castle in 1958. To these have been added three gardens of outstanding importance unattached to great houses, Inverewe and Pitmedden in 1952 and Branklyn, in a suburb of Perth, in 1967.

The total number is not large now, but it includes representatives of most types of garden and from these one can learn a great deal about the progress of gardening in Scotland and the thought-processes of the practitioners, past and present. Pitmedden, a Scots variation on Le Nôtre formality, has entered upon its fourth century. Culzean exemplifies the Grand Manner in contrast to the large-scale informality of Brodick and Inverewe. The splendid design at Falkland complements aptly the architecture of the Palace. From modest beginnings in about 1923 Branklyn, a small treasure, has assembled a remarkable collection of plants from nearly all the temperate parts of the world.

In general, Scotland has been as susceptible as England to changing vogues and styles. The Trust is fortunate in that it has inherited none of the worst results. It used to be fashionable to have the garden half a mile or so from the house. In some cases there may have been good architectural reason for this. (At Culzean the late-eighteenth-century walled garden, a monument to the Kennedys' first venture in practical horticulture, with flowers and vegetables as well as fruit, is a good quarter of a mile from the castle, but the Fountain Court garden is immediately adjoining its landward side.) All too frequently the garden, when one got to it, was merely a kail-yard. It might well be regarded as another tribute to the enduring influence of John Knox that gardens, other than those growing edibles, were regarded as unworthy frivolities. Luckily some enlightened lairds broke away from this gloomy concept. At Crathes, the castle by itself is a gem; the garden (which is of a much later date) is one of the finest anywhere, and it comes right up to the castle walls, harmonizing most beautifully.

Of the gardens which are not attached to great houses, Inverewe was offered to the Trust by Mrs Mairi Sawyer, the daughter of Osgood Mackenzie who began to make the garden in 1865. She presented it with an endowment, which was supplemented by well-wishers, in particular the Pilgrim Trust. Branklyn was willed to the Trust by the late John Renton with an endowment which, by itself, would not have enabled the Trust to accept, despite the generosity of the offer. An appeal was made and sufficient support was forthcoming to justify acceptance. A practical contribution by the City of Perth was decisive; without it the Trust would have been unlikely to take over.

The Pitmedden proposition differed in every way. There, in the sparse and bumpy plain of Formartine, north of Aberdeen, was a superb walled garden, full of potatoes *et al* at the appropriate time of year, with two entrancing pavilions at the north-west and south-west corners. (Other Trust gardens went through patriotic wartime potato phases, including the garden at Falkland, which, contrary to its appearance of maturity, was all planned and planted in its present form after the Second World War.) The original house at Pitmedden had been burned out many years previously and replaced by a comely building of no great pretensions. The property was given to the Trust, with a very handsome endowment, by the late Major James Keith of

Rhododendrons at Inverewe

Pitmedden, C.B.E. The walled garden, known as the Great Garden of Pitmedden, dates from about 1675, and the generosity of the endowment enabled the Trust to re-create the garden in its original style. This could not have been done without the scholarly researches of the late Dr James Richardson, formerly H.M. Inspector of Ancient Monuments in Scotland, who investigated such early records of the garden as could be found and also examined designs recorded as having been used in the garden of the Palace of Holyroodhouse at about the same date. It is not an exact copy of the original: the plants used are different (those of the seventeenth century would look pretty dull compared with the same plants after three centuries of improvement and the discovery and introduction of hordes of others); and there are first rate herbaceous borders round the inside of the perimeter walls. But one likes to think that it is now much as it would have been had it evolved over those three hundred years. (There were probably other potato interludes in its long history; such interludes have their uses in giving one a chance to get the ground clear of weeds.) Another garden in much the same style as Pitmedden, although of a more elaborate architectural order, is that at Edzell Castle in Angus, an old stronghold of the Lindsays, which is in the care of the Scottish Development Department (Ancient Monuments).

In gardening as in other matters the Trust is empirical and accommodating. One can perhaps best illustrate this by reference to Threave, Gigha and Ben Lawers.

Threave, in the Stewartry of Kirkcudbright, is a fine agricultural property with the additional advantage of having some of the best duck and goose wintering-grounds along the river Dee (a river so hydro–electrocuted that it hardly knows which way it is going – but the geese do not mind). The house is a solidly built edifice of the Victorian era. *Aere perennius*. The donor fully realized that, even with a substantial endowment, neither the house nor the garden had sufficient merit to meet the criteria which the Trust is accustomed to apply, so he suggested that the property be accepted and put to some worthwhile use. The result was the foundation of the Threave School of Practical Gardening. One must be of an age to appreciate how large a gap the school fills. In the spacious days, the head gardener was regarded by the apprentices as being about on a par with one of the major prophets: he knew his job and could impart his knowledge to others. There are very few gardens now where a young man can get a full training in all branches of the arts of gardening. This is what Threave supplies (see pp. 152–3).

In Gigha the Trust has one unusual but highly desirable

R. cinnabarinum,
Achamore House

possession, the collection of plants, including many rhododendron hybrids, in the garden of Achamore House. Gigha
is a small Atlantic island lying between Islay and the Kintyre
peninsula. The late Sir James Horlick purchased it in the late
1940s. There was no garden, but there was the essential
windbreak in the form of a planting of sycamores, described
by the new owner as 'the scruffiest trees I have ever seen'.
In the short space of twenty-five years he made a large-scale
garden or, as he preferred to call it, a series of small gardens.
These now have an appearance of maturity which is difficult
to reconcile with the known facts. He had a fine garden near
Ascot, and many big plants were moved from there to form
the nucleus of the Achamore garden. It was proposed at one
stage that the Achamore property be made over to the Trust.
In the end a mutually acceptable compromise was reached.
Sir James very generously made a gift of his collection of
plants, with an endowment for their upkeep. He wished
naturally that the products of his work as a plantsman, many
of them of singular beauty and interest, should live after his
death. In order to safeguard these, it was arranged that young
material should be propagated, either by cuttings or layers,
and that the resulting young plants should be moved to Trust
gardens, mainly to Brodick, where an area was cleared to
accommodate the Horlick collection. The risk has thus been

R. magnificum,
*Brodick (photographed
in February)*

spread and the new venture at Brodick is going well. No attempt has been made to move the big plants from Gigha. Sir James was so generous that a good many gardens in the west have propagations of his best things; so their future should be secure.

In this Guide the longest entry on the subject of Ben Lawers appears, rightly, under the heading of Countryside (see pp. 191–3). Lawers is a mountainous country property. It was purchased in 1950 by the Mountainous Country Fund, a creation of the late P. J. H. Unna which has the object of enabling the Trust to acquire and protect a proportion of our unspoiled uplands. The mountain's Alpine flora, however, makes it the largest and finest rock garden in the country. The 'wild flower' meets soon became field-days for botanists and instructive occasions for the gardener.

Alpine gentian, Ben Lawers

The point has been made that the Trust took to gardening as
a contingent obligation – that gardens came first as appendages
to great houses, then as individual properties. Mention has
been omitted here of gardens of the middling sort, charming
as they are, but they add their quota to the work-load, and
that taxes administration and resources to a degree which
would have been unimaginable in 1945. In addition, there is
constant concern to help in assuring the future of the living
garden in private ownership.

Meconopsis at Branklyn

The Trust has a Gardens Committee, constituted in 1950
with the late Lady Elphinstone as Convener. There is no fixed
'establishment' for the Committee, which normally consists of
about twenty-five members. They include representatives of
the Royal Horticultural Society, the Royal Caledonian
Horticultural Society, Scotland's Gardens Scheme and the
Institute of Parks and Recreational Administration. All
members are keen and knowledgeable gardeners; and they
are encouraged to keep in touch with the staff at any Trust
garden reasonably accessible to them. The Trust has a full-
time Gardens Adviser, one of the least of whose duties is to act
as Secretary to the Committee.

The post came into being as the result of an evolutionary
process. When Mrs Sawyer of Inverewe died in 1952 the late

133

M. campbelli,
Inverewe

Dr John Cowan, of the Royal Botanic Garden in Edinburgh, was on the point of retiring. He accepted the Trust's invitation to take charge at Inverewe and at the same time to exercise a general supervision of all Trust gardens. On his death in 1960 it was decided to have a whole-time Trust representative at Inverewe and to appoint a gardens adviser who would work from Trust headquarters in Edinburgh, for by this time Inverewe was becoming 'big business' and definitely a full-time job. Mrs Cowan, Dr John's widow, carried on at Inverewe for two years, and made a triumphant success of a difficult job (a success reinforced by Miss Alice Maconochie, M.B.E., S.H.M., before she passed the baton in 1974 to Mr and Mrs J. G. B. Gibson). Mr J. E. Robson was appointed Gardens Adviser, a post which he still holds and, one hopes, will continue to hold for many years to come.

The arrangement whereby Scotland's Gardens Scheme has a representative on the Trust's Gardens Committee is a reciprocal one; the Trust has representative members on the governing body of the Scheme. It is a most remarkable organization. There is a small headquarters in Edinburgh; and there are organizers in each county, whose job is to persuade owners of gardens of any merit to allow members of the public to enjoy their gardens. Most owners regard it as a compliment to their gardens to be asked to open them; and as a result approximately 245 gardens are open each year, some open once a year, some at intervals and a small number daily for six or more months. Large sums of money are raised. Garden owners can nominate their own favourite charity (in many cases they nominate the Trust) to receive a proportion of what they have collected. A substantial part of the balance comes to the Trust's Gardens Fund (normally the biggest single receipt by the Gardens Fund each year). Trust gardens, which are of course open regularly, nominate certain days when the money collected goes to Scotland's Gardens Scheme. The Trust is thus situated honourably on one side of the fence, and comfortably on the other.

There are some practical advantages in having a diversity of gardens under a degree of central control. Plant exchanges are simplified, and much of the propagation can be centralized. A good deal of the propagation is done at Threave, where it forms part of the training of the students.

One sometimes hears criticism to the effect that the Trust is altering the character of some of its gardens, even to the extent of veiled hints that 'it is making them like public parks'. *En passant*, one may say that this would have been taken as a wigs-on-the-green insult a generation ago, but that it savours of a compliment now, so greatly have the standards of public

parks in Scotland risen in recent years. But if one analyses the
reproach dispassionately, one has to admit that certain changes,
which one would have liked to avoid, have been inevitable.
Inverewe may be taken as an example. Before the Trust
acquired it, it was a garden enjoyed by the family who owned
it, and by their own friends. Now over 100,000 people go there
each year. If it had not been for the ruthless realism of John
Cowan, whose main alteration consisted of making proper
paths and roads (other regrettable essentials were public
lavatories), there would not be much garden left now. Of
course, some plants had to be moved, and probably some were
destroyed, and for some time the result looked a little startling
to those who had known the garden in earlier days; but this
had to be done, and it was done very well. Much criticism
is also received both because plants are properly labelled
('making the place look like a —— Botanic Garden') and
because they are not labelled enough!

The converse applies at Branklyn. The garden is small and
vulnerable, and a very delicate balance must be held between
the interests of the public and the interests of the paths, which
are mostly turf, and the plants. The exact degree of publicity
appropriate to the rather unusual circumstances is not easy
to determine.

*Branklyn:
rhododendrons, azaleas
and orange-stemmed
birch*

Brodick Castle: summer bedding in the formal garden

The Trust's west coast gardens, Brodick and Inverewe, are at their best from April to June, which is early for the main holiday season. Much has been done to lengthen the season, but it remains a fact that July and August are not good months for flowering trees and shrubs, which form the backbone of the display in these two gardens. It would be relatively easy to make a gay show with bedded-out annuals, but they would be entirely out of keeping in such places. By late August some of the autumn-flowering plants such as the eucryphias are making a show, and the autumn colouring can usually be trusted to help. Certain fairly late flowering plants from South Africa, such as the watsonias and agapanthus, have always been a speciality at Inverewe, whence they have been successfully exported to Brodick.

There is no doubt that an increasing intelligent interest in gardens is being shown by the public. Some Trust gardens, such as Inverewe, are on a main tourist route, and almost constitute an obligatory stop on the Grand Coastal Tour of the North. Others, such as Brodick, a garden of the highest merit, are not helped by geography, but many people manage to get there. Few private individuals can afford the upkeep of such gardens in these days, or certainly not to the high standards set by the Trust; and it is therefore all the more important that the Trust should be able to continue to look after the gardens which it holds. They give pleasure for the simple reason that they are beautiful in themselves. They move the mind because, though beautifully composed, they are composed of living things and so are never static; and individually and collectively they cover a fair section of the spectrum, social and historical as well as horticultural. One could wish that staffing problems everywhere were as simple as for Ben Lawers, where we need no gardeners at all. Man-made gardens have been more demanding from the time of the first of which we have any record:

Branklyn: the central path

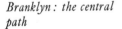

> Tomorrow ere fresh morning streak the east
> With first approach of light we must be risen,
> And at our pleasant labour, to reform
> Yon flowery arbours, yonder alleys green,
> Our walk at noon, with branches overgrown,
> That mock our scant manuring, and require
> More hands than ours to lop their wanton growth.

Things change little over the years – early rising, shortage of manure, too small a garden staff; nothing new in that. But there are rewards, of course.

Gardens

Dundee Road, A85

Just as a husband-and-wife team transformed the expansive gardens and landscape park of Crathes Castle in this century, John and Dorothy Renton established Branklyn. Having started in 1922 to build a house on the southern skirt of Kinnoull Hill, one of the agreeable equivalents on lower Tayside to the rocky bluffs above the Rhine, they went on to create what has been described as 'the finest two acres of private garden in the country'. He was the designer, she the botanist who devised the micro-climates and put in and tended many thousands of plants.

The soil, a good medium loam, afforded scope for apparently endless experiment with material from countries as far off as Japan. Among the shade trees is a magnificent orange-skinned birch, *Betula albo-seninsis septentrionalis*, which was grown from seed acquired in 1926. A celebrated place for meconopsis, both monocarpic and perennial, by the 1930s, Branklyn has enhanced its reputation since that time. One form of *M. grandis* raised in the garden received a first class certificate from the Royal Horticultural Society in 1963 (cultivar name, 'Branklyn'). Of the rhododendrons, the few large-leaved varieties are only less notable than the collection

Branklyn: the Renton touch – a diversity of plants and shrubs

Branklyn: a typical
group of meconopsis

of small-leaved plants. The latter includes many fine forms of
R. racemosum, *R. primulaeflorum*, *R. cephalanthum*, *R. david-
sonianum*, *R. schlippenbachii* and *R. wardii*; it also shelters a
selection of primulas. On two areas of scree there are *Acer
japonicum aureum*, possibly the finest specimen plant in the
garden, and a congregation of smaller things — *Stellera
chamaejasme*, *Corydalis cashmeriana*, *Primula forrestii*, *P.
marginata*, *Paraquilegia anemonoides* and Aquilegia and
dianthus in variety. Three well-grown magnolias, *M. sinensis*,
M. watsonii and *M. sieboldii*, stand side by side. The range of
viburnums gives bloom and fragrance over half the year, from
December onwards, and in autumn the downy leaves of *V.
alnifolium*, the 'Hobble Bush' of New England, turn the
colour of claret. The collection of conifers is extensive, and
the hydrangeas make a vivid display. But it may be the very
small things that truly make Branklyn much greater than
the sum of its parts.

Brodick Bay is situated on the east side of the Island of Arran and the castle is on the north side of the bay. The garden, which is large and occupies the slope between the castle and the sea, has just about all the natural advantages for which one could hope. There are no climatic extremes: more than seven degrees of frost is uncommon, the rainfall is fairly high (about seventy-two inches) and well spread over the year, the shelter is good and the soil is deep, slightly acid and rich in humus. These are perfect conditions for growing a very wide range of trees and shrubs. The few plants which insist on lime in the soil can have it given to them – one can add lime, though one cannot take it away.

Formality has its place in the walled garden immediately below the castle with fairly orthodox herbaceous borders and a modest area of well-planted beds. The wall itself is of red sandstone and dates from the eighteenth century. Below its south face the borders contain some interesting and tender plants. But the splendour of Brodick is in the garden which was made and planted at lower levels in the 1920s by the late Duchess of Montrose and her son-in-law John Boscawen, and the transition from walled garden to completely natural conditions is made very effectively. There is a small burn which has fine candelabra primula along it, backed by very good plantings of *Myosotidium hortensis* (when the rabbits do not get there first) and dwarf rhododendron species, all set in well-kept grass. This is bordered by a path, on the other side of which formality ends.

When the duchess began to make her garden the ground was bare except for a few big trees. In the earlier years the emphasis was on rhododendron species, particularly the big-leaved members of the *grande* and *falconeri* series. These found conditions so much to their taste that they frequently made two growths in a year and many of them, bearing in mind that few are as much as fifty years old, have reached a prodigious size. The majority of these are planted practically at sea level and within thirty yards of the bay, the protective windbreak being the worst weed in Arran, *Rhododendron ponticum* (introduced to the island about 1800, at great expense, by the then Duke of Hamilton). Some of the big-leaved plants have now overtopped the shelter belt and are growing as well and as vigorously as ever. Many of these big rhododendrons flower very early in the year (February and March) and are thus vulnerable in most gardens to frost; two of them, *magnificum* and *giganteum* (or has it now changed its name to *protistum*? – botanists will not leave well alone)

Brodick:
R. sinogrande

139

*Brodick: the pond in
the woodland garden*

even make their growth in February. It is a tribute to the
Arran climate that they are hardly ever damaged.

The main rhododendron display is from early April to
about mid-June. The collection is a good one. Apart from the
big-leaved species, the tender, sweet-scented plants of the
maddenii series are notable. Some, such as *cuffeanum* and
rhabdotum seem hopeless anywhere else in Scotland, with the
possible exceptions of two other great island gardens, Colonsay
and Gigha. There is a great deal of natural regeneration,
though rhododendrons believe in the permissive society and
the progeny seldom show much more than a family resemblance to their parents.

It must not be thought that the garden is a collection of
rhododendrons with a few other plants thrown in. Lists of
plants make dull reading, but some must be noted. There is a
group of plants of *Crinodendron hookerianum* which are probably as big as any in this country, and they are a great spectacle
in June when their Chinese-lantern-shaped flowers open.
Also from Chile are *Jovellana violacea* (formerly calceolaria),
which grows to around six feet and is covered with flowers of
about the same size and colour as a robin's egg, various
drimys species, eucryphias, azaras, and two of that splendid
trinity of shrubby gesnerads, namely *Asteranthera ovata* and

Mitraria coccinea (the third one, *Sarmientia repens*, is not easy to obtain, though efforts are being made). Rather strangely, there are no big embothriums, but plenty have been planted recently and are growing well.

Another genus originally rather poorly represented was magnolia. The defect has been made good, but it will be some years before the full reward comes. Until recently, there were very few of the great magnolias such as *campbellii* in Scotland. Cornwall had a near monopoly of them, but they are now well spread. The only snag is that *campbellii* itself takes about thirty years from seed to reach flowering size.

One rather special plant is *Clethra arborea*, from Madeira, which is growing well, though it cannot compare with the plants in some of the gardens in south-west Eire. New Zealand is well represented with leptospermums in many colours and several metrosideros.

No attempt has been made here to offer a tour round the garden. Paths radiate in all directions and the way to enjoy the garden is to wander at will. You may get lost, but uphill brings you to the castle and downhill to the sea.

14 miles west of Aberdeen and 2 miles east of Banchory on A93 **Crathes Castle, Grampian**

Crathes is not one garden but an enchanting series, covering an area of about six acres within the walls, subdivided by vast yew hedges, descending by well-defined steps towards a screen of great trees that protects all, to some degree, from the

Crathes Castle: an indispensable frame; the yew hedges date from 1702

caller airs of Deeside. Every part has the imprint of two remarkable people who started early in this century with the bare outline of an earlier formal garden – the yews date from 1702 – and acquired an expertise to match their imagination. Sir James Burnett of Leys, Bt., who presented the estate to the Trust in 1951, was knowledgeable and adventurous in the use of trees and shrubs (some surprising exotics went into the woodlands and are worth seeking). Lady Burnett, fascinated by colour, had an unerring eye for herbaceous plants and a talent for design. Situation, colour and diversity of content have earned Crathes a celebrity that it truly deserves at any time of the year despite the severity of the north-east climate.

The serenity of the Pool Garden, an elegant piece of formality under the very walls of the castle, is so apt as to be taken for granted on first acquaintance. There comes with time the realization that the means by which the effect is achieved, a seemingly simple arrangement of stonework and choice of plants, amount to genius. This, begun in 1932, was the last of a number of gardens which Lady Burnett made, introducing here a colour theme of red, yellow and purple.

Two yews of some antiquity form an arch over the garden entrance, on the same level as the Rose Garden and the Fountain Garden. The latter is strongly Victorian in character with a replica of a Florentine statue as the central feature and a colour scheme restricted to shades of blue. In the lower gardens Lady Burnett's flair for colour arrangement and Sir James's knowledge of trees and shrubs are immediately apparent. There was space in which to work. They made the most of it, with results which astonish the casual visitor in June, July and August. A host of things would merit mention in a plant list and simple causes for wonder are abundant. In the Trough Garden, where a graceful *Prunus serrula* overhangs a large stone trough, a group of lilies, *L. pardalinum giganteum*, stands all of seven feet tall and an *Acer griseum*, contributed no doubt by Sir James for good measure, sheds bark the colour of cinnamon. The Camel Garden, deriving its name from two raised beds, glows even in autumn, the red berries of a choice cotoneaster, *C. hebephyllus fulvida*, shining in company with the blossom of a tall viburnum, *V. lentago*, and lower-growing plants.

It is much to the credit of the Trust and a diligent and skilful staff that the herbaceous borders have lost none of their splendour. (The same may be said of Pitmedden where the borders, later in date, were designed by Lady Burnett when that garden was restored.) The 'White Border' and the 'June Border' are as magnificent in content as in scale, and there are rarities in the border along the bottom of the garden, including a grey-leaved honeysuckle from Spain, *Lonicera splendida* and a shrubby form from Manchuria, *L. maackii*. The making of a 'Golden Garden', a project favoured by Lady Burnett but not overtaken in her lifetime, has been in process since 1970.

There are two nature trails within the 595 acres of the estate, and some of the finest specimen trees border the avenues, in greatest number on the east avenue between the castle and the lodge.

12 miles south of Ayr on A719, 5 miles west of Maybole by B7023 **Culzean Castle, Strathclyde**

In the thirty years between 1762 and 1792 two bachelor brothers, Thomas Kennedy, ninth Earl of Cassillis, and David, who succeeded him in the earldom, put a fresh face on the Culzean estate. Runrig and moors and mosses were carved up to form new farms. Thomas, the innovator, eased or dragged tenants into the mainstream of agrarian reform and set in trees for shelter; and in so doing laid the groundwork for a superb achievement in gardening and landscape planting. Before his death in 1775 he went some way towards formalizing a seventeenth-century all-purpose garden in the deep hollow to the south of the old house. David thought enough of the project to have Robert Adam crown the terraces with crenellated parapets and pavilions while the new house and its ancillaries were building (1777–92). This was without doubt the genesis of Fountain Court, the formal garden which accords so happily with the great south front of Adam's

Culzean: the Fountain Court

Culzean: the Swan Pond

castle. The walled garden, primarily utilitarian, was established at a discreet remove in 1783.

As regards the antecedents of the landscape park which is spread over most of the 565 acres in the care of the Trust, there is little documentary evidence, but one may postulate the involvement of David, tenth earl, and three hired helpers. Two, Robinson and Whyte, were pupils or disciples of Capability Brown. The third, Alexander Nasmyth, a Scots artist who is represented in the castle by two masterly paintings of Culzean, had some skill in landscape architecture. It can be deduced that Brown's tree-moving device was used to shift semi-mature trees to new locations; and throughout the nineteenth century earth-moving and construction works kept pace with the social advancement of the family.

The Gothick Camellia House between the castle and the walled garden was built for Archibald Kennedy, twelfth Earl of Cassillis, whom William IV created a Marquess in 1831. Later the formal garden acquired an orangery and a fountain (hence the new name). Swan Pond was conjured up to accommodate decorative wildfowl and Swan Cottage, a delightful octagonal building, to accommodate a keeper; the latter also had in charge the residents of the adjoining aviary, yet another structure in the Gothick style.

The artefacts of the Victorian era were matched in boldness by introductions of plant material. Very large silver firs (*Abies alba*) in Silver Avenue on the way to the walled garden pre-dated single specimens of Mexican pine and Monterey cypress in the same area and many exotic trees and shrubs in Happy Valley. There, on the landward side of the walled garden, is a notable botanical collection put together by the third Marquess. Inheriting at the age of twenty-two in 1870 and dying at ninety in 1938, he was a man who did nothing by halves. It was he who gave Fountain Court its essential character. In 1910 Sir Herbert Maxwell of Monreith recorded 'an extensive collection of exotics'. In addition to the cabbage palms under the terrace, a few rarities defied time and vicissitude and many have been added by the Trust. On the opposite side of the garden a low stone wall built in 1960 (and weathered most beautifully) makes a terminal to formalism. The bank above it is planted with heathers.

Culzean is a year-round pleasance. Masses of snowdrops usher in the spring, hydrangeas bloom in autumn and thickets of bamboo prosper in all seasons.

11 miles north of Kirkcaldy and $11\frac{1}{2}$ miles west of Cupar on A912, 3 miles off A91 at Auchtermuchty, and 38 miles from Edinburgh via M9

The Royal Palace of Falkland, Fife

From the reign of James II (1437–60) up to the Union of the Crowns, Stuart kings took a constant interest in the garden of their palace of Falkland. It was enclosed by a stone wall in 1513, the year of Flodden and the death in battle of James IV, who was an exemplar of the 'new monarchy' in Europe, the man most likely to have made the Renaissance in Scotland a confabulation of poets, artists, architects and philosophers amid the roses. The garden as it stands today has an exuberance and sense of style worthy of his extraordinary court, but it is of vastly different date. New planting was ordered in 1628, five years before Charles I's one stay at Falkland. Then there was a lamentable hiatus until the arrival of a Crichton Stuart, the third Marquess of Bute, as Hereditary Constable, Captain and Keeper in 1887. It was he who identified, by scholarship and patient field-work, components of the royal precinct which had mouldered and vanished in the space of two centuries. Excavation of the sandstone ridge on which the palace stands revealed the foundations of the north range and the outline of an earlier castle of Falkland with a great round well-tower. The ridge was levelled and terraced, apparently in preparation for planting though this was not done. To the

145

Falkland Palace:
grass, skilful planting
and agreeable
stonework

third Marquess we also owe the long retaining wall under the ruined east range of the palace which restored the symmetry of the palace garden. It was, nevertheless, his grandson and present Keeper of Falkland, Major Michael Crichton Stuart, who fulfilled the grand design with refinements of his own invention.

The construction of stairways in Yorkshire stone to connect the terrace with the site of the main garden began before the outbreak of the Second World War. The evolution of a complete garden plan had to await its end. In the interim Falkland opted to 'Dig for victory' and the main garden became a potato field, fortunately without detriment to work which was to follow with the object of fixing a pattern to match the magnificent architecture of the palace. Major Crichton Stuart found in Percy Cane a garden architect of like mind. A design was accepted *in toto* in 1947 (and executed at the keeper's expense by 1952, at which date he put Falkland in the care of the Trust and provided an endowment for its upkeep).

At the upper level this design set pyramidal cypresses around the perimeter of the terrace, an Italianate conceit which is enhanced by the disposition of paving and the flights of stone steps. Below this the main garden gives an impression of amplitude out of all proportion to the dimensions of the parallelogram in which it is contained, an effect achieved by borrowing from architecture the device of voids and solids. The edges of herbaceous borders under the east and west walls run in parallel with the straight edges of half-moon shaped beds, three on either side, extending from north to south. Liberal use is made of shrubs. A belt of deciduous trees at the south end divides the garden proper from the East Port, the Trust centre by which the visitor enters.

In the view from the water-pool garden at the north end flowers and foliage and the long, smooth sweep of the East Lomond, highest but one of the hills of Fife, make a superb frame for the palace buildings. This was the purpose of the plan. The subtlety of the design appears as one moves around, and that is an easy exercise. There is a continuous grass path on the perimeter (and turf of such quality that one party of French visitors removed their shoes before venturing on it). Looking down from the terrace in summer what takes the eye at once is the herbaceous border along the east wall, the 'August border' dominated by reds and bright yellow, the colours of the Lyon standard which was raised whenever the monarch was in residence. On the west side, half of the border under the retaining wall is notable, especially in June, for a selection of lupins. The other half is devoted to bearded iris cultivars, and the wall itself supports interesting climbers, principally roses. The neighbouring border to the north is more subdued but fascinating in its range of pinks, blues and mauves.

Falkland is a modern garden without pretence at 'period'. Though there is much material of botanical interest, what is vastly impressive is the massing of colours in summer and at other times. It has been accomplished by skilful choice of plants – a choice sufficiently catholic to accept heaths and ornamental grasses as readily as delphiniums or roses, azaleas, viburnums, berberis, prunus and weigelas. Formality is restricted to one area in the south and one in the north, both contributed by the Trust since 1952. Paving (again in Yorkshire stone), camellias in white-painted tubs and plantings of thyme and lavender fill the enclosed space below the East Port very agreeably. The water-pool garden, with its lily ponds, is enclosed by clipped yew hedges and walls of grey stone.

Falkland Palace:
no pretence at 'period'

**Inverewe,
Highland**

85 miles west of Inverness on A832

The extent of the Inverewe collection, some 2,500 species in twenty-four acres of woodland and a similar area of gardens, would command respect anywhere in Britain. That plants gathered from both hemispheres could flourish in the open on a Highland headland (and on approximately the same parallel as Cape Farewell in Greenland) was an implausible proposition long after the foundations of the gardens were laid.

The essence of Inverewe is almost Asian; a great horticulturist once likened the woodland garden to some wild corner of Burma or Northern China. It was the invention of a remarkable Victorian who spent much of his youth on the Continent. Osgood Mackenzie, third son of the laird of Gairloch, a little way down the coast, had, in addition to a lively and inquiring mind, pertinacity and money, an intelligent and indulgent Hanbury mother. She took him early on his travels. Awakening interest in St Kilda drew them there in 1853. The estate at the head of Loch Ewe which was bought for him nine years later must have seemed to any but the eye of love only a little less unthrifty and unkempt than those rough isles of the sea.

*Inverewe : palm trees
by the shore of Loch
Ewe*

The peninsula (in Gaelic, *Am Ploc Ard*, the high lump) was a mass of red Torridonian sandstone, pocked by peat-

hags and bare of vegetation except for heather, crowberry and two dwarf willows (one of which survived for many years without cosseting). The new laird, however, did not have to ponder long on how to counter gales and driving rain (rainfall averages nearly sixty inches a year); he started planting in 1865. Once an outer windbreak of Corsican and Scots pines had been established, behind deer- and rabbit-fencing, he was exceptionally venturesome in setting out native trees and the exotics with which plant collectors were delighting and challenging gardeners in more southerly latitudes.

In *A Hundred Years in the Highlands* Osgood Mackenzie made no bones about the extent to which he was guided by trial and error. That fascinating memoir also identifies some of the factors which governed the rate of progress – the life-styles of laird and estate workers, the time spent with a gun (there were numerous and often extraordinary entries in his game book) and the benefits and disadvantages of residence in a Ross-shire mostly devoid of roads. Soil had to be carried in creels. It was needed not only to form beds but to fill deep nooks in the rock in which such species as *Sequoiadendron giganteum* were set. By 1880 it was possible to introduce eucalyptus and some of the best species of rhododendron. The latter were the basis of a collection of such size and diversity that it extends from the early flowering *R. praevernum* to the tender *maddenii* series which normally can be grown only in a glasshouse. One specimen of *R. giganteum* was raised from seed sent home by George Forrest. Among the other large species *R. sinogrande* at twenty-five feet high is overtopped by *R. hodgsonii*.

Inverewe: Am Ploc Ard *transformed – the tree screen is essential*

There are plants no less impressive than the rhododendrons. In a good year a very large *Magnolia campbellii* produces by late March or early April hundreds of large pink blooms, each about eight inches across. Beds of the giant Chatham Island Forget-me-not, *Myosotidium hortensia* (noted at Culzean Castle in 1910 but long vanished from there) owe their vigour to Mrs Mairi Sawyer who tended the garden for a lifetime, first with her father, then with sole responsibility after his death in 1922: she compounded the right fertilizer from sea-weed and herring fry left by the tide. In July and August the scarlet blossom of the Flame Flower of Chile (*Tropaeolum speciosum*) greets one on the drive. Mrs Sawyer lived to see many of the original trees entwined in creepers of similar provenance – the coral plant (*Berberidopsis corallina*) and the Glory Flower (*Eccremocarpus scaber*), together with clematis in variety, the blue-berried *Billardiera longiflora* from Tasmania and the climbing hydrangea, *H. petiolaris scandens*, from Japan.

149

In a design so artful as to appear artless, rock gardens, ponds and peat banks all serve to broaden the range of habitats; and among the things with which Inverewe has had conspicuous success American Avalanche Lilies (*Erythronium revolutum*) supply glorious colour in spring, as do *agapanthus* and *watsonia* from South Africa in autumn, and in the walled garden two fine forms of Kaffir Lily, *Schizostylus coccinea*, flower as late as December.

Pitmedden, Grampian

14 miles north of Aberdeen by A92 and B999, 11 miles north-east of Inverurie off A96

Setting to work in the latter half of the seventeenth century, Sir Alexander Seton, first baronet of Pitmedden, created a masterpiece, a garden in which formality in the grand manner of André Le Nôtre and Henry Wise, Le Nôtre's contemporary in England and possibly his peer, was allied with the practices of two preceding generations. When the estate was given to the Trust in 1952 all that remained of the Great Garden was the magnificent architectural frame. Time had obliterated the elaborate floral designs and had eroded pavilions, fountains and pools. In the space of seven years all was made anew, if not precisely in detail then certainly in spirit. The Pitmedden papers were destroyed in 1818 in a fire which consumed a large part of the house, but there were other texts on which the research and design team could draw.

The original inspiration came from three or four sources. Seton was reared at Winton in East Lothian. There, about 1620, his kinsman and guardian George Seton, third Earl of Winton, had 'founded and built the great house from the foundations, with all the large stone dykes about the precinct, park, orchards, and gardens thereof'. The garden patterns at Seton in the same county and Pinkie in Midlothian were designed at about the same time by relatives of Alexander Seton, whose land in Formartine was then a mossy, moorish waste between the rivers Don and Ythan. Later as a royalist much in favour and a lawyer who was frequently about in royalist company in Edinburgh, he became familiar with an enclosed garden which was laid out for Charles I at the Palace of Holyroodhouse in 1639.

Sir Alexander fell heir to Pitmedden in 1667 (his elder brother, like his father, died in the service of the Stuarts). By then new notions which Charles II and his court brought back from the Continent at the Restoration were reaching Scotland; and none who had seen Vaux-le-Vicomte during Charles's exile took up the Le Nôtre style of gardening or

Pitmedden

Pitmedden: in the vogue – the ogee roof alone would date the pavilion to the late 1600s

classicism in architecture more readily than Sir William Bruce of Balcaskie. (The French influence shows at once in the house and garden which he designed for himself at Kinross by Loch Leven, less clearly in the large additions which he made to Holyroodhouse, perhaps for the reason that the King's Master Mason was a home-based Scot, one whose work, as will appear, came to be represented much later in the Great Garden.) How much of Bruce's enthusiasm rubbed off on the laird of Pitmedden, or how far recollections of Charles I's garden and Seton gardens in the south helped him in determining the arrangement and planting of parterres, one cannot say precisely.

What is not in question is the brilliance of the split-level

Pitmedden: the Seton parterre adjoins the north-east pavilion

concept. It took full advantage of the lie of the land before the house. An upper garden, extended by terraces on north and south, was formed to overlook the Great Garden on three sides. The entry to the latter by pillared gates and a graceful semi-twin stair on the median retaining wall made (and makes) a perfect harmony with pavilions, two storeys high, in the north-west and south-west corners. The 'large stone dykes' which enclose the whole composition are dated to May 2nd, 1675.

July and August are the months in which to see the re-creation of the laird's great work. In four parterres, differentiated by box hedging and turf paths, some 30,000 bedding plants are ranked in the mode of his time. Two of the designs repeat the patterns in Charles I's garden as it stood in 1647. The centrepiece of the fourth, a parallelogram with insets of the Scottish saltire and the thistle, is Sir Alexander Seton's coat of arms. In each garden there is a fountain. When that in the Great Garden was re-erected seven of the sculptured stones which were built into it came from the Cross Fountain of Linlithgow, a structure designed and executed by Robert Mylne, King's Master Mason, to commemorate the Restoration of Charles II. Twenty-seven sundials, none with a margin of error greater than ten minutes, mark the passing hours. The pavilions, their ogee roofs re-set to the original line, afford more than shelter. For a floral key (and a sight of Sir Alexander's bath-house) turn to the north-west; the theme of the exhibition in the south-western pavilion is, un-surprisingly and very conveniently, the evolution of formal gardens.

Threave, Dumfries and Galloway

2 miles south-west of Castle Douglas on A75

Threave is a garden, more precisely a teaching garden, in the making. The exercise began in 1960 with the founding of the Trust's School of Practical Gardening, an object which the late Major Alan Gordon had much in mind when he presented and endowed the Threave estate. Few great gardens remained in which a young man could receive systematic training and acquire the skills which made the 'Scots gardener' acceptable around the world. Threave, supplying a two-year residential course and accepting annually seven entrants in the age range of seventeen to twenty, meets the deficiency to the extent of producing seven diploma students each year.

Threave House serves both as school and as hostel accommodation. The primary purpose of a syllabus which affords theoretical and practical instruction in equal parts is to teach cultivation and appreciation of a wide range of ornamental

plants. Subjects to which special attention is given include botany, genetics, classification of plants, soil science and control of pests and diseases. A prerequisite for entry is a minimum of one year's practical horticultural experience. Other Trust gardens make available a number of pre-training places each year, and their facilities may also be used for instruction during the course. Such arrangements are convenient but in no sense restrictive. Threave has a special relationship with Longwood Gardens, Pennsylvania, based at student level on a two-way exchange programme which is funded by the Scottish Heritage (U.S.A.) Inc. Threave, in common with the great gardens, also affords experience for graduate and post-graduate students from the United States.

Threave: 'a house of no great pretension'

Major Gordon's interest was concentrated, outside of the walled garden and the glasshouse, on daffodils. He had large areas of the woodlands and policies planted with many different varieties. They make a magnificent display in April.

The new garden, on a west-facing slope of some sixty-five acres, has been designed to serve the school. It incorporates as many facets as possible of ornamental gardening. The first of its subdivisions, the rock garden, was given priority because the Trust has few examples of this type of garden. A peat garden, first adopted at Logan in Wigtownshire and later at the Royal Botanic Garden, Edinburgh, as an addition or alternative to rock gardens, accommodates on its ledges rhododendrons, *Gultheria*, vaccinium, meconopsis and primulas. The rose garden contains a large selection of shrub roses (species, old-fashioned and modern). Other new creations are a woodland garden, a heather garden, an arboretum, a vegetable garden, a pond and herbaceous beds. A patio, an adjunct to the walled garden, was constructed in 1972 to demonstrate the use of stone in the garden and examples of plants which can be grown in paving. The nursery, to the north of the walled garden and the glasshouse, is used extensively for propagation.

Threave: the visitor centre

In anticipation of further growth of holiday traffic in Galloway, and a consequent increase in attendances and demand for information, a large visitor centre was built, with substantial financial aid from the Scottish Tourist Board, and opened in 1975.

IV · HISTORIC SITES

with an introduction by Gordon Donaldson

Introduction

A large part of the history of Britain has been shaped by conflict between the southern and northern parts of the island, for any ambitious ruler with the ample resources of the south at his disposal was tempted to try to extend his sway northwards, at least up the east coast where there is no obvious natural frontier.

This first happened in the eighties of the first century A.D., when Agricola, the Roman commander in Britain, conducted operations against the Caledonians and erected a line of forts between the Forth and the Clyde. For a time the Romans fell back to the Tyne–Solway line, where Hadrian's Wall was built about A.D. 130, but within a few years there was another advance, and in about A.D. 140, in the reign of Emperor Antoninus Pius, Lollius Urbicus erected the Antonine Wall between Forth and Clyde. It was held, with intermissions, for perhaps half a century. Thereafter, although the Emperor Severus (d. A.D. 211) again invaded Caledonia, the wall of Hadrian remained the frontier of the Roman province. But military operations were not the whole story, for some tribes north of the Cheviots received a tincture of Roman civilization through the proximity of the settled and prosperous Roman province, and Christianity reached them in the last years of the Roman Empire, at about A.D. 400. To that extent the Romans had lost the war but won the peace.

The same pattern frequently recurred. The Angles, Teutonic invaders from the Continent, whose kingdom of Northumbria stretched from the Humber to the Forth in the seventh century, failed to establish political hegemony over the Picts farther north, but their cultural influence extended into Pictland. From the middle of the ninth century, when the Picts were united with the Irish 'Scots' who had settled in Argyll about the year 500, the rulers of this united kingdom took the offensive and by the beginning of the eleventh century they had extended their frontier to the Tweed. But in acquiring the south-east, Scotland had acquired a channel for the renewed penetration of southern influence, which after the Norman Conquest of England was Norman influence. In the twelfth century the Scottish kings encouraged the immigration of Anglo-Normans and reorganized their kingdom more or less on the English model. From time to time Scottish kings were reduced by England to a state of vassalage, but the new institutions brought in from the south were to give the country a cohesion which, somewhat paradoxically, enabled it to resist later attempts at conquest in a way that the purely Celtic lands of Wales and Ireland could not do.

From the eighth century Scotland was under pressure from the north as well, for Scandinavians settled in the north and west and established principalities subject to Norway, one centred on the Isle of Man and embracing the Western Isles, and the other centred on Orkney and including Shetland and Caithness. It was only in 1266 that Scotland acquired the Western Isles, and another two centuries passed before Orkney and Shetland were added.

After the deaths of Alexander III in 1286 and his grand-daughter, the Maid of Norway, in 1290, Scotland was con-fronted with a succession problem. The two main candidates, Robert Bruce and John Balliol, were of Anglo-Norman descent and, like many other Scottish nobles, held English estates. At this time the relations between Scotland and England had long been peaceful, the royal families had inter-married generation by generation, English kings had more than once imposed kings on Scotland, and Edward I was respected for his sagacity. Quite naturally, the dispute was submitted to Edward's adjudication, and, equally naturally, the claimants agreed that whoever he selected as king of Scotland should be a vassal of England for his kingdom as well as for his English estates. Edward decided in favour of Balliol, but he goaded him into a rebellion which led to an English conquest and the removal to Westminster in 1296 of the sacred stone on which the Scottish kings had been inaugurated.

Within a year rebellions had broken out, under Andrew Moray and William Wallace. Victorious at Stirling Bridge (1297), Wallace was defeated at Falkirk (1298), but others maintained resistance, and only in 1305 was the country once more subdued. But within a year rebellion again broke out, this time under Robert Bruce, grandson of the claimant of 1290. Bruce had a rival in the shape of a 'king over the water' – the deposed Balliol, who had retired to his French estates but who was senior to Bruce by blood and had, unlike him, been inaugurated on the sacred stone. Bruce was no more a 'national' candidate than Balliol was, and he had to wage civil war against dynastic rivals as well as against the English. But he had not only to win military victories: he had to win the hearts of a people, which was perhaps the harder task. He could justify his kingship *de facto*, and did so magnificently at Bannockburn (June 24th, 1314). But he could justify it *de jure* only by claiming that he had been 'chosen' as king by 'the community of the realm'. His propaganda department made the most of his case. The Declaration of Arbroath

(1320) forcefully distinguished the dynastic cause of Bruce from the cause of independence by declaring that should Bruce waver they would cast him out and make another king, 'For it is not for riches, or honours, or glory that we fight, but for liberty alone, which no worthy man loses save with his life.'

Scotland's independence was formally recognized by England in 1328, but the liberator king died in the next year, and his five-year-old son, David II, was soon challenged by Edward Balliol, son of King John. The latter did have English support, but many Scots, too, preferred an adult Balliol to a juvenile Bruce, and there was another war in which Scottish castles were only gradually recovered from the English and their collaborators. The English, however, were from the 1340s involved in the Hundred Years War with France, and once that war was over were distracted by the Wars of the Roses (1455–85). Scotland was therefore in little danger of conquest by England, but a kind of ding–dong warfare at every level, from minor Border raiding to occasional large-scale invasions, was almost incessant.

After two centuries of Anglo–Scottish warfare, the sixteenth century opened with the promise of better things, for in 1503 James IV married Margaret, daughter of Henry VII, the first Tudor king, and concluded a 'treaty of perpetual peace'. The ultimate result was that a hundred years later the great-grandson of James and Margaret became King of England as James I. But the immediate results were less happy, for in ten years the two countries were at war again, in a campaign which led to James IV's defeat and death at Flodden (1513).

James IV had invaded England under pressure from the French king and in fulfilment of the Auld Alliance, first formally concluded by John Balliol in 1295 and many times renewed. While French forces had occasionally come to Scotland, far more Scots had gone to fight the English in France, and by this time the principal use France was disposed to make of the Alliance was to induce the Scots to invade England when France was threatened. After Flodden some Scots began to reflect that the Alliance had been a somewhat one-sided affair, and thought it time to reconsider Scotland's foreign policy. The growth of what may be termed a pro-English faction was soon stimulated by the Reformation, for Scots who were inclined to Protestantism looked for support to an England which under Henry VIII cast off the Pope.

Thus when, in 1542, James V undertook a campaign against Henry VIII in the interests of the papacy, the nation was divided, and the result was a disastrous defeat at Solway Moss. James died in the following month, and was succeeded by his week-old daughter, Mary. In her long minority both

France and England sought, by war and diplomacy, to make Scotland a satellite. France succeeded, to the extent that Mary went to France and married the Dauphin, who in 1559 became king as Francis II; but the undisguised attempts of France to use Scotland as a base for aggression against England and to make it a mere dependency of France provoked bitter resentment. In 1560, after the Protestants had started a rebellion, English help was enlisted to drive out the French occupying forces. At this stage, both the long war with England and the Auld Alliance with France came to an end.

That it should be replaced by a new alliance, between a Protestant Scotland and the Protestant England of Elizabeth Tudor, seemed logical, but the persistence of faction in Scotland and the irresolution of Queen Elizabeth combined to delay the making of a formal 'bond' until 1586. From that point it was ever more likely that James VI would succeed Elizabeth, and no one was surprised when he peacefully ascended the English throne as James I in 1603.

There were still two kingdoms, each with its own Parliament as well as its own law courts and Church. Such an association could work only if the two Parliaments found themselves in accord or if the Crown, which joined the two countries, was powerful enough to restrain two independent Parliaments from pursuing divergent policies. Concord and royal control alike vanished in the 1640s. A Scottish rebellion against Charles I had begun in 1638, after the signing of the National Covenant, and the English Civil War began in 1642. Some of the Covenanters thought that they should make common cause with the English Parliament, but others opposed this policy; and when a Scottish army crossed the Border to join the English Parliamentarians, the king commissioned the Marquess of Montrose to raise his standard in Scotland. Montrose won a whirlwind series of victories, but was defeated at Philiphaugh (1645) and his campaign did nothing to stave off disaster for his king.

The Scots soon found that in allying with the English Parliament they had miscalculated. For one thing, they wanted the English to adopt Presbyterianism, but the English army, which gained the ascendancy over the English Parliament, wanted a congregational system. For another, the English became hostile to the monarchy as well as to Charles personally, while the Scots, though rebellious, thought that his right to be their king was indefeasible. Thus when the English beheaded Charles in 1649 and established a republic, the Scots unhesitatingly proclaimed his son as king. The result of this complete breakdown in the personal union was the conquest of Scotland by the armies of Oliver Cromwell in 1651.

After Charles II was restored to both kingdoms in 1660, the Parliaments were more assertive than they had been under his father and grandfather, but the Crown was able to prevail and the tension never became intolerable. However, when Charles II's Roman Catholic brother, James VII and II, lost his throne to William of Orange in the Revolution of 1688–89, the Parliaments largely escaped from royal control and the Scottish Parliament in particular became aggressive at a time when there were only too many grievances against the new king's policies. After the Revolution, Presbyterianism had been restored, and the still influential and numerous Episcopalian faction felt that they had nothing to thank William for. But the Presbyterians were not happy either, for William was reluctant to sanction their intolerance. The new king did not understand the Scots, and he was dependent on agents who often had their own ends to serve and were involved in factious disputes. Then in the later 1690s came a disaster to Scottish commercial and colonial aspirations. Ever since Sir William Alexander, Earl of Stirling, had projected a colony in Nova Scotia and a few Scots had settled there in 1629, the Scots had intermittently planned a colony of their own in America, for they were not permitted to trade with the English colonies. In 1695 the Scottish Parliament authorized the establishment of a Company of Scotland trading to Africa and the Indies, which was to establish colonies, and the choice fell on a site at Darien, near Panama. This venture, to which Scots gave lavishly of their scanty capital, was a dismal failure; and William was blamed, because English assistance to the Scottish company and its colony had been forbidden. Scottish resentment was bitter, and the episode showed the weakness of a situation in which two Parliaments could pursue conflicting economic policies, and even conflicting foreign policies – for a settlement in Darien infringed the rights of Spain, a country with which William had been anxious to keep the peace.

Readjustment of the constitutional position became urgent owing to the state of the royal succession. At the Revolution the Crown was settled on the heirs of William and Mary and of Mary's sister, Anne. But William and Mary had no children and the last of Anne's family died in 1700. England then settled the Crown on the Electress Sophia of Hanover, a granddaughter of James VI, and her descendants. But no such Act was passed by the Scottish Parliament, which instead was disposed to emphasize its right to make its own choice. William died in 1702, to be succeeded by Anne, and in the same year the War of the Spanish Succession began. England was thus faced with the possibility that during a life-and-death struggle with France Anne might die and Scotland adopt a different sovereign from England, to become once more a French base. All in all, the personal union was again breaking down and the possibility had to be faced that there might again be civil war and even an armed conquest of Scotland by England. This time, however, another way was found. England was prepared for a bargain: she would concede commercial rights and other privileges to the Scots in return for a union of the Parliaments and the acceptance of the Hanoverian line as future sovereigns. The outcome was the Treaty of Union of 1707, which preserved Scots law and the Presbyterian Church of Scotland but set up a single Parliament in which there were forty-five Scottish members of the House of Commons and sixteen Scots peers.

The first Hanoverian king, George I, succeeded Queen Anne in 1714. The Hanoverian title was thus a statutory one, and, as with Robert Bruce, the element of 'choice by the community' had to be stressed to justify that title against the claims of a 'king over the water'. James VII and II, deposed in 1689, had his supporters, the Jacobites, and a rising on his behalf had at once been led by John Graham of Claverhouse, Viscount Dundee. Dundee was victorious at Killiecrankie, but was killed in the moment of victory and his army was subsequently checked by the spirited defence of Dunkeld by Colonel Cleland. Jacobitism was especially strong in the Highlands, from which Dundee, like Montrose, drew most of his support, and it was the reluctance of some Highland clans to acknowledge William as king which led to the massacre of Glencoe (1692). James VII died in 1700, and the Jacobites then recognized his son as James VIII. In 1708 a French fleet approached the east coast with this young man on board, but did not make a landing – though probably that juncture, even more than when the next Jacobite effort was made, in 1715, was singularly propitious for an appeal to Scotland on behalf of the exiled prince.

The fact is that the Union of 1707 was at first highly unpopular. Its ultimate results were to be in many ways beneficial to the Scots, if only because Anglo–Scottish co-operation in the economic field led to much new industrial activity in Scotland, but half a century elapsed before these advantages became apparent, and in the interval many issues arose on which the Scots felt that they were unfairly treated. The discontent occasionally produced riots – for example the Shawfield riots in Glasgow (1725) and the Porteous riots in Edinburgh (1736). Dislike of the Union probably gained supporters for the Jacobite cause in 1708 (the year after the Union) and in 1715 (the year after the accession of the first

Hanoverian king). The Fifteen (memorable chiefly for the battle of Sheriffmuir, which tactically was a draw but strategically a victory for the government) may have had a real chance of success, but its prospects were destroyed by the ineffective leadership of the Earl of Mar.

Thereafter, apart from a minor effort in 1719 in association with a small Spanish force which was defeated at Glenshiel, Jacobitism was dormant until 1745. By that time the Hanoverian line was firmly established, the Union was nearly forty years old, some of its benefits were becoming apparent and men had grown accustomed to a united kingdom. Thus, when Prince Charles Edward, grandson of James VII, landed in Scotland in 1745, he gained only very limited support. Attempts to make capital out of Scottish resentment against the Union now brought little return, and the surviving strength of Jacobitism arose largely from the ecclesiastical situation. Few Presbyterians were Jacobites, and most Protestant Scots preferred a Hanoverian ruler to an Italianate Roman Catholic. Yet there was an important body of Episcopalians, who were called non-jurors because they refused to take the oath to the Hanoverian kings, and who were denied toleration: their congregations (where prayers were said for King James and not for King George) were a chief instrument in keeping Jacobitism alive. Equally, Roman Catholics, who likewise suffered under certain disabilities, supported the cause of the Stuart claimant. Added to this ecclesiastical situation was the social structure and economy of the Highlands. Among Highlanders there was a long tradition of raiding the Lowlands – only by the proceeds of such raids, indeed, could the population of the Highlands be adequately fed; Highlanders therefore followed Prince Charlie, as they had followed Montrose and Dundee, out of a desire for loot. But the Highlands were divided, for inter-clan feuds and traditional enmities meant that some clans inevitably took a different side from others: notably, because Clan Campbell was Presbyterian and Hanoverian, the neighbours of Clan Campbell were Episcopalian and Jacobite. In the Forty-five, therefore, some Jacobite support came from the Episcopalian Lowlands, especially in the north-east and in Perthshire, and in the west its main recruiting ground was in the predominantly Episcopalian and Roman Catholic areas. The north, and the Western Isles, were in the main neutral or loyal to the government. It is perhaps significant that the standard for the Fifteen was raised at Braemar, in Aberdeenshire, that for the Forty-five at Glenfinnan in the remote west.

Never more than 9,000 men mustered under Prince Charlie's standard, and it has been shown that there were more Scots in arms on the government side. Owing to the lethargy of the administration and the spirited tactics of the Highlanders in the field, the Jacobites routed Sir John Cope at Prestonpans and advanced into England as far as Derby. But neither Lowland Scots nor Englishmen joined them in appreciable numbers, and they had to fall back, to be defeated in the end at Culloden on April 16th, 1746.

The significance of that battle is often exaggerated. Facile talk about 'the clans' being defeated at Culloden ignores the quarter of a million or so clansfolk who were nowhere near Culloden on that fatal day and those others who were on the winning side. And equally facile talk about 'the clan system' being destroyed at Culloden ignores the fact that Highland society was transformed and the clan system destroyed by social and economic changes some of which had started before the Forty-five.

Yet, despite the relative unimportance of the Jacobite movement as it actually existed at the time, Jacobitism as a legend has proved to be of some significance in Scottish history. In general the period since the Union of 1707 has seen an acceleration of the infiltration of southern influence and of the anglicization of Scotland – processes which had been going on in one way or another since the eighth century. Scotland, unlike Wales, had not been conquered by England as a preliminary to annexation but had entered into a union by free negotiation between two separate Parliaments. To that extent, England's many attempts at military conquest had failed and England had in the end lost the war. But there has always been a fear that England would yet win the peace, by imposing or infiltrating culture, customs, institutions, law and a belief that the two countries share the same historic heritage. Scots, by way of reaction, have therefore tended to foster not indeed the truth about their history – for the agreeable fiction always prevails over historical truth – but myths and legends among which such assorted characters as Wallace and Bruce, Mary Queen of Scots, John Knox and Bonnie Prince Charlie figure largely. At the time, the great majority of Scots, especially Lowlanders, utterly repudiated Jacobitism, and felt that it was an English slander to attach the taint of sedition to the whole Scottish nation. But in later times Jacobitism and the apparatus of romance which surrounds it have played a significant part in keeping Scottish sentiment alive.

Culloden: Old Leanach

Historic Sites

2 miles south of Stirling on A80

The Borestone sector of the battlefield of Bannockburn was **Bannockburn,** vested in the Trust 'on behalf of the Scottish nation' in 1932. **Central** Some thirty years elapsed before anything more than passive trusteeship was feasible. The area of chief historical importance was difficult of access, though bisected by a minor road. The way towards the resolution of this difficulty was opened in 1960 by the purchase of a small area (1·3 acres) with a frontage on the Stirling–Glasgow trunk route (A80). By that date historical research was pointing to the true significance of this extremity of the escarpment which borders the Carse of Stirling on the south; propositions which even then were theoretical have been confirmed by a growing body of scholarly testimony. It can be said with confidence that these fifty-eight green acres hold the key to one of the greatest battles in history.

Bannockburn, fought on June 23rd and 24th, 1314, was a victory of such dimensions that it may be called the watershed *Bannockburn: the* in the Scottish wars of independence against the Angevin *Rotunda*

Bannockburn: the Bruce statue

kings of England; nothing barbarous or disastrous which came after, and much did, could rob Scotland of national identity.

The conflict and the events leading up to it are recalled in vivid images and evocative sound in an audio-visual programme, *The Forging of a Nation*, in the auditorium by the entrance. A rotunda and an equestrian statue of Robert Bruce, King of Scots, crown the slight eminence on which he established his command post, his battle H.Q. There the contours have been restored so far as possible to the original forms — an undertaking which required *inter alia* the stopping-up and in-filling, with the consent of the Royal Burgh of Stirling and the Scottish Office, of the minor road to which reference has been made. The rotunda is so disposed as to command on one side a view of the route by which King Edward II hurried forward his army and on the other Stirling Castle, which was his objective.

It was on the Borestone sector that the battle opened on June 23rd. Bruce was short of front-line troops; he had an estimated 5,500 (5,000 foot and 500 light cavalry) against an enemy mustering nearly 20,000. Edward was short of time. Stirling Castle, the last great strength in English hands, had endured a siege and the garrison were under promise to surrender unless they were relieved by an English army by Midsummer Day — June 24th, the following day. The direct route from Falkirk to Stirling was on the line of a Roman road which descended into the shallow valley of the Bannock Burn, then rose diagonally across the Borestone brae to reach the top of the escarpment. It was here that Bruce chose to stand in a situation in which an English assault on a broad front would be impossible. Off the track the low ground was mostly bog, traces of which are discernible today. Improving on nature, the Scots dug pits to make booby-traps wherever there was firm footing for horse or man. Their position on the ridge, and astride the road, had a further advantage: it was within the New Park, a royal hunting forest, and scrub woodland gave at least partial concealment to the four units into which Bruce divided his forces. Edward's 'Great Van' — heavy cavalry (the armoured fighting vehicles of medieval warfare), foot and archers — forded the Bannock Burn and launched what, with good reason, they expected to be an irresistible attack. It failed; the Scots were not dislodged. A cavalry sortie on firm ground below the escarpment, in an attempt to bypass the Scots position, failed also. The decisive battle was fought next morning on the ground to the north-east, below the escarpment.

Fragments of the Borestone, a boulder with a socket in

which according to legend Bruce set his standard, are preserved in the auditorium. In 1967 the building gained for the Trust a commendation for enterprise in tourism from the British Travel Association. In 1972 the British Tourist Authority awarded a special commendation to the audio-visual exhibition, *The Forging of a Nation*. The Scottish Tourist Board contributed generously by grant and loan towards the capital cost of the latter. A further development in 1981 by the Scottish Tourist Board in association with the Trust is designed to create a National Tourist Information Centre at the site.

5 miles east of Inverness on B9006

Culloden, Highland

The Rising of 1745 was in its political antecedents in Britain and Europe, its conduct and its aftermath vastly different from the romantic legends and the songs. Culloden has become the most emotive of Scottish place-names. For many who make no claim to Highland ancestry it signifies a double tragedy. The last battle fought on British soil was a clamorous incident in an irreversible process which put an end to much besides the Stuart claim to the throne of Great Britain and Ireland. It hastened, because heads of a patriarchal society lost their nerve or turned resolutely to self-interest, the erosion and ultimate destruction of a social and economic order for which Whitehall and the Lowlands could not or would not supply an adequate replacement. The effects have been lasting.

The memorials and the ground on which they stand were conveyed to the Trust in 1944 by Hector Forbes, thirteenth

Culloden centre and Old Leanach

Laird of Culloden, a descendant of an earlier laird, Duncan Forbes, Lord President, who strove to avert the rebellion, then to contain it and had his advice ignored when it was over. The cairn, erected in 1881 by Duncan Forbes, tenth Laird of Culloden, is twenty feet high and eighteen feet in diameter. The legend inscribed on it is perhaps an expression of family feeling as it existed 135 years after the event:

THE BATTLE
OF CULLODEN
WAS FOUGHT ON THIS MOOR
16TH APRIL, 1746
THE GRAVES OF THE
GALLANT HIGHLANDERS
WHO FOUGHT FOR
SCOTLAND AND PRINCE CHARLIE
ARE MARKED BY THE NAMES
OF THEIR CLANS

It was on the personal order of Prince Charles Edward Stuart that the Jacobite army, exhausted by a night march and half-starved, formed up to await the advance of the Duke of Cumberland and the Government forces. What followed, from simple clansmen and from commanders who contended in vain that this was the wrong place and the wrong day, was heroic but foredoomed. All was over in an hour with the loss of more than 1,000 Jacobite dead. It is this moving chapter in a record of unexampled loyalty that has made Culloden a place of pilgrimage. The cairn marks an area where there was intense fighting. Very near to it are the mass graves of the clans, identified by simple headstones for which Duncan Forbes was also responsible. The green mound over the Mackintosh grave was originally fifty-four yards long – part of it was covered by a public road constructed about 1835. Another stone records 'The English were buried here'. The exact site of graves or trenches is not known, and the use of the word 'English' may not be wholly accurate. There were Scottish regiments in the Government forces and Campbells were not the only Highlanders who served with them.

Culloden: the memorial cairn

The gift made by Hector Forbes included, in addition to the principal memorials and the Well of the Dead, Old Leanach Cottage: this last was a farmhouse at the time of the battle and survived it. He also sold for a nominal sum the triangular field, to the east of Old Leanach and the Trust centre, in which is located the Cumberland Stone. From this large flat boulder the Duke may have made his first survey of the field; according to one account he returned to it after the battle to eat his lunch. Other gifts of land were made in 1937 by the late Mr Alexander Munro of Leanach Farm and in 1959 by his son, Mr Ian Munro. The Trust's care of the field and the memorials was preceded by many years of devoted voluntary effort by the Highland Society of Inverness.

By the roadside to the west of the battlefield there is the Irish Memorial erected by the Irish Military History Society in 1963. It commemorates the Irish soldiers of the French service, 'The Wild Geese', who fought on the Jacobite side and suffered heavy casualties in covering the retreat. King's Stables Cottage in the same vicinity was part of the Forbes gift of 1944. A small, simple dwelling, typical of the mid-eighteenth century it takes its name from Stable Hollow where Cumberland's dragoons were picketed while they guarded the battlefield.

The Culloden Centre was established in 1970 with sub-stantial financial aid from the Highlands and Islands Develop-ment Board. It contains a historical display and a lecture room with projection and audio-visual equipment in order to make full use of current methods of interpretation. Old Leanach Cottage, which served from 1959 to 1970 as a visitor centre, is the Battlefield Museum, exhibiting under its rough-hewn roof-timbers and heather-thatch a large collection of maps and relics. The provision of services and the gradual restoration of the historic ground proceeds with the counsel of the local Culloden Committee. The Forestry Commission, whose plantations occupy a large part of the battleground, and the local planning authority co-operate in the process of re-creating the eighteenth-century scene. Planning law could not prevent the erection in 1937 of a bungalow in the area between Old Leanach and the cairn. The building was purchased by the Trust in 1972 and demolished.

18½ miles west of Fort William on A830

Glenfinnan Monument, Highland

The Glenfinnan Monument, in a superb situation at the head of Loch Shiel, was presented in 1938 by Sir Wilfred Blount, the proprietor, on behalf of himself, the Trustees of the Glenaladale Estates, and the Roman Catholic Diocese of Argyll and the Isles. The late Mr A. MacKellaig entered into a Conservation Agreement in order to give permanent protec-tion to an area of twenty-eight acres around it.

The tower, of coursed stone rubble, was erected in 1815 by order of Alexander MacDonald, tenth Chieftain of Glenala-dale. Within it a spiral staircase ascends to a battlemented platform sixty-five feet above ground. The platform is

surmounted by a statue of a kilted Highlander. The latter was
commissioned by Angus, twelfth Chieftain of Glenaladale,
from the sculptor John Greenshields, of Carluke in Lanark-
shire, and set in place in 1834. An octagonal area around the
base is enclosed by a stone wall. The wall carries on the outer
face three large plaques of dedication in Gaelic, English and
Latin. Alexander was careful to record that on this spot Prince
Charles Edward Stuart first raised his standard in the Forty-
five, but what he sought to commemorate was 'the generous
zeal, the undaunted bravery and the inviolable fidelity' of
his own forefathers and 'the rest of those who fought and bled
in that arduous and unfortunate enterprise'.

Glenfinnan saw the bright morning of the Forty-five. This
was to be the third attempt to reinstate the Stuarts on the
throne of Great Britain and Ireland. The first was an abortive
enterprise, though it aroused genuine fear of invasion. It was
launched in 1708, nineteen years after the Revolution Settlement and the accession of William of Orange and Mary.
A French fleet, with which Louis XIV despatched 6,000
troops and the Chevalier de St Georges, the Prince's father,
in the general direction of the Firth of Forth, was held off by
the British navy and the weather, and returned without making
a landing. The Rising of 1715, a year after the death of Queen
Anne and the summoning of the Elector of Hanover to succeed her, was led by the Earl of Mar. It lasted six months,

had a bold beginning in the north-east of Scotland, an ill-directed middle period during which no help came from France, and a sad end in which the Chevalier played an ineffectual part. Thereafter the Scottish Jacobites came firmly to the view that another bid was impossible without massive support in military supplies and money. They did not reckon on yet another shift in the military and political situation in Europe and the irruption of the Young Chevalier at the age of twenty-four – gay, handsome and athletic, with enormous personal charm, hardihood as unshakeable as a gambler's nerve and manifest faith in his destiny. He brought a meagre supply of arms and seven companions instead of an army.

The clans came in reluctantly – first young MacDonald of Clanranald, then the Camerons. The entry of the latter was decisive. A rendezvous at Glenfinnan was arranged for August 19th, 1745, a Monday. (Alexander MacDonald, seventh Chieftain and great-uncle of the Alexander who raised the Monument, lodged the Prince at Glenaladale the night before the gathering.) The Prince ordered the raising of his standard in the presence of 1,000 to 1,500 clansmen, including a Campbell. Charles wore a 'red-laced west coat and breeches and a dun coat with a yellow bob at his Hat'. The company which heard the formal proclamation of his father as King of Great Britain and Ireland was not exclusively Jabobite: among those present were an officer of Guise's Regiment and some seventy Royal Scots, the first prisoners to be taken.

By September 17th the Prince was in Edinburgh and the proclamation had been repeated at the mercat cross. The first battle, Prestonpans, was a signal victory, but few recruits came in from Lowland Scotland, or from England as the march to the south proceeded. After Derby, from which the retreat began, nearly all was misfortune save for a skirmish at Clifton and the battle of Falkirk. The arrival of a small force from the French service was heavily counterbalanced by the return of the British army from the Continent, and the navy defeated belated attempts to run in French money and supplies.

The Trust centre, opened in 1966, provides an exposition of the Prince's progress from his first landing in Moidart to his escape from the same region five months after Culloden. A notable exhibit is a scale model of the *Du Teillay*, the French frigate which carried him from France to Loch nan Uamh (a name which now would have a less remote and romantic connotation had not the West Highland Railway, after an initial survey, decided to make Mallaig its terminal). The old loyalties find expression in a garden of the clans and

Glenfinnan: to commemorate zeal, bravery and fidelity

in bolts of Glenaladale tartan which are specially woven for the Trust. It was felicitous that the present Chief of the Camerons, Colonel Donald Cameron of Lochiel, K.T., should be elected convener of the local Glenfinnan Committee in 1952 in succession to his father, and similarly that the most consistent contributors to Glenfinnan funds should be members of a family, resident in Canada, who had close associations with the direct descendants of the MacDonald chieftains of Glenaladale.

Pass of Killiecrankie, Tayside

2½ miles north of Pitlochry on A9

Queen Victoria looked down on the Pass of Killiecrankie in 1844 and declared herself as much pleased with it. Earlier travellers would have wondered why. Up to 1723 the pass was one of the most forbidding of Scotland's river roads. A rough and narrow track on a precipitous slope above the river Garry was an unavoidable hazard on the route from Perth to Inverness via Atholl and Badenoch. Then General Wade built his military road on the eastern rim, more or less on the line of the present A9 trunk road. Last century the railway engineers, blasting and tunnelling, laid a track a little above river level. Nothing remained to indicate that this had been

The Pass of Killiecrankie

a natural obstacle to rank in military terms with the Pease Gorge, the double defile which was Scotland's static defence against any advance from England by the east coast.

There is nothing on the A1 between Dunbar and Berwick-upon-Tweed to hint at the toil and trouble with which Edward I in 1289 and Cromwell in 1650, both marching north, got their armies across the Pease Burn and Heriot Water. History is better served at Killiecrankie. The Trust centre here was the first to be built with interpretation and information as the main intent. It stands within a mile of the narrow ground on which the battle of Killiecrankie was fought in 1689, and the pass heard the first shot fired in the Jacobite cause, just as Culloden heard the last sixty-seven years later. It came from the gun of Iain Ban Beag Mac-rath (Little Fair John Macrae), an Atholl hunter and scout as wary and economical as Daniel Boone in the American wilderness. He had one bullet. It killed a cavalry officer who fell near the gully which bears the name of the Trooper's Den.

*Killiecrankie:
the visitor centre*

The Revolution of 1688 brought William of Orange to England in November and sent King James VII and II in flight to France two days before Christmas. There he was recognized by Louis XIV as King of Great Britain. In Scotland the only man prepared to lead an armed opposition against the Government was the king's Lieutenant-General, John Graham of Claverhouse, Viscount Dundee – 'Bonnie Dundee'. He sought recruits in the Highlands, then moved south into Atholl where Blair Castle had been seized and garrisoned for King James. In the interim King William, who gave scant attention to anything in Scotland but the Jacobite threat, had appointed Major-General Mackay to command his forces there. Mackay, at Dunkeld, was determined to recover Blair Castle and marched out early on July 27th, 1689. An advance party secured the pass. His 4,000 men – six regiments of infantry and two troops of horse – won to the north end, followed by a train of 1,200 baggage horses. They emerged on a little flat by the river, and found that Dundee and his 2,500 clansmen had the advantage of standing on higher ground. Mackay moved his army up to what seemed an adequate defensive position and awaited an attack.

Killiecrankie, like every major engagement in the Risings except Prestonpans, began as a set-piece battle. It was won by a Highland charge, though Mackay's volleys killed more than 600, and instantly it became a rout. Mackay rallied about 400 men and marched them over the hills to Weem Castle near Aberfeldy. Most of the rest were either killed or taken prisoner. One man evaded the slaughter in the pass by an incredible jump, from rock to rock, across the river at the

Soldier's Leap. But it was a Pyrrhic victory for the 'king over the water'. Dundee was mortally wounded, and resistance collapsed within a year.

The battleground, behind Urrard House, is on private property. The fifty-four acres of the Pass of Killiecrankie, formerly part of the estate of Faskally, came to the Trust in 1947 by gift from Mrs Edith Foster.

<table>
<tr><td>Rough Castle and the Antonine Wall, Central</td><td>6 miles west of Falkirk by A803, 1 mile south of Bonnybridge, off B816</td></tr>
</table>

For possibly half a century the Antonine Wall was the north-west frontier of the Roman Empire. It was constructed in A.D. 142 (across the narrow waist of Scotland, a full thirty-seven miles, from Bridgeness on the Firth of Forth to Old Kilpatrick on the Firth of Clyde) – and apparently abandoned towards the end of the second century. It represented a partial return to the 'forward' policy of which Julius Agricola, governor of Britain, was the first exponent (A.D. 79–84) backed by a tenth part of Rome's regular army, three legions out of thirty. After his departure, under orders, and the gradual abandonment of the fort system which he had created, there was great dubiety about what to do about the turbulent tribes of north Britain. The emperor Hadrian, having reconnoitred at least part of the terrain in person, decided to stop short of the Cheviot Hills. He strung his great stone wall from Newcastle to Carlisle (A.D. 122–28). Next, on the imperial instruction of Antoninus Pius, a new governor of Britain, Lollius Urbicus, moved up against the trouble-makers and established the frontier-line in Scotland. He too had three legions – the II, VI and XX, in which many southern Britons may well have been enlisted. They commemorated the governor's ritual victory, place and date unknown, in the dedication-tablets of the wall of turf which they built for him.

Rough Castle is by far the best preserved, though one of the smallest, of the forts which were erected at intervals of two miles to house a garrison of perhaps 7,000 auxiliaries. (Fragments of an inscribed stone on which the Sixth Cohort of the Nervii recorded that, under the charge of Flavius Betto, a centurion of the XX legion, the headquarters building was all their own work, were recovered on the site in 1903.) The fort, together with the sectors of the great defensive system immediately to the east and west, form a notable Roman monument in which all the basic components are visible within a short compass.

Antonine's Wall stood for most of its length on the lip of

an escarpment. It was a rampart of turf, laid on a stone
foundation fourteen feet broad. It stood at least ten feet
high and was probably surmounted by a wooden breastwork.
Twenty feet in front of the rampart there was dug a defensive
ditch, forty feet wide and twelve feet deep in the centre.
Behind the rampart, generally parallel with it, there was
constructed a hard-top road for the swift movement of troops
and vehicles. This, the military way, was about eighteen feet
wide, had a foundation of large stones embedded in clay and
a cambered surface consisting of rammed cobbles topped with
gravel.

*Rough Castle: the
ditch – investigation
and restoration, 1963*

The lay-out of Rough Castle, tucked behind the rampart,
high above a ravine through which the Rowan Tree Burn
slides down to the valley floor, is eloquent of the offensive-
defensive principle which dominated Roman military thought.
The main gate, a double gate facing north, was placed in the
wall itself. A patrol or a punitive force could issue on the
instant, crossing the ditch on a mound, taking care to avoid
the booby-traps beyond. These were ten parallel rows of
pits, or *lilia*. Each pit was seven feet long and three feet wide
at the top and two and a half feet deep in the centre, and had
in it a sharpened stake so positioned as to cause maximum
discomfiture to anyone who stumbled in. The fort had single

gates on the east, south and west. Its small size has been noted. It measured 215 feet within its rampart. The latter was also turf, twenty feet thick at the base and resting on a stone foundation. In addition to the headquarters building, excavation has located within the fort the foundations of the governor's house and a granary with a loading platform at the north end. These were all built of stone. The site of a barrack block, constructed of timber, has also been identified. An annexe, attached to the east wall of the fort, contained the bath-house which was an indispensable requisite in every Roman station. Fort and annexe were protected on three sides by ditches.

The site was excavated in 1903 by the Society of Antiquaries of Scotland. The defences were re-examined by Sir George Macdonald in the 1930s. The property is in the guardianship of the Scottish Development Department (Ancient Monuments).

The profile of the great ditch is also seen to advantage west of Falkirk and east of Watling Lodge on the Bonnyhill–Camelon road, B816. (From a fortlet on the site of the Lodge there issued the Roman road to the north which is mentioned in reference to Bannockburn.) To a third stretch of ditch and wall in Seabegs Wood, one mile west of Bonnybridge on the south bank of the Forth–Clyde canal, the Trust added by purchase in 1973 an area of fifteen acres. Seabegs, like the Rough Castle sector, stands on the edge of the escarpment and, scarcely touched by the hand of man since Roman times, bears only indigenous trees in an area which has been transformed by the extension of agriculture and by industrial development.

Rough Castle: excavation by the Scottish Society of Antiquaries, 1903

V · COUNTRYSIDE

with an introduction by W. J. Eggeling

Introduction

In few places in the temperate Western world is there within so limited an area so great a diversity of countryside as in Scotland. A glance at the map picks out the three main regions. First, the south or Lowlands, stretching from the border with England to the southern limit of the Central Highlands; second, the centre and east, with the Great Glen forming its northern march; third, the north and north-west, comprising the remainder.

Each of these regions is different and each has within it great contrasts. In the south: the remote fastnesses of Galloway; the hills of Carrick giving way to the lush dairylands of Ayrshire; the wide sweep of the Southern Uplands, series upon series of smooth, treeless hogsbacks and rounded summits separated by steep-sided valleys and cut by narrow rocky cleughs, beloved by raven and ring ouzel. These contrast, on the one hand, with the valley of the Tweed and the historic Borders – a land of wide, slow-flowing rivers, deciduous woodlands, warbler song in summer – and, on the other, with the high-yielding barley and potato fields of the East Lothian coast. Westwards from here, still greater contrast: the humming industrial hive of Scotland's midland belt abutting on the approaches to the Highlands – Loch Lomond, the peace of the Campsie Fells and the wooded splendour of the Trossachs.

The Central Highlands, unique for Scottish crested tits and a relic arctic flora, are a jumble of upland masses – the Breadalbane Hills, the Monadhliaths, the Cairngorms, and many more. They include the highest peaks and plateaux in Britain. Each separate range has its characteristics; no two have the same mixture of vegetation and underlying rocks, or the same level of fertility – or lack of it; each, scenically, is in part the product of man's usage of the land. Here, too, are some of Scotland's noblest lochs and rivers: Earn, Rannoch, Tummel, Dee, Don and Spey, all of them noted for their salmon, each with its own magnificent setting. Deeside and Speyside boast the largest and best-preserved, although much altered, remnants of the old Caledonian pinewood; and it is in the Grampians, notably within their eastern half, that the best of the Scottish grouse moors are located, and that the development of heather is at its finest. Almost all the higher ground throughout these Highlands is grouse moor or deer forest; nowhere in the centre is arable a feature of the landscape; but in the east there is again the pastoral contrast – the broad

179

belt of plough and pasture fringing the North Sea from Angus round through Aberdeen to Banff, and on to Inverness.

Lastly, the north and west: to many, because of its wildness and its remoteness, and for the breath-catching beauty of its coasts (cliffs, sea lochs, bays, beaches and islands) and for the individuality of its mountains, this region is the Scotland of their dreams – for holidays. But much, indeed the most of it, is barren, largely as a result of land misuse, although inherently the land is poor. The human population is scanty, except in isolated pockets near the coasts; Caithness is a waste of peaty bog; eastern and central Sutherland an empty land. Everywhere are ruined crofts, each with its small, abandoned fields. Sheep there are, and deer, but farming in the main is confined to the seaward fringe, mostly in Easter Ross. Seen from the summits of its mountains, most of the far north – Caithness, Sutherland and Wester Ross – is a mosaic of waters; here there is the greatest density and largest number of freshwaters in the British Isles. Ranging from large loch to tiny lochan, the majority are poor in nutrients and thus infertile – except in beauty.

These in brief sketch are the countrysides and landscapes of Scotland. Little in the scene has changed since the Countryside Commission for Scotland published the first edition of its official guidebook, *Scotland's Countryside 1970*, in European Conservation Year. By every assessment, those landscapes which involve mountains and water rate highest in scenic value; the rich pattern of farmed countryside comes next; anything that savours of uniformity, third; unrelieved industrial landscapes, last. Overall they rate as exceptional, not only because of the extent of wild upland and scattered waters but also because of the variety and sharp contrasts throughout the whole.

To what exactly do we owe this heritage? Obviously in the beginning, to the great earth movements and subsequent erosive processes that shaped the form, created the skeleton. But naked rock and bare earth alone are not enough; such landscapes are dead. It is the clothing of the bones, the covering of vegetation in all its permutations of life-form, plant associations and colour, changing with the seasons, and all the other life that is in the end dependent on this, that create the living pattern of countryside which transmutes mere lands form.

How did this pattern arise, what have been the factors in its shaping? One has overridden all the rest: the activities of man. There is not one single corner where he has not been the main creator of his surroundings. In the ice ages, succeeding glaciations erased all trace of vegetation from the face of

Scotland – except, perhaps, on one or two high hilltops. In subsequent millennia the land recolonized, and at length the whole of it, save probably a few lone hilltops, bore forest. Man, though present, had a negligible effect on the vegetation; he was a hunter and fisher.

Then came a time of increased rainfall. When it ended, about 5,000 years ago, man began to clear the land to grow his barley and to graze his cattle and his pigs. The early farmer was nomadic; and everywhere, he felled the forest. In the Bronze Age, the rate of clearance quickened; settlements replaced nomadic life; sheep and goats became important. And so it went on: more people, better tools, increasing stock, the widespread use of fire. Came the Iron Age, a time of vast deforestation; wood was used for smelting, wood the only source of power. There was no let-up. During the long wet periods, blanket bog had formed extensively in Scotland. When the rain had passed, and the climate once more favoured forest, the grazing of man's stock held back its spread. And so, from century to century, trees disappeared. Not until the eighteenth century, when only scattered patches of the woods remained, did man replant – in places. And only in the last half-century has there been large-scale reafforestation.

In the Highlands man has destroyed. He bared the hills of trees and denuded the Highlands of shelter; by excessive pasturing and the repeated use of fire he lowered the fertility of the grazings that replaced the forest; over the years, by misuse of the land, he drove his own folk from it, as the empty crofts now testify. And in place of the human population that might still be there we have wild, lonely places.

How different in the Lowlands, on the deeper soils, sustained through care. Here, with the options open, the covering of the land, the coat of landscape, can be varied; altered to meet man's changing needs; planned to suit – both for crop-yield and beauty. The lairds of the eighteenth and nineteenth centuries gave us the settled pastoral landscapes that we have today. The early eighteenth century brought the massive introduction to the Highlands of the sheep – the ultimate destroyer – but the same century saw, the great agricultural revolution which transformed the Lowland countryside.

Most of the pattern of that countryside – the lay-out of farms, steadings, shelter-belts, woodlands and rural communities – was created between 1750 and 1800. There was planning for river, stream and wood, for large farm and small farm, for arable cropping, pasture and sport; for the livelihood of builders, ditchers, hedgers, farm workers, blacksmiths, millers, woodmen and keepers; provision for the rural community. In the course of the nineteenth century and into the twentieth there was further, if slower, change: the gradual exclusion of the smaller unit, the creation of bigger holdings, the introduction of improved farm implements, fewer jobs for country people. Today there is still greater change; the break-up of the large estates due to high taxation and crippling duties; the mechanization of farming, with its demand for bigger fields, fewer hedges, the undergrounding of drainage, the clearance of small, wild places, and the use of herbicides and pesticides. The landscape problem now is to maintain the variety that constitutes scenic attraction; to avoid a singularity of use, the intensity of total farming; to retain a modicum of trees and other cover.

As we have seen, the history of the Highlands is a record of the human exploitation of very limited and delicate natural resources, with the inevitable consequences. A range of economic and ecological problems was created – many of them with us still. Agriculture in the Highlands has always been a struggle; today it depends, to an ever greater extent than farming in more fertile areas, on government subsidies for livestock and land reclamation. The Forestry Commission, ploughing and fertilizing hundreds of thousands of acres of hill, helps not only in the economic sense of making barren land produce timber, but also in the ecological sense, with a new planting policy and mass rehabilitation of bare landscape to a more diverse environment. But the unbalanced age-structure of the surviving crofting communities presents the Crofters Commission and others with a problem for which there is no simple solution.

In the twentieth century the people of Britain are struggling to find room as more and more countryside disappears under houses and industrial estates and as the coastline becomes developed for leisure and recreation. The desolate Highlands, with their beauty of space, colour and form, their exhilarating winds and their challenge, have assumed new importance; their use as the sporting perquisite of the few may have been acceptable in the past, but today every square mile of remote and uninhabited land is the potential recreational range of the British people as a whole, and this heritage of mountain landscapes and purple moors has become the Mecca of tens of thousands of visitors. There is something about wilderness which prompts people to participate; a drive to a viewpoint may satisfy the majority, but others wish far more than this. Man seeks to maximize participation in wilderness, yet wilderness can survive only where human influence is at a minimum. The conservation of wilderness must therefore involve planning to control the growing impact of human pressures on areas which are at present comparatively inaccessible to man, particularly by car. Constraints must also be applied to access by boat, pony and on foot. Within wilderness there must be zoning for different types of public pursuit, ranging from the viewpoint on the main highway to the sanctuary into which man may go only for essential management and surveillance. Between these two extremes visitor-pressure must be regulated to the precise needs of conservation, but as many people as possible must be allowed to take part in the wilderness experience. And on the periphery of the wilderness areas the indigenous population will surely reap the benefits of developing tourism, improved communications and an increase in other facilities.

Linked inescapably with the planning of the countryside is the conservation of its wildlife, the plants and animals of its fields, woods and streams. The quality and beauty of a countryside depend as much on its ability to reflect the lives of those that live in it, wildlife as well as man, as on anything else. This is something that the improvers of the eighteenth century recognized, and for which they catered in their planning; it is up to us to do the same.

Just as the countryside of Scotland has changed over the centuries, so too have the plants and animals that have enlivened it. Almost all the larger animals that inhabited the early forest have gone, never to return. In historic times, the lynx was amongst the first to disappear; the bear went in the sixteenth century; the wolf in the mid-eighteenth. The red deer, more adaptable – and valued for food and sport – has survived. The original wild cattle were replaced early on by half-wild herds and then domestic strains; wild pigs persisted longer, but they too had been largely exterminated by the seventeenth century. It has been the same with birds: species have been lost to Scotland by deliberate persecution – the sea-eagle is a recent example – but much more important in this context has been the loss of habitat, particularly perhaps through the drainage of marshes and fens. However, there have also been introductions. The rabbit, brought into Britain by the Normans, quickly spread throughout Scotland; it has affected our native vegetation more than any other animal except man and the domestic sheep, itself an introduction. Grey squirrel, mink, several species of deer, pheasant, these and others have been brought in, too. And what of plants? Changes profound, and continuing. Of the trees, by far the most and some of the commonest – the sycamore and the beech, for instance – are introductions. Scotland has only three native conifers, the Scots pine, juniper and yew, but dozens of other softwoods are now commonplace: larches, firs, cypresses, spruces. With hardwoods, shrubs and herbs, the same situation: newcomers everywhere. Some have been introduced deliberately and some by accident; others arrived by natural spread.

What are the agencies which have perpetuated and are still striving to sustain in the face of growing pressures the diversity of countryside in small compass which is the great charm of Scotland? To give credit where credit is due, we must first pay tribute to our planning system and, despite the occasional lapse, to our planners. Supported since establishment in 1968 by the Countryside Commission for Scotland, the latter have in the last few decades almost stopped the ribbon development which was spreading out into the countryside and have put a stop to other gross misuses. We have also to thank the past, not least the improving lairds whom we have mentioned and even the absentee landlords who, by excluding all development, have done what lack of water and the tsetse fly have done for so much of Africa – preserved countryside as it was, so that it may be used wisely in the future. Next there are the national agencies headed by the Forestry Commission, whose activities have produced in many places a much greater diversity of habitats than existed previously and have provided also for the nation that wonderful range of forest parks which include, in Scotland, the Glen Trool Park in Kirkcudbrightshire, the Argyll Park, the Queen Elizabeth Park in Perthshire and the Glen More Park in Inverness-shire. Then there is the Nature Conservancy Council, whose series of National Nature Reserves (over forty already notified in Scotland with many more, one hopes, still to come) seek to conserve typical habitats and the plants and animals which frequent them.

Just as it is wise not to have all the eggs in one basket, so too it is wise to have several examples of the same habitat conserved – and in different parts of the country. In this way as great a range as possible is preserved unspoiled within every region, for as many people as possible to see. It is for this reason that the activities of the National Trust for Scotland, the Royal Society for the Protection of Birds and the Scottish Wildlife Trust – whose Loch of the Lowes reserve is a model – are so greatly to be welcomed: together these bodies conserve and manage properly a large slice of Scotland's countryside and its wildlife content. Some of their reserves are of national significance – the Loch Insh Fens, just north of Kingussie, run by the R.S.P.B. is a good example – and not a few are important internationally.

In so far as the National Trust for Scotland is concerned we may mention especially Ben Lawers, which, together with adjoining sister National Nature Reserve of Meall nan

Tarmachan, is of international importance for its flora, and the quite unique oceanic island group of St Kilda with its native Soay sheep and its own island forms of fieldmouse and wren, as well as its unparalleled seabird colonies.

At Threave in Kirkcudbrightshire the National Trust for Scotland maintains a wildfowl refuge, in Fair Isle there is an internationally famous bird observatory and at the Corrieshalloch Gorge in Wester Ross there is one of the finest examples in Britain of a box canyon. All these places are out of the common but, although Fair Isle (like St Kilda) possesses some magnificent seascapes, these three properties would scarcely qualify as examples of countryside. It is not just a matter of size but of being typical: the Pass of Killiecrankie is not large (only fifty-four acres) and is perhaps best known for its historical associations, but it and the relatively tiny Linn of Tummel and the equally small Hermitage near Dunkeld are outstanding examples of a particular type of Scottish countryside and of the birds and plants which are found there, well conserved.

For barer, wilder countryside larger units are required in order to portray within the one holding the whole range from

St Kilda: a long haul still to Boreray

sea and river to foothill, corrie and peak. The Trust has all these at Balmacara, Kintail and the Falls of Glomach in the north-west Highlands (together totalling some 20,940 acres), at Torridon also in the Highlands (16,100 acres), with which should be listed the adjoining Beinn Eighe National Nature Reserve, and the Glencoe and Dalness property of 14,200 acres in Argyll. The Grey Mare's Tail and Loch Skene property in Dumfriesshire (2,383 acres) preserves typical Border countryside of the upper levels.

Glencoe :
Gearr Aonach

In a small country so indented as Scotland and with such a variety of off-shore islands, very little is far from the coast; and as many of the views are of the sea and its bays and islands as are of countryside in its conventional sense. Unspoilt sea-scapes are therefore important and it is fortunate that, as is stated in 'Good Intent, Good Offices' (pp. 303–16), the National Trust for Scotland has the power to enter into agreements restricting use. As is said there, the principle of these agreements is simple, the terms flexible. An owner does not divest himself of ownership, but no change of use is permitted without the prior approval of the Trust. Naturally

Torridon: Beinn Alligin from Shieldaig

Sangomore, Durness

it is essential that the Trust considers the area to be worthy of conservation in the national interest.

So far in western Scotland agreements have been signed for Fleet Bay, Kirkcudbrightshire; for five miles of seashore from the Heads of Ayr to the Croy Burn in Ayrshire; for a mile in a critical sector north of Oban; for half a mile on the east coast of Skye; for two miles of Loch Shieldaig to the south of Gairloch; and for thirty-four miles on the shores of Loch Broom and Little Loch Broom, also in Wester Ross. Agreements in Sutherland safeguard five miles of spectacular cliff scenery, sandy beaches and an adjacent island on the north coast at Durness, ten miles around Tongue and eight in the vicinity of Bettyhill. On the east coast, there is an agreement in Fife covering Elie Ness and Chapelgreen; and in East Lothian protection for the coast at Gosford plus the North Berwick Links and the Law.

At the very least, a beginning has been made.

Countryside

On A87 in the Kyle–Plockton area

**Balmacara Estate
Highland**

Of the two Trust properties on the main road to Skye (A87), Kintail is country for the hill walker and mountaineer, and Balmacara the nearest approximation to Lowland in all of Wester Ross. The estate was bequeathed to the Trust in 1946. In the previous hundred years two eastern mercantile fortunes set mixed woodlands around Balmacara House, created a home farm, and enclosed new fields. Today Balmacara's 5,616 acres, rising often to a smooth or craggy hump but never to a peak, occupy roughly half of a green peninsula bounded by Loch Alsh, the Inner Sound and Loch Carron. They comprehend Kyle of Lochalsh (a rail terminal and ferry port for Skye), the village of Plockton, three crofting townships and an airstrip. They look out on landscape and seascape of bewildering diversity – mountains, islands, islets, reefs, the great promon- *Balmacara Bay from* tories of Applecross and Glenelg, the long reach of the Inner *Lochalsh House*

Balmacara : 'a smooth or craggy hump but never a peak'

Sound and the narrows of Kyle Rhea across which the Skye drovers used to swim their cattle on the first leg of a long journey to a mainland tryst.

Kyle of Lochalsh arose somewhat haphazardly with the coming of the railway. Plockton, developed at an earlier date on a more orderly plan, is no longer a trading port but sits snugly on an enchanting bay; and the pleasure-craft in summer are no more colourful than the painted houses on the shore.

Balmacara House was acquired by the former County Council of Ross and Cromarty for use by the education committee. Lochalsh House, to the west, was conveyed to the Trust in 1954 by National Land Fund procedure and is both residence and office of the Trust regional representative. There is roadside parking space on the perimeter of the estate, and there are pleasant woodland walks and a woodland garden. Elsewhere there are lochans populated by brown trout, scrub and heather which harbour many species of birds, watercress in cool, clear streams, and the township of Drumbuie, to protect which the Trust fought the most stubborn and expensive amenity battle in its history.

Since 1970, road improvements, including the construction of a new length of A890 along the southern shore of Loch Carron to eliminate the ferry at Strome, have made communication easy. They have had the effect, however, of isolating

Strome Castle, one of the few ruins which the Trust owns. This stronghold of the MacDonalds of Glengarry was captured in 1609 by Kenneth Mackenzie, Lord of Kintail. Having granted the garrison safety of life and baggage, he blew the place up.

North of Loch Tay, 6 miles east of Killin and 20 miles west of Aberfeldy on A827

Ben Lawers, Tayside

Ben Lawers, soaring 3,984 feet above Loch Tay, is the highest peak in the Breadalbane range, a magnificent labyrinth of hills that enfolds Glen Lochay and Glen Lyon and such natural and man-made wonders as dwindling stands of indigenous Scots pine, traces of ancient bloomeries at which iron-workers toiled, and the shell of a school, a remote and mute memorial to the Scottish Society for the Propagation of Christian Knowledge and an eighteenth-century drive to promote morals and milder manners by teaching English to a population of Gaelic speakers. The vast bulk of Lawers is dissected by many glens; in distant view and on close acquaintance it is truly a mountain of great beauty. That was one reason which moved the Trust in 1950 to buy with 'Unna money' 7,420 acres on the southern face of Lawers and Ben Ghlas. There was another, just as

Loch Tay and Ben Lawers

cogent. The Lawers massif is singular in Britain for the range of its arctic-alpine flora.

How that came about cannot be explained precisely, at least at this date, in simple or even scientific terms. But the schoolboy who emerged from the Mountain Visitor Centre describing Lawers as the mountain that stood on its head was not completely off the mark. The folding of sedimentary rocks (the result of intense geological convulsions) and altitude and exposure were the main factors in producing a habitat which has survived since some point in the early post-glacial period.

By agreement between the Nature Conservancy Council and the Trust, an area of 8,530 acres consisting of the Trust's holding together with 1,110 acres in the Meall nan Tarmachan National Nature Reserve, established to the west of Lawers in 1964 with the consent of two private landowners, is now one National Nature Reserve. (These sectors and an adjacent 5,300-acre Site of Special Scientific Interest to the north are classified in the Council's 'Conservation Review' as a Grade 1 site of international significance because of the rich mountain flora.) This alliance is a logical extension of an arrangement made in 1963 whereby the Nature Conservancy combined with the Trust to establish an information centre; it accords perfectly with a joint operation which led to the construction of the Mountain Visitor Centre as the focal point for the interpretation and ranger services. To that enterprise the Countryside Commission for Scotland, the Carnegie U.K.

Ben Lawers:
unobtrusive and
indispensable – the
mountain visitor centre

Trust and the former Perthshire County Council all sub-scribed. The Centre, opened in 1972 and manned by Trust ranger staff, is supported in part by grant aid from the Countryside Commission and the Scottish Development Department. The Nature Conservancy Council continues to help in providing the information services.

The imperatives of a management plan go beyond the need to prevail on visitors to stay on the trails and refrain from picking or uprooting plants as specimens. Lawers is almost as notable for its wild life – invertebrates, birds and mammals, fishes and amphibians – as for its flowers. Of the old land-uses, grazing continues. Later variants include ski-ing and the Scottish Ski Club's lunch-hut at an elevation of 2,000 feet in Coire Odhar. Lochan na Larige, beside the hill road to Glen Lyon, and the smaller Lochan nan Cat are reservoirs for a North of Scotland Hydro-Electric Board power station. The Trust car park was a by-product of the tunnel works. It was constructed and presented by the Board and Cementation Ltd in 1952.

Ben Lawers:
Silene aucaulis

The principal plant communities, a continuum nourished by an abundant supply of fresh mineral matter, occur at altitudes from 2,500 feet to around 3,800 feet. Most spectacular, certainly in June and July, are the flushed grasslands and the sides of the corries, aglow with pink masses of moss campion yet affording room for the saxifrages, alpine mouse-ear chickweed, cyphel, gentians, globe flower and mountain pansy.

Corrieshalloch Gorge, Highland

At Braemore, 12 miles south-east of Ullapool near junction of A835 and A832

One of the pleasures of driving in Scotland is the experience of 'coming off the roof', dropping down from moorland to a green strath or a long arm of the sea. At Braemore the sparse vegetation of the Dirrie More (once 'the big oak forest') gives way to well-grown woods. And these conceal a chasm as awe-inspiring as the peaks on either hand, An Teallach to the west, Beinn Dearg on the east.

Corrieshalloch Gorge is a magnificent box canyon, 200 feet deep. For the length of a mile it marks the old boundary between Easter and Wester Ross. In places its width, 50 to 150 feet, is little greater at the top than at the bottom. The river which carved this channel through hard metamorphic rock ('psammitic granulite' to a geologist) plunges 150 feet over the Falls of Measach. A little way downstream from the falls a suspension bridge and a viewing platform make safe vantage

Corrieshalloch: the gorge and Falls of Measach

points – one has to take great care on all paths.

The gorge is a very special habitat for plant life. The latter must survive in conditions of high humidity and poor light. Here, though Corrieshalloch is deficient in lime, is a haven for species which might have vanished from the region because of moor burning and grazing by sheep. Sanicle flourishes at the lowest levels alongside ferns and feather mosses, and reappears on rills in company with opposite-leaved saxifrage, mountain sorrel and germander speedwell. The narrow horizontal ledges harbour five species of fern, and greater woodrush, tufted hairgrass and woodmillet, a plant rare in north-west Scotland. The trees which find a foothold include wych elm, birch and hazel and naturalized sycamore, Norway maple and beech. The most numerous shrubs are goat willow, bird cherry and guelder rose.

There are trout in the deep pools. Most species of woodland birds are represented, and ravens nest on a ledge opposite the viewpoint. The suspension bridge would merit an entry in any inventory of industrial monuments; it was constructed by Sir John Fowler (1817–98), joint designer of the Forth railway bridge, who bought the estate of Braemore in 1867. Detailed annual inspection confirms the durability of the main components.

By agreement, the Trust property is incorporated in a National Nature Reserve.

1½ miles north of Pitlochry on A9

Craigower, Tayside

The summit of the beacon hill of Craigower (1,300 feet) is reached by a right-of-way across a golf course.

It has at its back the rough heather-clad slope of Ben Vrackie (2,757 feet). In the panoramic view to the west man-made and natural landscape are adjusted in happy balance, much as they appeared in 1845 when Sir James Clark, Queen Victoria's physician, signified approval of Pitlochry and its environs and so assured the place of a future as a resort. The confluence of the rivers Garry and Tummel is marked by well-grown woods. Both rivers are elements in an extensive hydro power system of which the ancillaries are visible as far north as Dalwhinnie and Loch Ericht. Here the effects on landscape

Craigower, Pitlochry

have been considerable and agreeable. The broad expanse of Loch Tummel has grown slightly broader; and there is a new creation in the south-west, Loch Faskally, formed by the damming of the Tummel. Its outflow drives the turbines in the Pitlochry power station. But the sculpted symmetry of Schiehallion (3,547 feet) owes nothing to artifice, and sight of the tops of the Glencoe range on the far horizon is an intimation that larger features of the Highland scene can never be domesticated. The prospect to the south-east across Strathmore and Tayside, is closed felicitously by the Lomond Hills in Fife.

At Linn of Tummel (see pp. 205–6) one has the freedom of fifty enchanting acres by the banks of the two rivers.

Culzean Country Park, Strathclyde

12 miles south of Ayr on A719, 5 miles west of Maybole by B7023

Culzean Country Park, the first in Scotland, occupies the grounds of Culzean Castle and the range of home farm buildings which was designed by Robert Adam, like the castle itself, and built in 1777. The park was established in 1969 by agreement between the Trust and three local planning authorities, Ayrshire County Council and the town councils of Ayr and Kilmarnock. Since the reorganization of local government in 1975 new authorities form a 'consortium' with the Trust – the District Councils of Kyle and Carrick, Cunninghame, and Cumnock and Doon Valley, and Strathclyde Regional Council.

The boundaries encompass 565 acres of woodlands, gardens, cliff and seashore. (The gardens and the original landscape plans are described on pp. 143–5.) Outdoor facilities for visitors include picnic places, nature trails (one of which was formed by clearing a disused railway line) and guided walks in company with ranger-naturalist staff. The Park Centre in the home farm buildings provides, in addition to a restaurant and shop, audio-visual sessions, an exposition of topography and social and economic history, lecture rooms, classrooms and numerous teaching aids. Programmes devised in consultation with education authorities in the region make extensive use of the centre and the park for interpretation and the teaching of fieldcraft to school groups.

The restoration and adaptation of the home farm complex – formerly a hollow square of stables, byres and barns – was a major project in which the external elegance of Adam's buildings and entrance archways was regained by the replacement of eroded stonework. The cost, some £233,000, was met by a Government grant of 75 per cent made available under the

Culzean: the Country Park Centre – the courtyard

Countryside (Scotland) Act 1967 by the Countryside Commission for Scotland and the Scottish Development Department, the balance being borne in equal proportion by three 'founding' authorities. Numerous items for the historical exhibition—harness, agricultural implements, hand tools, dairy equipment and household plenishings – came, most appropriately, as gifts from local sources: a main theme is the vigorous movement towards land improvement in Ayrshire in the eighteenth and nineteenth centuries.

What the 'improvers' accomplished by muscle-power and horsepower, on good and indifferent ground, is apparent within the park and in the Ayrshire countryside.

Culzean: the Country Park Centre – adaptation gave back to Robert Adam's home farm complex its original outline

14 miles north of Tyndrum, 16 miles south of Fort William on A82

Glencoe and Dalness, Highland

Beyond Tyndrum the A82, the Glasgow–Inverness trunk road enters a landscape wilder than any on the southern sectors. Loch Tulla, encircled by mountains, is a prelude to the long slope of the Black Mount and the apparently endless expanse of Rannoch Moor. That ancient watershed ('as waste as the sea', said R. L. Stevenson in *Kidnapped*) has for a backdrop to the north a line of peaks extending from Ben Nevis to Ben Alder. Far to the east there is an end-on view of Schiehallion, a silhouette as improbable as that of Stac Polly or Canisp on the western margin of Sutherland. Yet nothing short of a first

Glencoe

sighting of Stob Dearg, the vast north-eastern shoulder of Buachaille Etive Mor (the Great Shepherd of Etive), prepares one for the grandeur of Glencoe.

At high noon in high summer the great defile can and often does look like a cold, wet corner of hell – a cleft in rocks indifferent, inimical to man; a place to spark a flashing crack of recollection or apprehension. The modern highway is paralleled by an old military road. When it was driven through, in about 1750, the wilderness began at Callander, Crieff and Dunkeld, and the massacre of Glencoe was within the memory of man.

On a crisp, clear day there are no superlatives too extravagant for this 'through valley', so stark in beauty and, with the Forest of Dalness to the south, so apt for walking, climbing, field studies, self-study or a sun-warmed drowse beside a clattering burn. It was regard for wilderness, a regard with contemporary roots, which put 14,200 acres of Glencoe and Dalness into the hands of the Trust between 1935 and 1937. These form a rough triangle with sides some six miles long enclosed by the river Etive above Dalness, the river Coe above Clachaig, and the Aonach Eagach ridge, the north wall of Glencoe. This area contains, in addition to Buachaille Etive Mor and the long, serrated Aonach Eagach ridge, Bidean nam Bian (at 3,766 feet the highest summit in Argyll) and Buachaille Etive Beag.

At the head of the glen the road makes a spectacular entry between tumbling streams (the Meeting of Three Waters) and the rocky upthrust of the Study (named in old Scots the 'stithie' or anvil). At lower levels there is green pasture around Loch Achtriochtan, Ossian's Cave is visible on the north face of Aonach Dubh (but not the book in which rock climbers record their visits), and the river Coe turns northward past Achnacon and the Signal Rock into a broadening strath. It was in small townships in these areas and around Carnoch that thirty-eight MacDonalds died at the hands of Robert Campbell of Glen-lyon and a company of 120 men of Argyll's regiment in the massacre of 1692.

Some of the most celebrated rock and ice climbs in Britain are located on Buachaille Etive Mor and Bidean nam Bian. The latter has a notable twin peak, Stob Coire nan Lochan (3,657 feet) and three outliers, the 'Three Sisters of Glencoe' – Beinn Fhada (3,120 feet), Gearr Aonach (2,500 feet) and Aonach Dubh (2,849 feet). The mean annual rainfall is approximately 90 inches, so Glencoe may be shrouded in mist and rain on any day of the year. October brings the onset of frost. Heavy snowfall is most frequent in January and February. The best prospect of settled weather occurs in May and June.

The territory is not especially rich in wild life, but it is ranged by red deer. Wild cat, golden eagle, ptarmigan, golden plover, dotterel, mallard and teal may also be observed. Of the flora, moss campion, saxifrages, crowberry and Alpine alchemilla are most prominent.

In pursuit of the common conservation aims of the Country-

Glencoe:
the townships have gone,
but memories of the
Massacre abide

side Commission for Scotland and the Trust, the farm of Achnacon (1,390 acres) was purchased in 1972. One of the buildings is now the Glencoe mountain rescue centre. The Glencoe visitor centre at Clachaig, erected by the Countryside Commission for Scotland, is by agreement operated by the Trust.

Grey Mare's Tail, Dumfries and Galloway

8½ miles north-east of Moffat and 20 miles south-west of Selkirk on A708

The Trust's one property in the southern uplands was acquired in 1962 in order to ensure continued access for the public to White Coomb (2,695 feet), Loch Skene and the Tail Burn which, cascading 200 feet to join the Moffat Water, forms the waterfall of the Grey Mare's Tail.

It is a wedge of 2,383 acres in rough country, more primitive than any feature visible from road level in the valley of the Moffat Water would suggest. Around the waterfall is an area rich in wildflowers. There, visitors are urged to exercise the utmost care. A similar warning applies to the route to the loch by a narrow, unmade path on the steep eastern bank of the Tail Burn: a slip on an apparently innocent grassy slope can

Grey Mare's Tail

have dire consequences. The trackless hinterland has changed little since the days when the Covenanters sought sanctuary in it, or the day on which fog descended and Sir Walter Scott went down, horse and man, into a bog-hole and was hard put to it 'to get extricated'. Nothing to the westward, where three rivers – Clyde, Tweed and Annan – 'rise a' oot o' ae hill-side', approximates more closely to 'wilderness'. The hazards and discomfort of the boggy areas alternate with rough going over mounds of moraine. The latter are deposits from glaciers which shaped and smoothed not only the Peeblesshire 'Laws' and the great grass hills beyond Megget Water and St Mary's Loch but the whole extent of Ettrick Forest away to the north-east.

Loch Skene

That was sheep country, exporting wool to Europe through Berwick-upon-Tweed as early as the thirteenth century. This is sheep country, too. A summary of land-use and current methods of sheep husbandry, together with notes on flora and wild life, is set out on information boards on the inner wall of a 'stell' (stone-built sheepfold) by the roadside. The sheep are not aggressive. It is best to leave the wild goats to their own devices.

The Hermitage, Tayside

2 miles west of Dunkeld off A9, by the village of Inver

The Hermitage, a charming folly set above a fall on the river Braan, was built in 1758 for the third Duke of Atholl. It was presented in 1943 in fulfilment of a wish of the eighth duke, the Trust's first President.

Ducal notions on how to embellish this retreat, a rectangular pavilion in random rubble masonry with a slated roof and a circular look-out platform, varied from generation to generation. Originally it was surrounded by a wild garden, 'with flower beds and borders about the rocks'. In 1783 the building was renamed 'Ossian's Hall' and furnished in honour of the mythical Gaelic bard to whom James Macpherson attributed his 'translations' of the epic poems *Fingal* and *Temora* which he published in 1762–63.

Restored in a more simple form in 1952, the Hermitage is set in thirty-seven acres of fine woodlands. It has been necessary to reinforce the rock on which it stands. The river has dealt less harshly with the adjoining rusticated saddleback bridge, the other main component in the third duke's creation. There is a nature trail.

The neighbouring village of Inver was the birthplace and home of a non-controversial contributor to Scottish culture.

The Hermitage

Neil Gow, a celebrated eighteenth-century fiddler, composed many of the country's familiar airs.

Kintail and Falls of Glomach, Highland

30 miles west of Invergarry and 20 miles east of Kyle of Lochalsh on A87

The contiguous properties of Kintail and Falls of Glomach cut a broad swathe for year-round access to splendid mountain country in which, for good reason, a casual entry to private land may be unwelcome and during the deer-stalking season (approximately mid-August to mid-October) positively fool-hardy. The need for a 'good neighbour' policy has never been in doubt, and the Trust does more than encourage use of Trust ground in preference to adjacent territory. Care is taken in Morvich visitor centre at the head of Loch Duich to show that stalking is not merely 'sport'. (The deer forests are demon-strably important units in the national economy in terms of

food supply, exports of venison and local employment.) *Kintail*

A gift of £7,000 by the late P. J. H. Unna enabled the Trust to purchase Kintail in 1944 and add its 12,800 acres to Glomach (2,200 acres), which had been presented three years earlier by Mrs E. C. Douglas of Killilan and the Hon. Gerald Portman of Inverinate.

The southern and western boundaries of Kintail rest on Glen Shiel, Loch Duich and Glen Lichd. The Glomach ground carries the northern march across the head of Glen Affric (in which a natural cross-country 'river road' alongside the east-flowing Affric was formerly as heavily trafficked as the track beside the west-flowing Shiel). Within these limits there is a marvellous expanse of summits, glens and lively waters. (It makes the perfect foil to Torridon, the Trust's great mountainous country property farther north – fifty miles by road – in Wester Ross.) The Five Sisters of Kintail rise abruptly from road level in Glen Shiel (sea-level at the head of Loch Duich) to a chain of pointed peaks. Four of them top 3,000 feet, and the summit of Scour Ouran (3,505 feet), the highest, is a celebrated viewpoint. All can be counted among the steepest grass-sloped mountains in Scotland. Beinn Fhada (or Ben

*Loch Duich and the
western end of the
range*

Attow), severed from the Five Sisters by the upper arm of
Glen Lichd and the river Croe, also has attractions in equal
proportion for the climber and the hill-walker.

The Glomach, a relatively short mountain burn, runs
northward from Beinn Fhada to the river Elchaig. Its beginnings are modest. It almost loses its identity in a succession of
small lochs between Beinn Fhada's northern neighbours. Then
it enters a high, narrow glen and starts over a shelf of rock on
a plunge of 750 feet. In the Falls of Glomach the water drops
sheer for more than 300 feet, hits a projecting rock ledge and
drops a further fifty feet into a pool which often, and always in
times of spate, is occluded by spray. The marvel about the fall,
one of the highest in Britain, is that erosion by so small a
stream should have produced such a fearsome channel.

Kintail, within the area of Atlantic influence, has generally
a moderate range of temperatures. The flora of the corries of
the Five Sisters and Bhein Fhada include alpine rue, dwarf
willow, mountain azalea, starry and alpine saxifrages, and
dwarf cudweed. On Beinn Fhada all of these species appear
even on the summit ridge (2,000 to 3,000 feet), plus marsh
marigold, moss campion, clubmoss, and cloudberry. In early

summer the nests of meadow pipit may be found at high elevations, companions to golden plover and ptarmigan. Badger is uncommon, fox and mountain hare less so, and short-eared owl, merlin, greenshank, black-throated diver and three or four species of duck are present.

From the fourteenth to the mid-eighteenth century this was the country of the Clan Macrae, 'Mackenzie's shirt of mail'. For generations Macraes were Constables of Eilean Donan Castle and Chamberlains of Kintail.

Linn of Tummel, Tayside

3 miles north of Pitlochry on A9, at junction with B8019

Under the high-level bridge which carries 'the road to the Isles' across the river Garry two Trust properties meet. Like Craigower, each is, physically and historically, characteristic of the Perthshire Highlands. Upstream is the Pass of Killiecrankie which saw the first and only set-piece battle in the first Jacobite uprising in 1689. Downstream, on the true right bank, a path through wild-wood and stands of oak, sycamore, Douglas fir, spruce and larch leads to Linn of Tummel. An obelisk commemorates a visit by Queen Victoria in 1844. At that date the Tummel made a plunging fall to join the Garry.

Linn of Tummel

The fall became the Linn (Gaelic – 'linne', a pool) when the level of both rivers was raised in 1950 by the creation of Loch Faskally, the lowest reservoir in a multiple development of water power in the Tummel–Garry basin by the North of Scotland Hydro-Electric Board.

The path is part of a forest nature trail established in 1970, European Conservation Year. The Linn and an area of some fifty acres were presented in 1944 by Dr G. F. Barbour of Bonskeid. (By agreement with the trustees of the Bonskeid estate the last section of the nature trail passes over their ground.) Beside the Linn there is a very early example of a fish pass which formerly enabled salmon to by-pass the falls. It consists of a tunnel, forty feet long, in which pools are formed by a series of boulder weirs. Upstream there is a fascinating rough corner replete with Scots pine, bracken and heather, and on the Bonskeid estate a splendid specimen of a Douglas fir. A good example of natural regeneration of the same species, which was introduced to Britain in 1828 by a Scots botanist, David Douglas of Perth, occurs on Trust ground a little to the north of the Linn.

The nature trail booklet, available at the car park by the bridge, is a first-rate guide not only to the flora and fauna of Linn of Tummel but to the country around it.

Threave Wildfowl Refuge, Dumfries and Galloway

2 miles south-west of Castle Douglas on A75

Over Scotland the flightways of migrant wildfowl, southbound in autumn, northbound in spring, are so numerous that no country child can suppose for long that the grey goose is solely a figure of myth in an old rhyme. There is cause for concern, nevertheless. A mounting interest in ornithology is barely keeping pace with the extension of agriculture and a consequent reduction in the area of wetlands. The natural habitat for geese in particular is shrinking. The Threave wildfowl refuge supplies, under the greatest practicable degree of protection, winter feeding and roosting grounds for both geese and duck.

This attempt at conservation, in a critical area bounded by Castle Douglas, Loch Ken and the river Dee, fulfils one object which the late Major A. F. Gordon, D.S.O., M.C., had in mind when he gave the Threave estate (1,490 acres) to the Trust in 1948. He wished to see the whole property made free from disturbance by wildfowling. The farms are leased on this basis. The project succeeded with the support of local people and the co-operation of Colonel Walter Ross, C.B., O.B.E., M.C., T.D., proprietor of the neighbouring estate of Netherhall.

Threave: observation post near Threave Castle

Public access is permitted within limits between November *Threave Castle*
1st and March 31st. There are four observation posts – two
beside the river Dee, a third on an island in the river, and a
fourth roughly midway between the river and Carlingwark
Loch at Castle Douglas.

The most common goose is the greylag, averaging about
1,500 a year and observed most frequently from the riverside
and island hides. Inland, whitefronted geese (Greenland form)
often occur in small parties, with bean geese and pink-footed
geese in lesser numbers, and there have been single records in
recent years of barnacle, brent and Canada geese. Whooper
swans are regular and Bewick swans occasional visitors.
Widgeon are the most numerous duck in winter. Mallard and
teal breed locally. Pintail and shoveller appear in smaller
numbers, and with great good fortune one may sight gadwall,
scaup or smew. Goldeneye and goosander are the most regular
of the diving ducks, and one may almost rely on seeing heron,
little grebe and cormorant.

11 miles west of Kinlochewe on A896

**Torridon,
Highland**

To this territory W. H. Murray gave top place in the survey
and assessment of Highland landscape (see p. 310) which he
made for the Trust in 1961: 'Glen Torridon, its loch and the

Torridon

mountains on either side exhibit more beauty than any other district of Scotland, including Skye.'

In accepting such a judgment one is not necessarily lending covert support to a 'lobby' for rigid hierarchical classification of landscape or joining the 'wha's like us?' brigade, though to resist the latter impulse may be difficult. By world standards Beinn Alligin, Liathach and Beinn Eighe are modest hills. But even in short perspective, across Upper Loch Torridon, they move this contributor no less deeply than sight of the Rocky Mountains from far off on the plains in eastern Colorado – a magical experience as Pike's Peak and then the Rampart and Front Ranges break the horizon's rim, take shape and put on majesty beyond Colorado Springs and the interstate highway to Denver. Torridon, of course, has no toll road or cog railway to the tops. Anyone choosing a direct line of ascent must pray that handholds and toeholds are sufficient at least for the day.

On Liathach, a five-mile, east-west ridge with seven tops capped partly by quartzite, an intricate and awesome pattern of corries, crags and pinnacles has been sculpted from red-brown Torridonian sandstone 750 million years old. Its neighbours to the west and north, Beinn Alligin and Beinn Dearg, would be notable in any less superlative company. To the east Beinn Eighe is divided in ownership between the Trust and the Nature Conservancy Council but managed in unison for conservation and recreation. It matches Liathach in nearly all respects – nine peaks, an elevation of 3,309 feet on Rhuad-stac Mor and 3,217 feet on the summit of the Sail Mor ridge, the Trust's eastern boundary, in comparison with the 3,456 feet of Liathach's Spidean a' Coire Leith. It differs mainly in that it is sheathed in Cambrian rock of later date. The hard, white quartzite, which on Liathach is merely the icing on the cake, is here in sufficient depth to contain and exhibit fossils of some of the earliest animals on earth – worms of up to half an inch in diameter.

On foot one can admire, without so much as an arduous scramble, the western, northern and eastern aspects of Liathach from a track connecting Coire Mhic Nobuil with Coire Dubh, and also get some impression of Beinn Dearg and the corries and craggy eastern flank of Beinn Alligin. Coire Mhic Fhearchair, a superb example of rock scenery, almost without parallel, can be reached by a relatively short diversion to the north round the base of Sail Mor, the western outlier of *Torridon: lochan in* Beinn Eighe. In this deeply eroded corrie the Triple Buttress, *the hills*

a vast and astonishingly shapely mass of light grey quartzite, leaps from a base of red-brown sandstone, and from a lochan at its feet a string of cascades spill out towards the valley floor.

The Torridon estate (14,100 acres) was accepted by the Commissioners of Inland Revenue in part settlement of estate duty following the death of the fourth Earl of Lovelace. It was transferred to the Trust in 1967 by National Land Fund procedures. A few months later the Alligin Suas property (2,000 acres) immediately to the west was given in memory of Sir Charles Blair Gordon, O.B.E., and Lady Gordon by their sons, Blair, Howard and John Gordon.

The Trust visitor centre at the junction of A896 and the Diabeg road has an audio-visual exposition on local wildlife and a red deer museum.

VI · ISLANDS AND COASTLINE

with an introduction by James Shaw Grant

Introduction

According to the dictionary an island is a small area of land surrounded by water, but personally I cannot conceive of an island in physical or structural terms. To me, an island is a community living in circumstances which intensify all aspects of life – including the difficulty of surviving at all.

There are, of course, uninhabited islands – and if they were inhabited at one time, they have the sadness of man's retreat from a frontier he once maintained. If they have never been inhabited and are incapable of supporting human life at any tolerable level, they lose a good deal of interest for me, although they may be correspondingly more interesting to the ecologist studying the balance of a hierarchy of inter-acting and inter-dependent communities – plants, microbes, insects, birds and animals – where the equilibrium is not disturbed by man.

To say that an island has an insulating effect on its inhabitants, whether human or not, is a pleonasm; and while it may be a simple statement of fact in so far as an uninhabited island is concerned, in implication it is misleading as regards most inhabited islands, for insularity has positive as well as negative consequences.

I suppose we all, as children, live in an 'island' of our own making to the extent that our horizon is limited and we either ignore its existence, regarding our own little circle as the complete universe, or we wonder what lies beyond. On either basis we regard it as separating us from others. But when we are bounded by a physical barrier like the sea, breaking on beach and cliff, and when anyone approaching from the world outside must first appear as a tiny speck on the horizon, gradually taking shape as a vessel with a plume of smoke or a spread of sail, or merely a white forefoot and a hiss of broken water, the sense of belonging to a community which is separate from other communities, and of sharing a life with one's fellow islanders, however one differs from them in religion, politics, recreation or temperament, is greatly strengthened. So too, I think, in most instances, is the desire to explore what lies beyond the sea. The islander tends to be more intense both in his wandering and his coming home.

The effect of an island on its inhabitants is a function of its size and distance from the mainland and also of the existence or non-existence of navigable harbours (and what is navigable changes with the technology of seafaring and with the threshold of acceptable discomfort set by the standard of living of those with whom we compare ourselves and to which we consequently aspire). St Kilda became uninhabited largely because of improved communications and the rising standard of living elsewhere. Stroma was abandoned almost as soon as the county council provided a pier which made it easy for people to get out.

I remember some years ago listening to a discussion on Highland development in which one of the participants illustrated the importance of leadership by contrasting the islands of Scarp and Scalpay, both in Harris, one of which was fast losing its population while the other prospered on fishing and the coastal shipping trade. The difference between the two he found in the existence on Scalpay of one enterprising family. Although his reasoning was at fault, I did not disagree with him openly at the time because we were of the same side of the general argument; but the fact is that the difference between Scarp and Scalpay is that the one lies on the exposed Atlantic coast of Harris and has no anchorage of any sort, while the other lies in the Minch and has several anchorages where small boats can lie with safety, if not with convenience. There are certainly islands where communities have been sustained in difficult situations by the initiative and stubbornness of one or two leaders and there are islands which have failed to prosper despite natural advantages; but, in the long run, the physical considerations are generally decisive.

When seventeen families from Boreray were resettled on the mainland of Uist one determined crofter remained behind with his family. He tried to ensure himself a postal service in his isolation by placing an order for the *Scotsman* to be sent to him daily and he kept up a voluminous correspondence with St Andrew's House about the difficulties of his existence, as well as pursuing a notable course of litigation in the Scottish Land Court. On one occasion he sent a peremptory telegram demanding that the Secretary of State should come to Boreray to see the situation for himself. After his death, however, the pressure of geography prevailed and Boreray is now given over to sheep.

The more complex life becomes, the larger is the population required in any island to maintain a viable community. Apart from the lack of employment for young people, families leave because they do not wish to be without doctors or schools; and while at one time the women were bound to the land though the men might roam in search of work, it is now probably the women who are the more anxious to leave.

In the 1920s the island of Scarp was frequently cut off from the mainland of Harris because there was no road to Huisinish, the nearest point on Harris to Scarp, and small boats which could be handled on the beach at Scarp were unable to venture into the open Atlantic, as they must, to get farther round the coast of Harris to Tarbert or the road-end at Amhuinnsuidhe Castle. Bolls of meal and other household necessities were carried by the Scarpaich in creels on their backs for eight miles or so across the hills to get to sheltered water where a boat could meet them. They complained of their isolation, but at that time there was little thought of leaving. Lord Leverhulme eased their situation by making a road to Huisinish, but they were still occasionally cut off from immediate medical aid. The celebrated Scarp twins were born, one in Scarp and the other in Stornoway, in different islands, in different counties and indeed in different weeks, because the mother's ordeal began on Saturday and was not over until twenty-four hours later on the Sunday by which time she had been taken by boat and bus and ambulance to Stornoway. A German scientist suggested in the mid-1930s that mail and medicines could be delivered to remote islands by rocket and he carried out a demonstration at Scarp. The British Post Office sent officials to watch the demonstration; but it failed, and the inventor returned to Germany where he helped to develop the rocket bombs which did so much damage in London in the latter part of the war. The situation of Scarp was considerably alleviated in the 1950s by the building of a massive pier at Huisinish, but the island was finally evacuated when there was no longer a boat's crew left.

A few years ago I would have said that many of Scotland's inhabited islands would quickly go the same way, but it is different now: there are signs that people are deliberately seeking to return to the remote islands, in spite of the hardships, in an attempt to escape from the even more irksome constraints of the industrial cities.

Papa Stour in Shetland had reached the point at which the school was closed and there was imminent danger of the post office going as well, which would have meant the withdrawal of the ferry service to the mainland and the complete isolation of a small, ageing but lively and tolerably contented community. At that time the local postmaster began to encourage new families to move to Papa Stour, and in an island where the school was closed in 1972 there are now eight children under school age. It is perhaps too early to say whether this is a permanent turn of the tide or an insignificant eddy which conceals but does not interrupt steady decline.

Life on Papa Stour has been described by Stella Shepherd, the wife of the last Church of Scotland missionary in a charming book, *Like a Mantle the Sea*. She wrote before the turn of the tide, if so it is, had begun, and she lamented the steady decline in population from the peak of 351 a century ago when there were fifty-six pupils in the local school to her own period as teacher in the 1960s when the school roll dropped from eight to seven, then from seven to four, from four to two, and finally to one. When the last pupil was due to go to Lerwick, the school in Papa Stour was closed and the teacher and missionary were both withdrawn. But even in a decaying island, which she looked at objectively, with no hint of romanticism, Mrs Shepherd was able to write, 'the thing that struck me very forcibly when I first came to live on Papa Stour was the fact that everyone, men and women, worked so hard and also played hard. If they were vigorous in their work they were exuberantly energetic at the socials.' Elsewhere she refers to 'merrymaking, energetic dancing, lively music and easy good fellowship, the revelry lasting, undiminished, until morning.'

Life in a small intimate community like Papa Stour is different in many ways from life on the mainland of Shetland just across the water, for there each township has ready access to neighbouring townships, and to the burgh of Lerwick with its frenzied peak of social life each January in the 'Up Helly A' festival. But both, I believe, have a heightened sense of interdependence, community and, paradoxically, individuality, compared with mainland populations of the same size, and the pull of the small island is probably stronger than that of the large. Referring to the second generation emigrants who used to come to Papa Stour from Australia and New Zealand, Mrs Shepherd writes, 'I always marvel at the threads, tenuous yet enduring, which bind these folk to the land of their forebears and can pull them back from half a world away. So strong is the appeal of Papa Stour, that most of them wish to make a little part of the island their very own. Some take away with them small phials filled with sand from one of the beaches; others take fragments of stone from the ruins that were once their grandparents' croft house.'

When I got to know Shetland first I found it was very like Lewis and yet very different from it. At that time Lewis and Shetland had the same problem of unemployment, the same crofting and seafaring traditions, many of the same attitudes and aspirations, but there was a sharp cultural and linguistic contrast, although language may have concealed deep-lying affinities. Geography has made Shetland the Charing Cross of the North Atlantic, with the ships of many nations seeking shelter in its voes, whereas Lewis, apart from the town of Stornoway, has been in a relative backwater: Lewis people have gone out into the world but the world does not come to their doors.

Now Lewis and Shetland are both in the midst of a rapid transformation which no one foresaw even five years ago.

Orkney, too, is feeling the effects of oil. Many islanders are fearful for their way of life, and fearful too of a period of hectic growth followed by a disastrous slump when the wells run dry. But for those of us who remember the emigrant ships after the First World War, and the desolation which spread through the townships with no young men, and the problems for the women who stayed at home to look after aged parents and missed the chance to marry and make lives of their own, the prospect of an overflowing cup is not so daunting: it is a less depressing problem than the one we have lived with all our lives.

Other changes are taking place, less dramatic than the developments consequent on the discovery of oil, but in some ways just as significant. Five separate islands of the Uist group are now one, linked by causeways and bridges which, with the ebb and flow of the tide changing the landscape from hour to hour, provide one of the most fascinating motor journeys in Britain if not in Europe. It is a great convenience to get from North Uist to Balivanich airport by car instead of by the old ferryboat which wandered crazily across what looked to the visitor, wrapped in his oilskins in the stern, an open stretch of water, but which the ferryman knew was crisscrossed by hidden sandbanks through which he had to pick a route which was carefully adjusted to take account of the depth of water and the set of the current. Apart from the convenience of getting from one island to the other, the causeways are beginning to make five separate communities into one, although the process is by no means complete. In the same period Uist has felt the impact of the rocket range, which has strengthened the island community greatly by providing jobs but at the same time has introduced a competitor to Gaelic which many of the locals fear.

Tourism, and the proliferation of second homes, are also having their effect on the islands in varied and sometimes contradictory ways. Whether one welcomes the money that tourism pumps into the local economy or frets over the commercialization of aspects of island life, tourism is a fact with which we have to reckon. Its impact is more severe in small islands like Iona, which is almost an obligatory place of pilgrimage, than in large islands like Skye; but the places most at risk are probably the mainland machairs of Argyll and Sutherland where the caravans descend like locusts in July and, like the locusts, devour the fields.

In a situation of change affecting many islands and large areas of coastline, one of our major safeguards is the vigilance of the National Trust for Scotland which can not only mobilize public opinion but act in so many effective ways as custodian

St Kilda : Boreray
and Stac an Armin

of national treasures or areas of importance, as watchdog over successive private owners under conservation agreements, and by active intervention in planning inquiries.

Conservation agreements in crofting areas present special problems because of the unusual relationship between crofter and landlord and the right the crofter has been given by law to acquire the ownership of all or part of his croft. These difficulties have been discussed in a series of meetings between the Trust and the Crofters Commission and have been very amicably resolved in so far as the uncertainties of a tenancy which can be transformed into ownership permit.

The work of the Trust in specific areas like St Kilda and Inverewe is beyond praise. In both these instances the Trust has maintained part of our inheritance which might otherwise have been lost, and has made them accessible to thousands of people whose lives have been enriched thereby.

In Fair Isle, too, the Trust has done an excellent job, both for the native population and for the visitors who come to study the migrant birds. But wherever the Trust controls a living community rather than an inanimate property, problems of a new dimension arise and the boundary becomes somewhat blurred between the functions of the Trust and the functions of other organizations involved in conservation in a different way.

The revival of the West Coast fishing fleet, for instance, begun by the Macaulay Fund, along with the Highland Fund and the Highlands and Islands Advisory Panel, and expanded much more effectively by the Highlands and Islands Development Board, is one of the most important works of conservation which has been carried out in Scotland in recent times. It has helped to preserve Highland communities like Eriskay and Scalpay which might otherwise have disappeared, and it has enabled them to evolve without any fundamental break in the native tradition.

Tourism is a rather flyblown word, but again it is difficult to draw a firm line between, for example, the opening up of Fair Isle for bird-watchers and the work of many of the island tourist associations; and although in a commercial activity like tourism there may well be a shading off into the unacceptable, as we have seen, the fact that it is often gradual makes it all the more difficult to draw a line and erect the necessary defences.

There is a close parallel between the Trust's adaptation of old buildings to new uses to preserve our architectural heritage and the work of the Highlands and Islands Development *Rough Island, Castle Point and Rockcliffe from the Muckle Hill*

Board and the Crofters Commission in the remote communities. Change and growth are essential features of life, and declining communities can only survive if they are enabled to evolve. In the north-west and the islands, where the population has been declining for generations and the age structure is unbalanced, there is nothing more important than the building up of a network of employment and service centres within commuting distance of the crofting townships. This the Trust recognizes.

In dealing with their Torridon property the Trust set a notable precedent by encouraging the establishment of a working party in which all the interested organizations, such as the local authority, the Countryside Commission for Scotland, the Highlands and Islands Development Board, the Nature Conservancy, the Forestry Commission and the Crofters Commission pooled their knowledge and their resources to work out a common plan of action. The results were not dramatic because Torridon does not lend itself to easy solutions, but it was a valuable discipline for bodies with different and sometimes conflicting roles to sit round a table and try to work out the highest common factor of agreement between them. The measure of the achievement was the extent to which differences were resolved or found to be illusory and attitudes modified in the course of the discussion.

Torridon

Although the Trust is sensitive to local needs and opinions, a recurring difficulty arises from the fact that, by and large, the indigenous population in any community is more interested in development than conservation (Drumbuie, because of its scale, was a special case), while visitors to the area are more interested in conservation than development. In some coastal and island communities the conflict is compounded by the fact that people who have retired, or established holiday homes, incline to conservation rather than to development; and, being more articulate and less inhibited, drown the voice of the real locals.

Two things are required to resolve the conflict between conservation and development. We need a well publicized code of land-use to explain to residents in the sensitive areas the basic principles of planning and the things to be avoided. Those who live in an area of great scenic beauty tend to take it for granted and difficulties can arise from thoughtlessness as well as from a real conflict of interest. The Crofters Commission has made a small contribution to the resolution of this difficulty through the Highland Village project which has engaged schoolchildren actively in improving the amenities of their own townships, but a much more vigorous and continuous educational or public relations exercise is needed.

The other requirement is that those who, because it is their chosen role or because the role has been conferred upon them by statute, are opposed to certain classes of development should actively interest themselves in encouraging, in areas where the range of possible developments is limited, those projects which can be harmonized with the landscape. Pressure groups and statutory bodies are both prone to deal with only one part of a problem so that their influence is negative; and indeed our rigid adherence to the principle of *ultra vires* makes it difficult for statutory bodies to do otherwise.

The National Trust for Scotland is readier than most organizations, and freer than most, to see its problems and responsibilities in the round; and it is important that others should follow its lead. It would be unfortunate if, in preserving Scotland's coastline, we were to imperil the fragile human communities which now inhabit it.

Islands and Coastline

Bucinch and Ceardoch, Loch Lomond, Central

The 'bonnie, bonnie banks' of Loch Lomond, largest of Scotland's freshwater lochs, are known the world over as a concomitant of Jacobite minstrelsy and legend. Wordsworth was attracted by the islands and had the good fortune to make his landing on the most northerly; the ruined keep of Island I Vow is almost certainly the hermit's cell of his poem. There are thirty islands in all. Bucinch and Ceardoch give the Trust a presence. They are among the smallest, minuscule by comparison with Inchfad which is occupied and farmed, less important ecologically than five in the care of the Nature Conservancy Council. Neither figures in recorded history. But Bucinch, heavily wooded, has its share of yews. Robert the Bruce is said to have ordered the plantings, in Inchlonaig in the first instance, in order to provide material for bows – he was desperately short of archers at the battle of Bannockburn in 1314.

Loch Lomond and its environs have been an area of special planning control for some thirty years. Bucinch and Ceardoch were presented to the Trust by Colonel Charles L. Spencer of Warmanbie, Dumfries, in 1943.

Loch Lomond from near Ardlui

The Burg, Mull:
Allt Airigh nan Caisteal

25 miles west of Craignure, off B8035

The Burg, Isle of Mull, Strathclyde

In the south-western quadrant of Mull, largest island of the Inner Hebrides, the upthrust of the Ardmeanach peninsula demonstrates in an agreeable way that the broader the expanse of wild landscape, the narrower is the base for food production. The Burg is Ardmeanach in microcosm. Situated at the west end of the peninsula, it is severed by the broad waters of Loch Scridain from the Ross of Mull and the road to Fionphort and the Iona ferry (A849). Ardmeanach was never so favoured or populous as tracts on the southern shore. It has affinities with harder, harsher samples of the earth's crust, in particular with Staffa whose smooth black columns of basalt stand a few miles out to sea.

223

This is sheep and deer country. Pockets of deeper soil once grew crops. As lately as 1938 Sir David Russell prevailed on the West of Scotland College of Agriculture to start a pilot project to eradicate bracken and improve the land. But economic fact and difficulty of access were decisive in the end. Vehicular access to the Burg ends five miles out at Tiroran, the terminal of a Forestry Commission road running westward from the B8035.

The property was bequeathed to the Trust in 1932 by Mr A. Campbell Blair of Dolgelly. Following the death of the last agricultural tenant, a shift of policy towards conservation of wild life and adventure camping is being considered. School groups are able to make use of existing facilities, and on application to the Trust camp sites for small parties may be provided.

In the Burg's western cliffs McCulloch's tree, a fossilized imprint possibly 50 million years old, can be reached at low tide. There, on a rugged shoreline and on 2,000 undulating acres, there is scope for adventure and potential for a genuine 'wilderness' reserve. The territory is a natural haven for red deer, wild goats, otters and other fauna. A sparse surface may offer somewhat less to the botanist than to the geologist, but both areas are rich in birds. Golden eagle, harriers, peregrine, sparrow-hawk and buzzard are resident; so too are ravens in number and golden plover. There are also numerous small birds. In summer, snow buntings can be observed on the tops. All the tits are present in quantity, with the exception of the bearded tit. Among the finches the only absentee is the hawfinch.

Fair Isle, Zetland

The National Trust for Scotland acquired Fair Isle in order to guarantee a secure base for a bird observatory, and discovered in ornithology a partial guarantee of prosperity for Britain's most isolated inhabited island.

Fair Isle, midway between Orkney and Shetland, situated on one of the major migration tracks, is a natural haven in a waste of seas. Victorian travellers – Fair Isle once had regular steamer services – first noted the number and variety of species to be seen on passage in spring and autumn or nesting on the cliffs in early summer. The resolve to set up a station for systematic study was not made until the 1940s, and then not by any institution but by two Lowland Scots in a German prisoner-

The Good Shepherd *off Fair Isle*

Fair Isle: the Sheep Rock

of-war camp. George Waterston supplied the scientific know-how for the enterprise and Ian R. Pitman the business acumen. The island was purchased and the first observatory established in 1948 in the huts of a wartime naval encampment.

The Trust made its entry in 1954 in the knowledge that in serving the cause of ecology it was accepting a considerable social responsibility or, alternatively, a statutory obligation as landlord which could be very costly. In terms of population and economic viability, Fair Isle was on the razor's edge. If the islanders should decide to leave, each crofter tenant would require to be paid compensation for the fixtures on his holding (except the house, his own property) and such improvements as he had made. The Dulverton Trust gave a grant of £5,500 by way of insurance against calamity, and the process of rehabilitation began with immediate and imaginative support from the Scottish Office, Zetland County Council and other agencies.

In 1969 the Fair Isle Bird Observatory Trust moved to new buildings, architect-designed, purpose-built, with accommodation for larger numbers of visitors. Towards the cost of this project the Highlands and Islands Development Board made a substantial grant and the Trust contributed £10,000 from the Wildlife Fund: it had been demonstrated that economic benefit to the island was increasing in direct ratio to the holiday accommodation available.

To ornithologists the justification for the observatory was never in doubt. Since 1948 the staff have recorded more than 300 species of migrants, of which approximately 190 occur annually, and these include a number of species rarely seen elsewhere in Britain. A programme of capture, ringing and release is producing significant and sometimes surprising results. Of birds ringed in Fair Isle, an arctic skua was reported on the coast of Brazil, a snow bunting in Arctic Canada, a rustic bunting in the Greek islands and a bar-tailed godwit in Siberia. The island has breeding colonies of great and arctic skuas, storm petrel, fulmar, kittiwake, razorbill, puffin, gulls, shag and eider. Many of these can be observed at close quarters, especially in the narrow geos. Other nesting species include raven, hooded crow, rock dove, Fair Isle wren (a distinctive sub-species), wheatear, rock and meadow pipits, ringed plover, oyster catcher and occasionally peregrine.

For the visitor who does not normally tote a bird list there are uncovenanted benefits. This is 'Frideray' of the Norse sagas, the beautiful, the fair isle. In summer little spouts of colour erupt from the great grey sandstone cliffs – roseroot, red and white campions, scurvy grass and bird's nest trefoil. *Fair Isle: shags*

Elsewhere, according to date, there are drifts of blue squill, sea pink and heather. The island is small. At rifle-regiment pace one could walk its length, three miles, in an hour and its breadth in half that time. Much more stamina, mental and physical, is needed to get a right understanding of the seemingly simple facts of geography, geology and weather. The effects of endless assault by the sea on cliffs and common grazing, are very variable. And this is the latitude of the 'simmer dim', the verge of the Arctic's sun's dominion, where at the peak of the year day can run beguilingly into day under a luminous sky.

Standing also in the track of shipping, Fair Isle has a long history of shipwreck. One of the first casualties on the rough bounds (A.D. 900) was a Norse longship. In 1588 *El Gran Griffon*, flagship of twenty-three hired transports in the Spanish Armada, was driven into Stromhellier, a gash in the cliffs in the south-east of the island. Of her company three hundred men survived. In 1868 the barque *Lessing*, bound from Bremen for New York with 465 emigrants aboard, was driven across the mouth of Clavers Geo. The islanders in their yoals brought every soul ashore.

Today the people of Fair Isle live in many technological ages

Fair Isle: North Haven

at once. The women, knitting into garments, gloves and other *Fair Isle: the landing* woollens the intricate, inimitable Fair Isle patterns, have the *strip* blessing of 'the light': a chain of small diesel-powered generators installed and run by corporate effort. The rhythm of crofter farming does not change either in the inbye fields in the south of the island or the skattald (common grazing) in the north; but methods do, with increasing mechanization. Up on Ward Hill a composite transmitter is beaming colour television to Shetland and enabling the Post Office to extend telephone coverage in the north. The island mail boat, the *Good Shepherd*, may need all the inherited skills of a six-man crew to get her through Sumburgh Roost on passage to or from Grutness at the southern tip of Shetland, but she ties up at a new jetty in North Haven. The passenger service which she provides is supplemented by charter flights by Loganair. All but a fraction of a community which now numbers seventy occupy houses which have been modernized with the help of rotating teams from International Voluntary Service. This work continues.

For guidance of seafarers there are two lighthouses. Two churches minister in equal measure on the Sabbath to the spiritual needs of islanders and incomers. On weekdays the latter have a share in a notably vivid social life.

229

From Iona there was launched a prodigious enterprise of the Dark Age in Scotland, the mission of the Columban church to the peoples of northern Britain. Seventeen centuries after Columba set up his monastery Dr Samuel Johnson was moved to observe: 'That man is little to be envied whose patriotism would not gain force upon the plain of Marathon, or whose piety would not grow stronger amid the ruins of Iona.' The memory of the saint, the ambience of the place, touches minds and hearts as readily today. So vivid is one's sense of light and space and colour that the true dimensions of this tiny platform – three miles long, no broader than the strait that separates it from the Ross of Mull – seem irrelevant.

Columba, whose love of beauty may be inferred from Adamnan's account of his travels, had practical reasons for choosing Iona. A Gaelic-speaking Scot from Ireland and a member of a princely family, he came in A.D. 563 to settle among people of his own race. High on the ends, low in the middle, Iona had at the centre land capable of tillage and on the west a substantial machair for the pasturing of stock. A man prepared, as he was, to make the sea his highway had a clear route via the Firth of Lorne and Loch Linnhe to the Great Glen, the central Highlands and the river routes to the north-east and Strathmore.

There were political consequences. Columba's presence gave prestige and cohesion to the Scots kingdom of Dalriada. Planted somewhat precariously in the southern Hebrides and what is now Argyll, on the flank of Pictland, Dalriada had need of both. Nearly three centuries were to elapse before Kenneth MacAlpin, king of Scots, gained the Pictish throne and united the two kingdoms under the name of Scotia, but here was the starting point of the story of the Gael in Scotland.

To primitive societies, including the apostate Picts whom St Patrick had abhorred, Columba and the missionary monks carried a new culture in addition to the new religion. Iona became a centre of learning and instruction in many things besides the preaching of the Word. It extended widely a civilization which had evolved in numerous monasteries in Ireland. The Columban church too exulted in craft skills, applying them with as much care and devotion to farming and the baking of bread as to building, sculpture, metal work, writing and the illumination of exquisite books.

The first buildings were probably erected in the vicinity of the present abbey church. According to Adamnan, a later abbot of Iona and Columba's biographer, writing a century after the death of the saint, they consisted of a church, a cell for the abbot, huts for the brethren, a refectory and a guest house, all enclosed by a palisade or a wall of boulders and

turf. Adamnan also records that they were constructed of *Iona, looking north* wattle and turf and roofed with thatch. If this was indeed the *to the village* case, it is difficult to believe that more substantial replacements were not made within measurable time. In Ireland building in stone was superseding wattle; the art of preparing lime for the making of mortar appears to have reached that country with Christianity itself. There are on the site of a slightly older and lesser monastery on Eileach an Naoimh in the Garvellachs, examples of beehive cells of stone in the Irish manner – that is, built like a drystone dyke but with each course projected beyond the last until the aperture at the top became narrow enough to be bridged, and roofed, by flagstones.

Columba had thirty-four years in Iona – he came in his prime and died in his own church in 597 at the age of seventy-seven. How he looked, what was the force of his oratory and personality are matters of conjecture, but there is no question of his constancy of spirit and ability as an organizer. The work went on. It was halted only temporarily by Viking raids. In the first, in 794 or 795, the abbey buildings were plundered and destroyed. In a third in 806, sixty-eight monks were murdered at Martyr's Bay. The Columban church retreated to Kells in Ireland (with what, if any, treasures is not known). Within a few years the monastery was built anew, almost certainly in stone, but the Norsemen had not yet done. Another raid followed in 825 and a fifth in 986. By that date the Scoto-

Pictish kings had moved their mother church to Dunkeld. Differences between the Celtic and the Roman forms of religion – an issue which had arisen less than a century after Columba's death – were being resolved in favour of the latter. The intervention of Queen Margaret, Malcolm Canmore's Saxon queen, was decisive. When, in 1074, she restored the monastery, it was not for the Celtic church, but for the Roman Catholic Order of Augustine.

The Augustinians may have suffered only a little less disturbance than the Columbans. Power struggles within Scotland were compounded by Norse, Danish and English pressure. Though Somerled, ancestor of the great Clan Donald, seems to have been well disposed towards Iona, it was an act of grace by his son, Reginald of Islay, King of the Isles, that ushered in the longest period of uninterrupted occupation. Reginald rebuilt the monastery at the turn of the twelfth and thirteenth centuries for the Benedictine Order. (The abbey church was dedicated to the Virgin Mary.) A nunnery of the same Order was also founded in about 1203. How robust was monastic life is apparent from the extent of rebuilding in the late fifteenth and early sixteenth centuries. Iona was then the seat of the Bishop of the Isles and from 1507 until the Reformation, the monastery had the dignity of a cathedral.

Iona was not 'purged' as was Dunkeld Cathedral in 1561. Abandonment and neglect caused the ruin which so affected Dr Johnson. It has a different aspect now. In 1899 the ecclesiastical buildings and other sacred sites were given in trust to the Church of Scotland by George, eighth Duke of Argyll. Since that date they have been administered by the Iona Cathedral Trust. (The trustees are *ex officio* office-bearers of the Church of Scotland and Scottish Universities.) In fulfilment of the duke's wish, the abbey church was largely restored between 1902 and 1910. A stipulation that members of other Christian denominations be allowed to worship there has had vivid significance since 1938. In that year the Iona Cathedral Trustees gave permission to the Rev. George MacLeod (the Very Rev. Lord MacLeod of Fiunary), on behalf of the Iona Community Trust, to begin the restoration of the monastic buildings with the object of housing a living community and receiving Christians from throughout the world. The integrity of the environment is ensured by the relatively late involvement of a third party, the National Trust for Scotland.

In 1980, at the request of the Secretary of State for Scotland and the Hugh Fraser Foundation, the Trust accepted the remainder of the island as a gift to the nation in memory of the late Lord Fraser of Allander.

Access to Iona has never been easy. For road vehicles the route runs from Oban to Craignure by car ferry, then some thirty miles south and west across Mull to Fionnphort. There the road ends. The final stage is by passenger ferry across the mile-wide Sound of Iona. There is no hardship if one has to wait. For the abbey church, which is plain in view, the rose-pink granite for the massive walls was hewn at Tormore half a mile up the coast from Fionnphort, the paler sandstone for dressings at Carsaig farther back on the Ross of Mull.

The church is cruciform in plan. The short square tower was capped originally by a gable roof. St Martin's Cross exhibits outdoors the vigour and inventiveness of Celtic design which was used up to a much later date in internal decoration. The cloisters were restored in 1958–9 by the late Ian G. Lindsay as architect for the Iona Community Trust. Of the other buildings, the oldest is St Oran's Chapel, the most noteworthy the shell of the nunnery, singular in Britain as a record of mediaeval building for such a purpose.

None of these may bring into clear perspective the interaction of church and state, but consider the Reilig Odhrain, the graveyard of the kings. The first to lie here, in the oldest Christian burial ground in Scotland, was Kenneth MacAlpin. In time he had for company forty-eight kings of Scotland (among them the murdered Duncan and Macbeth), four kings from Ireland and eight from Norway, together with Reginald of Islay and many a clan chief from the Highlands and Islands. 'The Celtic Church gave love; the Roman Church gave law.' Each added a new dimension to individual and national life.

The Graveyard of the Kings

Of the island which Columba knew, the Trust holds for the nation 1,087 acres, consisting for the most part of two farms and fifteen crofts and their common grazings. There are still, nevertheless, moorland and bog and sandy bays, a multitude of wild flowers, vast prospects seawards, and a clarity of air unequalled anywhere, north or south, on the rim of the Atlantic.

7 miles south of Dalbeattie, off A710

In the lexicon of the Scottish Trust 'Rockcliffe' signifies the success of a corporate policy for conservation and recreation in which local residents and local government participate. Territorially, it comprehends four small, contiguous properties on the eastern shore of Rough Firth, the estuary of the Urr, in the Stewartry of Kirkcudbright. The properties are the Mote

Rockcliffe, Dumfries and Galloway

of Mark, Rough Island, the Muckle Lands and Jubilee Path, and Auchenvhin in the village of Rockcliffe.

On Mote of Mark the history of human activity reaches almost as far back as in Whithorn to the west, where St Ninian set up his Candida Casa (White House), possibly the first Christian church in Scotland, about A.D. 400. Rough Firth, one of many mouseholes on the northern margin of the Solway, has legends of smuggling and records of a significant coastwise trade. In the last century Dalbeattie, at the mouth of the river Urr, the limit of tidewater, sent cargoes of the lustrous local granite all over the world (London got enough to pave the sidewalks and form the balustrades of the Thames Embankment). An inward trade in groceries and other commodities for the hinterland was equally large. The railways put an end to that without coming near Rockcliffe. But in summer pleasure craft, outnumbering by far the ghosts of the tall ships, now occupy the estuary. On shore the extension of the motorway system, bringing Rockcliffe within range of the large towns of central Scotland and north-west England, made an end of remoteness and seclusion.

Kirkcudbright County Council responded by not merely supplying the normal appurtenances of a small resort – car park and toilets – but choosing the sites for them in consultation with the Trust and the people of the village.

Mote of Mark, an area of twenty bumpy acres around a Dark Age hill-top settlement, together with Rough Island was given in 1937 by Messrs John and James McLellan in memory of their brother, Colonel William McLellan, C.B.E., of Orchard Knowes. The Mote is a granite outcrop 100 feet high. The site of the settlement is in a hollow on the summit ridge between two peaks. In 1973 excavations directed by Mr Lloyd Laing for Liverpool University dated it to c. A.D. 475–625 and produced evidence to indicate that it was possibly a princely stronghold of the Britons in the sixth century. In that period the Mote, fortified by a timber-laced rampart of stones and earth, was a centre of ornamental metal-working of a very high degree of skill, not only in bronze but conceivably in gold and silver. The intensity of activity at that time and in the following century may be deduced from the artefacts recovered then and subsequently. These, considered in relation to ample evidence which was adduced earlier of metal- and glass-working on sites in Kent, Wales, Ireland and the Outer Hebrides, are providing new information about early Christian Celtic art and about the movement of population, in particular the northward drive of the Angles. From the summit there are wide views to the south and west – over the Solway to the Cumberland coast, the hills of the Lake District and St Bees Head;

The Gelston shore from Rough Island

234

across Rough Firth to the wooded parks of Orchardton.

Rough Island, a bird sanctuary, is twenty acres in extent and is accessible on foot at low tide. Observation is being made on the fluctuating numbers of nesting terns and other species. The botanical interest of the island is also considerable.

The gift of the 51½ acres of the Muckle Lands, which are bisected by the Jubilee Path, put all of the rough coastline between Mote of Mark and Kippford in the care of the Trust. It was made in 1965 by Miss Hilda G. Longworth of Greywalls, Rockcliffe. Along most of the strip the conifer plantations of the Forestry Commission made a disciplined backdrop to a luxuriant growth of scrub and wild flowers. Bridle paths, established for the benefit of pony trekkers, require to be cleared at least once a year.

The 7½ acres of Auchenvhin, bequeathed in 1969 by Major J. I. A. McDiarmid, complete the Trust's coastside holdings, and fill the space between the village of Rockcliffe and the Mote of Mark. There is a picnic area on the frontage of the property. Auchenvhin House, the two adjoining cottages, and the lawns and garden ground are not open to the public.

In 1971 Mrs M. E. McLellan of Glenluffin, Rockcliffe, presented 9½ acres of coastline south of Rockcliffe and the Merse. The object was not to enlarge the area available to visitors but to provide a relatively remote location for a sewage disposal plant and sufficient land for a programme of screen planting.

3 miles north of Coldingham, off A1 by A1107 or B6483; St Abb's Head, approach by path from village of St Abbs Borders

The Great North Road (A1) and the east coast railway (Edinbugh–King's Cross) get round the bumpy knuckle-end of the Lammermuir Hills by way of the Eye Water valley. St Abb's Head, a few miles to the north, is Lammermuir's magnificent terminal.

The headland rears 300 feet above an unchancy North Sea. For the comfort of mariners it has had a lighthouse since 1862. (At a height of 225 feet the latter is on a lower elevation than the keepers' cottages.) It is a place of very old habitation, and was so before St Ebba, daughter of Ethelfrid, first King of Northumbria, founded a religious house in the seventh century and the place took on her name.

The site of St Ebba's Chapel is on a rocky promontory west-north-west of the lighthouse. The building was destroyed by the Danes in A.D. 870.

St Abb's Head

The property extends to 192 acres. It forms part of a Site of Special Scientific Interest – Grade I. The Nature Conservancy Council describe it as 'a fine series of sea cliffs with considerable botanical interest and the most important locality for cliff breeding sea birds in SE Scotland'. Of the breeding species, kittiwakes, guillemots, razorbills, shags, fulmars and herring gulls may be listed as 'regulars'. Frequent visitors include skuas, terns and shearwaters. The headland also has its quota of birds of field and hedgerow – only a shallow valley and the Mire Loch, a man-made feature, separate it from the hinterland – and rare species may be noted among the migrants, especially in autumn. There is not, at least not yet, a bird observatory as in Fair Isle; a ranger service supplies information and advice.

The rock formations are of perennial interest to geologists. The inlets make formidable mouseholes for a boat, not excluding Pettico Wick which used to be the port for the lighthouse. A similar word of warning applies to the numerous caves. They are accessible only from the sea, and then only at low tide and in calm conditions, but that has been no bar to the growth of smuggler legends.

Of the adjacent antiquities, Fast Castle was a cliff-top fortress, five miles to the west across inhospitable moorland. Its outline is no more easily discernible than that of St Ebba's Chapel or St Abb's Kirk (the latter less than half a mile south-south-east of the lighthouse). On the other hand, the choir of Coldingham Priory, restored in the middle of the nineteenth century, serves as the parish church, and Norman and thirteenth-century work has been preserved with care.

236

Given the sensitivity of Mr James Shaw Grant one can feel in an empty island what he described in his introduction to this section: 'the sadness of man's retreat from a frontier he once maintained'. It strikes in unlikely places. There were losses even in Orkney in the 1950s, at a time when a proportion of the county's farmers could see no option but to disclose in their tax returns a gross product per acre as high as any in Britain. For want of adequate communications small islands went empty. A change of circumstance could reverse that movement: places which have been farmed intensively may be farmed again. In St Kilda the train of events was irreversible.

For centuries a small, primitive, patriarchal society subsisted in almost total isolation in an inhospitable environment. It died of perplexity, lethargy and induced desires when contact with a meddlesome, mechanistic civilization was thrust upon it. The remnant of that community, thirty-six in number, left on August 28th, 1930, having petitioned the Government to remove them because life had become insupportable.

St Kilda – four islands and five great rock stacks – is a distant outlier of the British Isles. Its aspect from the sea has no equal in the North Atlantic. In Hirta, the main island, three peaks rise to over 1,000 feet. On the north face of Conachair (1,397 feet) the highest sea cliffs in Britain look to Soay and Boreray, whose rock walls rise to 1,225 feet and 1,245 feet respectively. Stac an Armin at 627 feet is the highest rock stack

St Kilda, Western Isles

St Kilda: village street, Hirta

St Kilda : Dun from
Ruival, Hirta

in the British Isles. Stac Lee, its near neighbour to the west of Boreray, lifts its stupendous mass to 544 feet and affords space for the largest gannetry in the world with a population of 44,000 breeding pairs annually.

The only practicable anchorage is in Village Bay on the south coast of Hirta. The bay is sheltered on the west by Dun, the fourth island of the group, but exposed to gales from any point between east and south. And it lies 110 miles west of the Scottish mainland, not much less than half that distance from Griminish Point in North Uist, the nearest landfall in the Outer Hebrides.

In this habitat, perpetually damp, the St Kildans evolved an economy that gave them subsistence and a margin with which to pay the rent – originally in kind, only latterly in money. The bases were wildfowling – young gannets for meat, puffins for feathers and meat, fulmars for oil – and an elementary form of crofter farming. They ran cattle and ponies in Hirta, sheep in Hirta and Soay, and worked the sea fisheries occasionally.

To British governments St Kilda was, until the middle of last century, an unregarded anachronism; not so to others. A tacksman or the MacLeod factor from Dunvegan in Skye came each year to collect the rents and deliver the meagre supplies which the islanders bought from outside sources. Word got round of the existence of this hold-over from the Middle Ages,

Martin Martin, reporting in 1698 on a visit from the previous year, described a happy, Gaelic-speaking people, fond of song and poetry if somewhat uncouth, ill-instructed in religion and ignorant of reading or writing. In 1705 the Society for the Propagation of Christian Knowledge sent a missionary. James Boswell had a thought of buying the place. Henry Peter Brougham published his judgment on it, in *Tour in the Western Isles Including St Kilda in 1799*, by the end of the century, thirty years before he reached the Woolsack or ordered the horse-drawn carriage to which, not unwillingly, he gave his name. The steam yacht enabled aristocratic travellers to make the treacherous passage in relative comfort. In 1860 the sixth Duke of Atholl set a precedent, which few followed, by spending a night in Hirta and eating an island meal.

Then John McCallum appeared on the scene in S.S. *Dunara Castle*, to be followed closely by Martin Orme with whom he formed the company of McCallum Orme; and St Kilda was taken over each year, at least for the duration of the 'steamer season', by the travel trade. From 1877 a tourist could have for £10 cabin-class accommodation, full board for up to ten days on a cruise from the Clyde to the Western Isles and – Tom Steel's comment in *The Life and Death of St Kilda* is not too bitter – 'an opportunity of viewing the only human menagerie in the British Isles'. Mainland Britain, so long indifferent, began to fill some of the voids in public services; but from that point the old order began to founder. Selling souvenirs to tourists was an easier trade than wildfowling or tending and gathering sheep in Soay.

St Kilda: Boreray from Hirta

So many artefacts remain in Hirta that the tragedy of the St Kildans – their utter failure, perhaps inevitable, to adjust to new circumstances, the total failure of even the well-intentioned stranger to comprehend the island mind – becomes a manifest reality. Early in the 1860s MacLeod of MacLeod financed the building of a line of sixteen new cottages along the village street, possibly the best houses of their time in the Western Isles: there they are. There, too, are the church, the manse, the school and the factor's house. Pre-dating all of these, the black houses which the MacLeod's cottages superseded turn their ruined gables to the street; latterly they served as byres. The boundary dyke that enclosed the inbye land clings to the hillside, and about a thousand cleits punctuate the lower and the upper slopes. The cleit, a beehive cell of rough stone, built with infinite care, was larder and wardrobe and storehouse. There was always sufficient wind to guarantee a circulation of air which preserved the seafowl taken for food and kept clothes and gear dry.

St Kilda was bequeathed to the Trust in 1957 by the fifth

Gannets off St Kilda

St Kilda: a cleit

Marquess of Bute. The Trust has leased the group to the Nature Conservancy Council (who, with Trust consent, subleased a portion of Hirta to the Department of Defence in order to provide a location for a missile-tracking station). Volunteer work parties toil year by year at maintenance and restoration.

The scientific interest of St Kilda is perennial – and of international significance in relation to the study, *inter alia*, of the vast colonies of seabirds. Soay sheep, an indigenous breed, continue to inhabit Hirta as well as Soay. The group has subspecies of wren and fieldmouse, a seal population and many things of botanical interest. More investigation is needed to determine the history of earlier settlements, including a fort site in Dun and three ecclesiastical sites in Hirta. But in the tiny graveyard, amid the nettles and the irises, one may well reflect that the bones of the cragsmen-boatmen-crofters, the women who bore the burdens, a shipwrecked sailor or two and innumerable children who died in infancy of tetanus are well rested now. That also is relevant to the story and the fable of human habitation through a millennium or longer.

Off Shieldaig, 15 miles south-west of Kinlochewe on A896

Shieldaig Island, Loch Torridon, Highland

Shieldaig is another island in a loch, in this instance a sea loch. It takes the eye because of one characteristic which is singular in the outback of Wester Ross – a tree canopy. The island's twenty acres were planted in the middle of the nineteenth century with Scots pine, clearly from excellent seed. The trees are even in height and straight-grown to a surprising degree. Their only competitors, a few rowans and some holly, lend colour and diversity. The floor is a mat of moss, heather, bracken and blaeberry. There is a heronry on the north-west corner, and the island has two small outliers, Sgeir an Fian to the north-west and Sgeir Shalach to the south-east. A long-term forestry plan is being applied in co-operation with the Nature Conservancy Council.

Shieldaig Island was purchased in 1970 by the Trust's Coastline and Islands Fund. In 1974 Mr and Mrs Armistead Peter III of Washington, D.C., 'adopted' it and contributed to the Fund the full equivalent of the purchase price in order to provide for maintenance or the purchase of other islands.

Shieldaig and Shieldaig Island

241

VII · RURAL LIFE AND FAMOUS MEN

with an introduction by T. C. Smout

Introduction

Among the possessions of the Trust is one group not immediately as impressive as the mountains, the gardens, the mansions and the battlegrounds, yet at least as significant in the Scottish story. Most of the properties of which this group consists are cottages; all are small in scale, humble in appearance and rural in location; several are cherished for their associations with poor men who became famous. Up in the northern burgh of Cromarty is a white harled cottage of 1711 which was the birthplace of Hugh Miller (1802–56), the stonemason who achieved a national reputation as a geologist, journalist and lay leader in the Free Church after the Disruption, only to shoot himself in tragic and mysterious circumstances at the age of fifty-four. At the opposite end of Scotland, at Ecclefechan in Dumfriesshire, is another, slightly more substantial, white harled house, built with his own hands by the father of Thomas Carlyle in 1791: his great son was born there four years later, and in his will refused a burial in Westminster Abbey in order that his body should be returned to the village of his birth. Carlyle's history and political philosophy are quite justifiably in eclipse today, but their impact on his Victorian contemporaries was enormous, and as an example of a lad o' pairts who made it to the top he ranked in Victorian estimation with David Livingstone and even Andrew Carnegie himself. At Kirriemuir in Angus is a weaver's cottage that was the birthplace of James Barrie (1860–1937), author of the sentimental but undeniably ageless *Peter Pan* and of several books in which his home town won repute under the pseudonym 'Thrums'. In Ayrshire there are two buildings with associations with Burns, Souter Johnnie's Cottage at Kirkoswald where the 'ancient, trusty, drouthy crony' from 'Tam o' Shanter' lived, and the Bachelors' Club at Tarbolton where the poet in 1780 formed a debating club for himself and six other young men. The first subject discussed, a good one as Burns was in love with Alison Begbie who was in service down the road, was whether to marry for looks or fortune.

Carlyle's birthplace, Ecclefechan

All these buildings were preserved from major nineteenth-century alterations because of their literary associations, and we may appreciate them doubly for their rarity value as survivals of the old Scottish vernacular architecture of the countryside. Hugh Miller's cottage, for instance, is all that is left of the fishertown houses of Cromarty. The two Burns properties are almost equally unusual as small eighteenth-century houses in Ayrshire. The thatched roofs of all three are

245

Kirkwynd Cottages,
Glamis

exceptional survivals of what was universal in many country districts before the nineteenth century railway brought cheap slate to everyone's road.

Along with these we should consider some buildings of a similar architectural character, not blessed with famous associations, but rather with memories of the humble forgotten who are the ancestors of us all. There is the Angus Folk Museum, a superb collection of tools and country plenishings gathered by Lady Maitland and displayed in a charming row of cottages at Glamis. There is the weaver's cottage of 1723 at Kilbarchan in Renfrewshire, housing the utensils and furniture of the handloom weavers whose trade flourished so exceedingly in the west of Scotland in the late eighteenth century, and only slowly went under before factory competition in the nineteenth. There is the old, conical, pantiled watermill at Preston Mill, East Linton, East Lothian, as ancient as the Act of Union and now restored to full working order by a benevolent firm of millers. To these one might add two fine doocots, one at Phantassie by Preston Mill, the other at Boath in Nairn, tower blocks for the pigeons that ate honest men's corn and in turn fed the fat laird who might have been content with one rent.

The importance of these structures is that they all recall the peasant past, when perhaps seven, eight or nine Scots out of ten got their living from the land, and many of the remainder won it by the spinning-wheel or the handloom. When we see the plain, scrubbed wooden chair where Hugh Miller's mother sat to nurse her baby, or marvel at the wally dogs in the Angus Folk Museum which were once the pride of someone's but-and-ben, or finger the working shuttles at Kilbarchan and watch the cumbrous wheels and cogs in motion at Preston Mill, we cannot but ask ourselves what it was like when almost everyone was so poor and technology was so simple. And how did it happen that a poor rural society like this turned out so many famous men, not only literary figures like Miller, Carlyle, Barrie and Burns, but practical men like Telford, a shepherd's son from Eskdalemuir, David Dale, who dominated the factory organization of cotton spinning in the early days of the Scottish industrial revolution but who started as a herd boy, or David Livingstone who was born at Blantyre in a factory village deep in the countryside? Almost all these great sons of humble country parents were born between the middle of the eighteenth century and the middle of the nineteenth. As the majority of the contents of these National Trust for Scotland properties are of the same period even when the building itself is a little earlier, we can readily see the kinds of household object and workaday tools they would be familiar with as children.

Let us try to understand the rural life which produced the great men. To do so we need to take account of two fundamental institutions of the countryside, kirk and school: the buildings of neither are represented among Trust properties, but they are worth seeking out. Eighteenth-century kirks are actually still fairly common in the countryside, though few escaped Victorian embellishment. One good example is the circular church at Bowmore in Islay, another the steepled church of Catrine in Ayrshire. Early village schools are harder to find, partly because they have altered their use as school accommodation became more demanding – but there are examples, for instance at Cramond in Midlothian and at Pencaitland in East Lothian where the stone statue of a child reading still sits above the doorway. Surely it would be appropriate to restore one old school to its original appearance, as a museum of Scottish rural education. The minister and the dominie set their stamp on the country community, and imprinted thereby something very distinctive in the Scottish national character.

What it was, however, is neither simple nor readily explained. The eighteenth-century Church, for one thing, was deeply divided. The local minister – after the middle of the eighteenth century – might be described as either a moderate or an evangelical: if the former, he would probably be devoted to the fashionable ideas of agricultural improvement as much as to the preaching of the gospel, as anxious to please the laird as the Lord; if the latter, it was likely he would be an old-fashioned Puritan, stern in his theology and religious life. But not everyone now belonged to the Church of Scotland: there were seceders, Presbyterians who believed the established Church as a whole had fallen away from its pristine purity and was not stern enough. To a degree they were the psychological heirs of the Restoration Covenanters, fanatical about God but contemptuous of man, whatever his degree. Carlyle's father was a seceder: 'Man's face he did not fear,' said his son; 'God he always feared: his reverence, I think, was considerably mixed with fear. Yet not slavish fear ...' Such a contentious, various and mottled sectarian background to eighteenth-century rural life was nevertheless part of a general context of deep seriousness and probably almost universal church-attendance, by the peasants if not always by the lairds. Men were profoundly impressed by the importance of their relationships to eternal purposes. But while the seventeenth-century Church had been a totalitarian and monolithic system bent on the extirpation of error, the eighteenth-century Church gave men room to breathe and to pick their opinions without being persecuted for them. It could even tolerate a man as heretical as Burns when he proclaimed 'the Religion of Sentiment and Reason': or, at least, if it did not like him, it had perforce now to put up with him. There must have been something extraordinarily stimulating to the intellect in this combination of freedom, diversity and seriousness in the kirk.

Schools, too, were of many different kinds, if only because the capacity of schoolmasters was infinitely various. Carlyle detested his education at Annan Grammar: '... the first two years of my time in it still count among the most miserable of my life. Academia! High School Instructers of Youth! Oh, ye unspeakable!' Hugh Miller, on the other hand, found at Cromarty Grammar a schoolmaster who 'was a scholar and an honest man, and, if a boy really wished to learn, he certainly could teach him': but there was little discipline. Bedlam ruled in the class-room, the boys brought in fighting-cocks, and Miller ultimately concluded (after being sent to another school) that 'the only school in which I could properly be taught was that world-wide school which awaited me, in which Toil and Hardship are the severe but noble teachers.' But great men will seldom admit they were ever taught anything worth learning either at school or university. What we should rather emphasize is that the parish schools produced universal literacy right across Lowland rural society, something very exceptional by international standards. 'However humble their condition,' wrote Burns' first biographer, 'the peasantry in the southern districts can all read and are generally more or less skilful in writing and arithmetic, and under the disguise of their uncouth appearance they possess a laudable zeal for knowledge ... not generally found among the same class of men in other countries of Europe.'

Hugh Miller's Cottage, Cromarty

The gift of knowledge was used in many ways. Some read only the chapbooks, homely or coarse tales written often in Scots and peddled by the travelling chapmen at the kitchen door. Others read the literature of agricultural improvement, and learned from the printed word of a new drainage plough or a better breed of sheep. Many read religious books, and even subscribed money to enable their favourite minister to publish: works of Scottish divinity from the middle of the eighteenth century may contain lists of tenants, weavers, and sometimes even coalminers, who put down their pennies so that wisdom could see the light of day. Certain books were wide favourites and were to be found on the shelf in very humble homes: Thomas Boston's *Fourfold State* was popular among the seceders, along with the verse of Erskine's *Godly Sonnets* – not to be regarded as easy reading today. The secular-minded were fond of old Scottish poetry, especially the works of Sir David Lindsay, Barbour's *Brus* and Blind Harry's *Wallace*.

Hugh Miller remarked that it was the last-named great tale of nationalism which, at the age of ten, first made him thoroughly conscious of being a Scot. A more modern tale of adventure was *A Voyage to the South Seas, and to many other parts of the world, performed from September 1740, to June 1744, by Commodore Anson, in his Majesty's ship the Centurian* – and it was enormously popular, with its vivid, science-fiction-like descriptions of exploration, mutiny, torture, strange natural history and even stranger human societies set in the palms and surf of the Pacific. In all this reading no doubt there was a large element of escapism from the drudgery of country life – to God, to the past, to the cannibal isles. But there was also liberation in literacy: books provided sources of authority other than the village wisdom and the *obiter dicta* of minister and laird. When the French Revolution came, the weavers sat down to read the seditious works of Tom Paine and Burns wrote 'A man's a man for a' that': the ministers felt the social order was being challenged on their own pulpit steps, and many agreed with their colleague at Dunbar that more church-going from the lairds and their associates would be 'a cheap and easy antidote against anarchy and disorder'. But in honourable contrast to England, few in authority wanted to close the schools in case the bairns learned the wrong things.

Liberation, however, is only meaningful in terms of opportunities open to the individual in his social context, and Scottish peasants were heavily circumscribed by an environment of poverty best summed up as bad housing and too little food. Even when you visit the Trust cottages it needs a great effort of the imagination to see them as they once were. The Trust keeps many things, but not the lice which lived in the farmer's hair, carrying typhus germs to kill him with 'famine fever' when failing supplies of meal lowered his resistance in the winter. The houses are not now shared by a cow, and we have no experience of a home (like one described by an eighteenth-century Galloway labourer) where the wife knows it is time to put the dinner on when she hears the cow urinating for the second time. Similarly, we have little concept of the monotony and debilitating nature of a diet like that on which the minister of Bathgate said the common people subsisted in the 1790s: 'oatmeal, pease meal, barley, potatoes, milk, chiefly buttermilk, greens, a little butter or cheese, sometimes the offals of beef, mutton, lamb or veal, or a small piece of beef, and on a particular occasion a leg of lamb or veal. For three-quarters of the year potatoes constitute nearly two-thirds of the food of a labouring man's family.' This was after forty years in which it was generally agreed that food had been becoming more plentiful for the agricultural classes.

The Angus Folk Museum is crammed with interesting objects tempting us to linger to do them all justice. But eighteenth-century peasants, even those who were tolerably well off, could certainly not afford to cram their homes: and the poor had astonishingly little. It was the law in Scotland, if you accepted poor relief from the parish, that your household possessions be made over to the kirk session. In 1741, Herbert Paine, pauper, died in the parish of New Abbey, Kirkcudbrightshire, and an inventory was made of his movable goods. The session agreed that his widow should have the use of them during her lifetime, after which they would be sold. The contents of this cottage were two old beds, two coverings, two pairs of blankets, two tubs, two chests, a 'sowing kite' (probably for sowing seeds) with 'crook chips and a pair of tongs', evidently for the fire. That seems to have been all the two old people had in this world.

There were two main paths that might lead a man out of this society, provided he had ambition, brains and luck. One was that of the traditional lad o' pairts, clever at school, who won a bursary to one of the Scottish universities: but it was a hard road beset by loneliness and many failures. Most who took it probably aimed at becoming ministers: many went half-way and ended as parish schoolmasters on a salary, at the beginning of the nineteenth century, barely better than the wages of a ploughman. In either case, they often never really escaped rural society, but merely re-entered it at a higher level of status. Paradoxically, one of the consolations of the peasant world was that its leaders had often risen from the ranks but had not risen far. It tended, therefore, towards a greater degree of equality than would be found among country people today, to some mutual understanding, to a strong community feeling and a ready help for neighbours, and to an absence of bureaucracy. The kirk session would not sell up Mrs Paine because they knew no one could cope without a bed, a meal-tub and fire-irons: and if she did run into trouble, the support of family and friends as well as the scanty bawbees of the poor box would be forthcoming.

The other path was that of the agricultural improver, but this needed, apart from ability, the co-operation and approval of the laird. The eighteenth and nineteenth centuries were a time of transformation in Scottish farming, an age of consolidation of the old, intermingled holdings, of enclosure, fencing and planting, of new rotations and crops, proper drainage, better animals, implements and buildings, and of all the paraphernalia of change that goes by the name of the Agricultural Revolution. In the Lothians it came early, with large farms well established by the Napoleonic wars. In many places it came much later: Aberdeenshire was still a county of small tenants working largely with family labour in the middle of the nineteenth century, recognizably the peasant world celebrated in the works of Lewis Grassic Gibbon even later.

The improving tenants who became the new farmers often began as peasants picked out by the landowner or his agent for their ability as husbandmen and receptivity to new ideas, and given a long lease of a large, newly enclosed holding. Alternatively, they were peasants who had already saved enough capital by thrift and industry to pay the *grassum* on entering the lease and the ensuing high rents. What happened thereafter depended on their own skill. Some perished after a few seasons, perhaps because they raced too hard after the latest novelty, introducing turnips on land where they would never grow or English sheep on hills where the winters were too severe; others gave up because they were still too cautious, and could not raise the productivity of their land to meet rents as high as their neighbours'; others succeeded triumphantly, adapting innovations rather than merely adopting them, and then pushing out the frontiers of agricultural knowledge by new implements of their own design suited to a local soil, or a new balance of rotations to produce heavier crops without exhausting the land. The Lothian farmers in the first third of the nineteenth century had become world leaders in agricultural technology, their farms centres of pilgrimage for young students from England and the Continent wanting to see model husbandry. In material terms the rewards were great: an East Lothian farmhouse, two or three storeys high, with Georgian fenestration and slate roof, walled gardens, yards, arcaded barns and row of labourers' houses is another world from Souter Johnnie's cottage. And the farmer's family, in their rustling silks, with their wine-coolers, pianos and carriages, had moved out of the world of Burns altogether.

In few other counties did the lucky minority move so far or fast to affluence as in the Lothians; but by the end of the nineteenth century the improvers had everywhere brought to an end peasant society as we have described it. The new world was one of capitalist farmers and landless labourers, of middle-class incomes and status for the former, and low earnings for the latter which nevertheless enabled them to live with more food and more material goods than their forebears. Everywhere after 1850 there was a drain from the countryside – from the farming villages went labourers and servants, going to higher wages and better prospects in the towns; from the weaving villages went displaced craftsmen, moving to urban centres of factory production.

As peasant society declined, the rural poverty, disease,

Souter Johnnie's House, Kirkoswald

malnutrition and bad housing that accompanied it were also slowly mitigated. But the sense of rural community also declined, accompanied and exacerbated by a cooling of enthusiasm for local institutions. By the 1890s popular church-going was more lukewarm: the General Assembly heard how the young ploughmen of Aberdeenshire were buying new bicycles and making for the glens on Sundays instead of making for the church. School too lost some of its local flavour after the 1872 School Boards Act; compulsory and, later, free state education (tightly controlled by Scottish Education Department inspectors) raised formal standards but also seems to have diminished the rural population's 'zeal for knowledge'.

The truth of the matter was that the countryside was becoming a satellite of the outside world. The state and the town were the dominant entities. Jobs and amusements were sought in the town; children grew up and left home to move scores or hundreds of miles away; the government, not the kirk session, came ultimately to decide about old-age pensions and sickness benefits. The country was still where you lived, but not as in the old days, where you had your being.

So peasant society came to an end, partly destroyed by the success of its sons, partly by external forces; in its hey-day some of the greatest men Scotland ever produced were rocked in its cradle. The Trust cottage properties, therefore, stand both for the deprivations, and for the less tangible gifts of that old rural life. Let us visit again the Bachelors' Club at Tarbolton and the white house at Cromarty. We cannot return to that eighteenth-century world, and we would not wish to do so if the choice was ours. But do we now so readily breed in Scotland the genius exemplified by a Robert Burns or a Hugh Miller? How in an industrial urban environment do we provide the psychological and intellectual stimulation that was somehow theirs? History gives no easy answers, but it prompts sobering questions when we drive back to town.

Rural Life and Famous Men

$7\frac{1}{2}$ miles north-east of Ayr, off A758

Tarbolton stands high amid the windy pastures and plough-land of middle Ayrshire, a near neighbour to two farms on which Robert Burns worked diligently to the formulae of eighteenth-century 'improvers'. It saw him in his hour of ease and shared with Mauchline, a slightly larger village to the east, the discovery that the man was a poet.

For some eight years this seventeenth-century thatched house of two storeys was a focal point in Burns's life. Here in 1780 he and his friends formed their Bachelors' Club; and here in 1781 he was initiated into Freemasonry. The upper room which the club and the Tarbolton Freemasons used as a meeting-place has been returned to use, furnished with an old oak refectory table, country chairs and other items of the period. Since 1971 a local Burns club has met here each year to celebrate the anniversary of the poet's birth. The lower room,

Bachelors' Club,
Tarbolton

253

The kitchen

the kitchen, is also of absorbing interest, but is not truly
equipped to cope expeditiously with a dinner party – the
plenitude of culinary appointments dates from the latter part
of the eighteenth century and the beginning of the nineteenth.

In 1780 Burns was twenty-one. He had been in Tarbolton
parish for three years. The early rhymes, not all of them rustic,
were jigging and wheeling in his large dark head, though there
was little enough in his circumstances to cheer him. His father
had entered on a lease of the farm of Lochlie in 1777 with
consequences which ultimately were almost ruinous. The
Bachelors' Club was an unpretentious society which could do
little to enhance his social or economic prospects: it admitted
to membership any 'cheerful honest-hearted lad, who, if he has
a friend that is true, and a mistress that is kind, and as much
wealth as genteely to make both ends meet – is just as happy as
this world can make him'. The Tarbolton Freemasons were a
company of a different kind. Burns soon found a friend in
Gavin Hamilton, a prosperous country lawyer in Mauchline.
Not only did Hamilton gain a welcome for him in circles in
which little note would normally be taken of a tenant farmer's
son; at the father's death he saved the Burns family from
bankruptcy and contrived their move to Mossgiel farm in the
parish of Mauchline.

From Mossgiel, as from Lochlie, Burns jogged into Tarbolton to join the Masons. The verses that preceded the great
poems began to flow more urgently. His mastery of language
became more sure – the racy Scots which he first learned from

his mother, Agnes Brown, the less tractable English of which John Murdoch had had time to impart a modicum. From a summer at Kirkoswald (see Souter Johnnie's House, p. 268) he got much besides a rudimentary knowledge of land surveying; in a year at Irvine he discovered the existence of wide boys and pretty, light-minded girls; the attempts of the Tarbolton schoolmaster to play apothecary inspired the first satire, 'Death and Doctor Hornbook'; in Mauchline he met Jean Armour. By 1788, when he left Mossgiel for Ellisland in Dumfriesshire, Burns was, in Catherine Carswell's measured phrase, a people's poet of full stature.

The house was renovated and re-thatched in 1971 with the aid of a financial grant from the Scottish Tourist Board; it is one of the most northerly points on the Burns Heritage Trail, a happy device inspired by the Board to help one comprehend the life and times of Scotland's national poet.

In Brechin Road, Kirriemuir, 6 miles north-west of Forfar on A926

James Matthew Barrie was born and had his home for eight years in No. 9 Brechin Road in the Tenements, Kirriemuir.

Barrie's Birthplace, Kirriemuir, Tayside

Barrie's birthplace

The parlour

The modest two-storeyed house was built of local stone and roofed with slate. It had four rooms. In the yard there stood a communal wash-house also of stone. Mr Duncan Elliot Alves of Bryn Bras Castle, Caernarvon, purchased both structures in 1937, soon after Barrie's death, and presented them to the Trust.

The oral history of Angus is insistent that but for this intervention neither would be there now. Barrie's American connection (established in company with Charles Frohman, who first produced *The Little Minister* as a stage play, in New York in 1896) was thought to justify the removal of the house to the United States and its re-erection stone by stone as a Barrie museum. A similar project had the object of transferring the wash-house, with all of its ascribed associations with *Peter Pan*, to Kensington Gardens, London.

Out of consideration for the lady who occupied the house, a friend of the Barrie family, restoration was deferred until 1961. Work then began to give back to the birthplace its former character, outdoors and in, and to provide accommodation for a resident representative. (The second purpose was achieved by a sensitive architectural operation which 'twinned' the adjoining house, No. 11, with No. 9.) In rooms rearranged to the pattern laid on them by Barrie's mother, Margaret Ogilvy, there stand examples of her furniture including the braw

chairs which she had installed on May 9th, 1860, the day
Barrie was born. There are also significant trophies of Barrie's
London days and his triumph as a playwright – his desk, the
couch and settle from his Adelphi Terrace flat, original manuscripts, his warrant of baronetcy and coat of arms and their
seals, a portrait in oils by Sir John Lavery, *Peter Pan* jerkins
worn by Pauline Chase and Jean Forbes Robertson, a selection
of letters, proof copies, photographs and press cuttings, and a
complete collection of his books.

Kirriemuir, alias Thrums, the town of the handloom
weavers, furnished Barrie with much of his material as author
and dramatist. Though he received his schooling in Glasgow,
Forfar and Dumfries and graduated at Edinburgh University,
he returned to the place again and again. However, Thrums
never had a playhouse; the young Barrie had his first sight of
the professional stage in the Theatre Royal at Dumfries, for *The wash-house,*
which in the previous century Robert Burns had written *Barrie's first 'theatre'*
prologues.

2 miles east of Nairn at Auldearn on A96

**Boath Doocot,
Highland**

The seventeenth-century doocot, on an eminence which was
crowned by a castle at an earlier date, is an excellent piece of
masonwork and accommodated a large number of birds. The
site has a double interest at this date. It overlooks the ground
on which Montrose, making a northern foray in his whirlwind
campaign (1644–45) for Charles I, defeated a Covenanting *Boath Doocot*

force under Hurry on May 9th, 1645. He flew the king's standard on the hilltop. There is a battle map on display.

The property was presented to the Trust by Brigadier J. Muirhead of Boath, M.C., in 1947.

Carlyle's Birthplace, Ecclefechan, Dumfries and Galloway

9 miles north-west of Gretna Green, 6 miles south-west of Lockerbie, off A74

Thomas Carlyle was born on December 4th, 1795, in this arched house on the main street of Ecclefechan in Annandale, an ancient river-route by which one wing of the Roman army invaded Scotland in A.D. 79 and by which the A74 highway and the London–Glasgow railway-line swing west and north from the Border. The house was built by his father and uncle. Both were master-masons, working in a south-west Scotland which knew almost as much of turbulence as of the rule of law. Carlyle wrote of the buildings which his father raised, 'they stand firm and sound to the heart all over his little district.' This is certainly true of the family home. It is built in two wings over a pend. The treatment of the façade is done with a workmanlike flourish which leaves no doubt that the 'fighting mason' who could protect himself and his property in lonely places had a right understanding of proportion and the mechanical properties of his materials.

Carlyle's birthplace, Ecclefechan

The room in which Carlyle was born is furnished as a writer's study. It contains part of the collection of his personal belongings and a valuable series of his manuscript letters. The most prominent items in the adjoining bedroom are his crib and a box bed. The kitchen, on the ground floor, has furniture, fittings and equipment of the kind to which his parents were accustomed – a swey above the fire, iron pots and pans, a meal ark and cloutie rugs.

It was from here that Carlyle at the age of eleven – 'a lang, sprawling ill-put-together thing' according to his mother – was convoyed by his father to Annan Academy. At Annan he met Edward Irving. It was Irving who put him on the road to Edinburgh University (to which he walked, all of a hundred miles, on the eve of his fourteenth birthday in the November term of 1809) and so not only to fame but to his marriage to Jane Welsh.

20 miles north-east of Inverness on A832

Hugh Miller's Cottage, Cromarty, Highland

Cromarty, a royal burgh for seven centuries, a port sheltered by the great headland of the South Sutor at the mouth of the Cromarty Firth, has but this one house surviving from a bustling eighteenth-century fishing town. The long, low, thatched cottage with its tiny upper windows 'half buried in

Cromarty and the mouth of the Firth

the eaves', was built for John Fiddes, a seafaring man, and his bride Jean Gallie. Their initials flank the date 1711 on a mantel in the principal lower room. It is probable that the house was paid for in Spanish gold – John's business in great waters included a spell of buccaneering.

The cottage has many of the features for which hundreds of its kind have been condemned, *inter alia* inadequate daylighting and ventilation, a low doorway. There is no damp course; the flagged floors of the lower storey are below ground level. But it served John Fiddes and was still trig when on October 10th, 1802, his great-grandson Hugh Miller was born in the room on the right at the head of the stairs. That event alone, as Professor Smout suggests (see p. 245), was the salvation of the place. Cromarty lacked nothing in pride or affection for the 'Cromarty stonemason'. The house was opened to the public as a museum in 1900 and handed over to the Trust by Cromarty Town Council in 1938. It is now as eloquent of the stonemason's early domestic circumstances as of his later attainments.

Hugh Miller, son of yet another seafaring man, owner and

master of a Cromarty trading sloop, clove to the land – possibly for the reason that his father was lost at sea when he was five. At the age of seventeen he declined an uncle's offer to send him to college, was apprenticed to the mason's craft and made in time his first significant geological discovery, the fossil specimens in the rock faces of the Old Red Sandstone quarries in which he worked. He became in turn a contributor to the *Inverness Courier*, accountant in the Cromarty branch of the Commercial Bank of Scotland, editor of a religious journal and author of a number of books on subjects other than geology, though now his best-known work is *The Old Red Sandstone*, which was published in 1841.

The Birthroom

The room in which he was born contains not only a scrubbed-wood nursing chair but such articles as the stone-mason's mallet and the shepherd tartan plaid which made him easily identifiable on the streets of Edinburgh as the editor of *The Witness*. In an adjoining room are papers which he held often in his hands, beginning with the last letter written by his father to his mother and spanning his career as journalist and author; the collection includes manuscripts and letters from Richard Owen, Charles Darwin, Thomas Carlyle and Thomas Chalmers.

In the geology room fossils of the ancient armoured fishes, taken from Miller's collection, are tagged by extracts from his descriptions of the specimens. Renewal of the plasterwork in the kitchen has made good the ravages of time, and in the garden a sundial which Miller hewed for his uncles testifies that his 'skill as a stone-cutter rose somewhat above the average of the profession in those parts of the country in which it rank. highest'.

Kirkwynd Cottages, Glamis, Tayside

6 miles south-west of Forfar off A94, 5 miles south of Kirrie-muir on A928

Kirkwynd Cottages have housed the Angus Folk Collection since 1957. When it was conveyed to the Trust for this purpose, by feu charter from the sixteenth Earl of Strathmore, the group consisted of a range of five one-storey houses and a communal wash-house. It had its origins in the intent of the seventeenth-century Patrick, third earl, to build four 'lodges' for the use of old men; the draft deed is noted in the *Glamis Book of Record*.

Built at the very beginning of the nineteenth century, the cottages are in every outward characteristic native to Angus and Strathmore, the great central lowland of Scotland in which high farming has sometimes been synonymous with high living but thrift and modesty have always kept creeping in. The men who christened the adjoining hamlets of Jericho, Zoar and Padanaram had at least some knowledge of the Scriptures and regard for the wrath of God.

The process of restoration and adaptation for new uses involved pointing the rubble walls, re-slating the entire roof with the original heavy slabs ('Auchmithie slate'), renewing wooden rones, replacing wooden floors with flagstones, and making openings in internal walls to afford easy circulation for visitors. An architect, craftsmen and artisans of native stock made a perfect job of it.

The collection was gathered by Jean, Lady Maitland who with her late husband, Sir Ramsay Maitland of Burnside, has devoted a lifetime to preserving in tangible form much of the domestic, agricultural and social history of Angus over two centuries and more. There are upwards of 1,000 items. They flow, as has been truly said, through all but two rooms with the exuberance of a farm roup – *anglice*, auction sale. Of the two static rooms one is a cottage kitchen, lifted straight out of a but-and-ben which was built in 1807 and demolished in 1960;

Kirkwynd Cottages

the other is a Victorian manse parlour. One part of the collection recalls vividly the old cottage craft of linen weaving. In Glamis as in Kirriemuir almost every household had its hand-loom. A less likely vocation is brought to mind by a work-bench and turning lathe from the manse of Carmyllie. It was there that the parish minister, the Rev. Patrick Bell, constructed the first reaping machine; he demonstrated it at a public trial in September 1830. Another utilitarian exhibit is the copper boiler in which Peter Reid, merchant in Forfar and benefactor extraordinary, made his celebrated Forfar rock and in due time a fortune. Out of the latter he financed for his native town a public hall, a public park and at the last a chain of public lavatories (cast-iron constructions from the Saracen Foundry in Glasgow, for men only).

In 1974 the Angus Folk Collection Trust asked the National Trust for Scotland to take the contents of the folk museum into its care in order to ensure that the collection shall never be broken up, or removed from the locality to which it relates, and shall retain its local character. The Trust's acceptance of the contents and a new building to house agricultural implements was made possible by the gift of a substantial endowment fund by a resident in Angus who wishes to remain anonymous.

Farmhouse kitchen with equipment of eighteenth- to nineteenth-century date

In Menstrie village 5 miles north-east of Stirling on A91

Menstrie Castle was the birthplace of Scotland's first imperialist, Sir William Alexander of Menstrie, Earl of Stirling and Viscount of Canada (1567–1640). The Nova Scotia Room commemorates not only his effort to found a Scots colony overseas but the foundation of the baronetage of Scotland by King James VI and I and the subsequent enlargement of the order down to the Treaty of Union between Scotland and England in 1707.

'His Majesties royal colony' of Nova Scotia or 'New Scotland' as defined by Sir William, the King's Lieutenant, was a vast tract of land lying between New England and Newfoundland. For its development finance and a large force of 'artificeris or labourers' was needed. The king hoped that the conferment of a baronetcy of Nova Scotia and the grant of 'ane proportioun of ground within New Scotland' (later set at 16,000 acres), to be purchased at a specified price, would induce a hundred 'knichts and gentlemen of cheife respect' to support the enterprise. In this he and his son Charles I were disappointed, but the latter confirmed the baronets' privileges and gave them

*Nova Scotia Room:
the baronets' shields
and portrait of King
Charles I*

the right to wear a distinctive badge – the arms of Nova Scotia with the motto *Fax mentis honestae gloria* suspended on an orange-tawny ribbon.

In the Nova Scotia Room the main composition consists of approximately one hundred shields bearing the arms of the Nova Scotia baronetcies which are still extant, in so far as they have been matriculated. There are maps to show the geographical location of the estates in Scotland from which the baronets took their titles and the position in Eastern Canada of the grants of land in 'New Scotland', though only a few of these can be identified as grants to individual baronets. The portraits in the room are those of King James and King Charles. In addition to the baronets' badges, the heraldic devices include the arms of Scotland and Nova Scotia, the badge of the Pilgrim Trust and the coats of arms of the former County Council of Clackmannan and the National Trust for Scotland. The motifs of the moulded plaster ceiling are the thistle and the maple leaf.

The castle, a sixteenth-century house, is not a Trust property. It was conserved and adapted to modern use by Clackmannan County Council with the support of the Province of Nova Scotia, the city of Halifax, the Pilgrim Trust, H.M. Government and the National Trust for Scotland. It contains four flats and is the focal point in an attractive housing estate created by the local authority. The apartment which has been converted into the Nova Scotia Room was presented to the Trust. It relates directly to the life of the village. The Menstrie branch of the county library was established there in 1963.

Preston Mill and Phantassie Doocot, Lothian

In East Linton, 24 miles east of Edinburgh, 5½ miles west of Dunbar off A1

Preston Mill springs from the rich East Lothian earth with as much exuberance as the great trees in the parks and policies of Tyninghame or the barley, wheat and oats in the brae-set fields of the lower Tyne. It is a rarity and a delight: the kiln with its conical roof and wind vane, the mill building and the out-buildings, all happed in red pantiles, make a perfect harmony. It is the sole survivor of roughly a score of mills which throve for centuries beside the shining river.

Grain has been milled on this site since the twelfth century. A substantial part of the existing fabric dates from the seventeenth. In a note on its maintenance Andrew Meikle, millwright and inventor of the threshing-machine who had his workshop at Phantassie (see below), has recorded that from

Preston Mill

The kiln and the mill   May 8th–27th, 1749, one Patrick Dawson 'wrought three weeks at Preston Mill'. An extensive renovation followed in 1760. The great iron wheel, 13 feet in diameter and 3 feet 2 inches wide, was cast in that year, probably at the Carron foundry beside Falkirk which supplied the carronades for Nelson's ships. But for one relatively short interruption the mill has been in service ever since, and one can still see how the miller worked – from the drying of the grain to its emergence as oatmeal from under the millstones, ready for bagging.

Preston Mill was presented to the Trust in 1950 by the trustees of the late Mr G. B. Gray of Smeaton. It had survived one of the greatest floods in its history – on August 12th, 1948, the river rose as high as the roof line of the mill building – and local effort came near to restoring it to full working order. Salvation came in 1966 when Messrs Rank Hovis McDougall Ltd, one of the largest and most modern milling organizations in Europe, resolved to 'adopt' what is unquestionably one of the smallest and oldest mills in Scotland. They did more than renew and repair machinery; the company have prevailed on experienced millers as they reached the age of retirement to serve as custodians and keep the wheels turning.

Phantassie Doocot, the mill's near neighbour to the south, was given to the Trust in 1961 by Mr William Hamilton, owner of the celebrated Phantassie farm. It is a massive structure with nesting places for 500 birds. The walls, four

266

feet thick at the base, project upward in horseshoe form to enclose a sloping roof. The latter was designed to give the 'doos' the benefit of a southern exposure, which suggests that the builder was either a Scot who knew southern France or was advised by someone who did.

It was in his workshop at Phantassie that Andrew Meikle tutored John Rennie (1761–1821) whose achievements as a civil engineer included the London and East India docks, the naval dockyards at Chatham, Portsmouth and Plymouth, and Waterloo, Southwark and London bridges over the Thames. A brother, George Rennie (1749–1828) made so many innovations in farming practice that a stream of visitors and inquirers from England, Ireland and Europe beat a path to his door.

Phantassie Doocot

13 miles south of Ayr, 4 miles south of Maybole on A77

John Davidson, the village cobbler of Kirkoswald, moved into his new thatched house in 1785. Five years later he had immortality thrust upon him. Robert Burns composed 'Tam o' Shanter' in the space of a winter day at Ellisland in Dumfriesshire, and there as a central figure was the cobbler – Souter Johnnie, 'the ancient, trusty, drouthy crony'. The dramatis personae of that enchanting, and enchanted, narrative poem, walked straight out of a Kirkoswald of an earlier time.

In 1775, at the age of sixteen, Burns was sent there to study mathematics and land-surveying under Hugh Rodger, the Kirkoswald dominie. He found himself amid a more raffish society than any he had encountered around Alloway, Ayr or Mount Oliphant. The prototype of 'Tam o' Shanter', Douglas Graham, tenant of Shanter farm on the Carrick shore, was celebrated as a roysterer even in the heart of the smuggling district. In the fifteen years between 1775 and 1790 Burns's genius came to full flame – in songs and love poems that speak to all humanity, satires like 'Holy Willy's Prayer' (unpublished until after his death) and the narrative poems. 'The Jolly

Souter Johnnie's House

268

Beggars' was conceived in the alehouses of Mauchline in company with younger cronies and tinkers, fiddlers and trollops. The stuff of 'Tam o' Shanter' was also drawn from experience which other men had shared. But in all that he did and wrote, the passion and compassion, the energy and indignation, the acute observation and the rollicking sense of fun were his alone.

The work of mason and joiner that went into the building of the cobbler's house has proved its worth. And the living-room-kitchen with its box-bed and local country furniture would look like home to Souter Johnnie. There are, however, a number of bonuses. The Burns relics include the poet's Masonic badge. A collection of Glasgow blue-and-white china which came to the Trust as a gift is added adornment for the old place. Out of doors, on a green sward which has replaced the kaleyaird in which the first occupant grew his vegetables, the Souter, Tam, the innkeeper and his wife are memorialized in stone. The figures, one and a half times life size, were sculpted by James Thom, a native of Tarbolton, where also Burns left the impress of his power.

In Kilbarchan village 10 miles south-west of Glasgow, north off A737, south off A761

Weaver's Cottage, Kilbarchan, Strathclyde

In this sturdy eighteenth-century cottage 'history on the spot' takes on a domestic and immediate aspect. Handloom weavers lived and wove here until 1940. The looms in the basement

The Weaver's Cottage: the kitchen

workroom are still serviceable and put to use.

The Weaver's Cottage in the Barngreen of Kilbarchan was built in 1723 by Andrew, John and Jenet Bryden. Their initials appear on the lintel over the front door. After them successive generations of two families followed the same craft and never thought it necessary to make radical structural alterations. The northern half of the building is in effect a 'cruck' cottage; the weight of the roof is carried within the house by pairs of trusses, formed of curved timbers, instead of by the external walls. The walls themselves were built of 'land gatherings', boulders collected from the moor and roughly dressed, just as the stones dug out of new-formed fields were used to build the farm dykes of Scotland some little time later.

The creation of the 'memorial museum of the local weaving industry' was inspired by the people of Kilbarchan. They contributed many of the items with local associations with which the Trust has restored the original character of the cottage since 1957. On the ground floor the contents of the living-room are as notable for validity as for diversity. A second room is devoted to pictures and portraits of weavers. In a third the history of Kilbarchan weaving and the refinement of Kilbarchan work is exemplified in a brave show of tools of the trade, shoulder shawls, shirt patterns and a few of the numerous tartans which came off the looms. The fabrics which the village produced included silks (in common with Paisley, whose 'pine pattern' was reproduced to perfection), cambrics, muslins, lawns, gingham and repp, in addition to linen and woollens.

Locally woven shawls are in use as covers on the box-beds, of which there are a prodigious number by comparison with the size of the cottage. The cruck structure can be seen in some detail in the attic. In the garden one feature indicates how much more truly rural was Kilbarchan of the weavers. There is in the wall a bee bole to take three skeps; and now there are three wicker skeps or 'ruskies' there.

The Weaver's Cottage: sound mason-work in random rubble

VIII · LITTLE HOUSES

with an introduction by Robin Prentice

Introduction

'There's the kingdom o' Fife, frae Culross to the East
Neuk it's just like a great big city. Sae mony royal
boroughs yoked end on end, like ropes of ingans, with
their hie-streets, and their booths, nae doubt, and their
krames, and houses of stone and lime and forestairs.
Kirkcaldy, the sell o't, is longer than any town in England.'

Andrew Fairservice in *Rob Roy*

Scotland's little houses, an extraordinary architectural
achievement by ordinary, relatively humble folk, survive in
many a small town and a few large ones. Medieval monarchs
and feudal magnates built castles. Merchants and tradesmen
and fishermen made the burghs. They were a long time at it.
David I began to establish burghal communities in the first
half of the twelfth century. One object was to add to the royal
revenues by an expansion of trade; but the burghs were also to
be art and part in a deliberate political ploy. The 'sair sanct',
the seventh ruler in the Canmore dynasty, whose roots were
part Scots and part English, was as firm as any in his resolve to
make of a primitive and predominantly Celtic Scotland an
organized feudal state. Of the main props in the grand design,
the barons had the task of enforcing the royal writ (and putting
down rival claimants to the throne); the Church, enriched by
large grants of land, would exert a stabilizing and civilizing
influence on lords and commons; the commons would have
their chance to participate and to profit in the king's burghs.
These were planted in locations, beside a royal castle, an
Anglo-Norman strength or a prelate's palace, where they could
most plausibly be expected to extend the influence of the
Crown.

Over the years an idea which David borrowed from England
took some unexpected twists. A royal burgh had by virtue of its
charter a monopoly of crafts and local and foreign trade, and
an exclusive right to hold fairs or markets, within a prescribed
area. Theoretically at least all inhabitants were freeholders of
the king. So they started on a fine egalitarian footing. By the
time the merchants formed a merchant guild, and long before
the craftsmen made a concerted bid for a say in local government through the craft guilds, some social and economic gaps
had opened. Not only were there freemen and unfreemen; it
was apparent that among the freemen the merchants were more
equal than others and that the royal burghs, especially the
ports with a royal charter, were first in royal favour. The latter

maintained a total monopoly in overseas trade until the second half of the seventeenth century – in consideration, no doubt, of the volume of revenue from the burgh 'mails' and the customs dues and the ease with which the king's officers collected it. This monopoly was a privilege for which the king's burghs had soon to contend with later creations.

Magnates and prelates in their turn were given power to set up 'free' burghs. In 1225 Alexander II granted Walter, Bishop of Glasgow, the right of having a burgh at Glasgow with a market on Thursdays. By 1400 Crown, kirk and baronage had raised the total number to just under sixty. In most if not all there was a lively mix of population, Flemings and Scandinavians in addition to Scots, but progress was very variable. Of the places which constituted the original 'Court of the Four Burghs', Berwick was lost to England, Edinburgh became the capital of Scotland, Roxburgh foundered, and Stirling prospered in a modest way. The ecclesiastical burghs of St Andrews, Brechin, Arbroath, Glasgow and Dunfermline gained in time the same status as the royal burghs, were represented in the consortium which later took the name of the 'Convention of Royal Burghs' and sent commissioners to Parliament. All of these five stood on 'Lowland' sites. Indeed, central and southern Scotland had four-fifths of the early creations. The rest, except for Tarbert in Kintyre, were strung like beads up the eastern coastal level from Inverbervie in Kincardineshire to Wick in Caithness. Tarbert in Kintyre was established as a king's burgh in an attempt to 'colonize' the Highlands and the Hebrides; the enterprise was no more successful in political or military terms than a later plantation at Stornoway in Lewis.

The 'sair sanct' and his successors achieved much of their purpose, nevertheless. The royal burghs might be, often were, wholly dominated by the merchant guild, who elected the town council from among their own number. Burghs of barony and ecclesiastical burghs had differing measures of independence. Yet the system brought order and discipline, a sense of continuing purpose and of community – 'we're a' Jock Tamson's bairns'. The corporate life style was far from elegant; yet it had some concern for civic dignity and also for the unfortunates in local society. The fact that the system worked even moderately well encouraged its enlargement. By the end of the seventeenth century more than 300 burghs could boast that they had been 'erected' by charter, and in the eighteenth it was a self-electing council which promoted and regulated the building of the New Town of Edinburgh.

The motive for the high concentration on the Forth, on the Lothian as well as the Fife shore, was simple: there was the prospect of revenue not only from trade with Europe but from the fisheries of the Firth. The results can never have been spectacular. Scottish merchants traded in a smaller way and within a shorter radius than the merchants of England. The burghs grew slowly; with the exceptions of Glasgow and Edinburgh, none grew big until the onset of the Industrial Revolution in the early years of the nineteenth century. But from the Middle Ages there was a two-way traffic with Scandinavia, the Baltic ports and the Low Countries. In Holland, Scots merchants had special privileges in their 'staple' at Veere in the province of Zealand, and there was a comparable arrangement in respect of the wine trade with Bordeaux (hence the Scotsman's inherited taste for claret). The effects of this to-ing and fro-ing were first noticeable within burgh boundaries. Men who came to be familiar with European ports and cities assimilated some of the culture, the entrepreneurial skills and the manual and mechanical skills of Continental societies. Ultimately a tincture of enlightenment and intellectual curiosity was bound to filter through to the neighbours, even the neighbours in the countryside, for the trading area of an individual burgh was often very wide.

The first call on new-found expertise had to do with money, how to make it, how to save it, how to spend it to best advantage. This was no bad thing. Much could be done without benefit of the higher mathematics or double-entry bookkeeping. A man must gather cash before he could gather gear, and gather gear the merchants did. It showed in household plenishings and apparel and at table. It showed most durably in architecture, the most practical of the arts. European influence gave to an economical vernacular style of building a touch of panache, almost a new dimension. Fondness for embellishment, modest embellishment, set in in the sixteenth century and survived the Reformation and an age of Calvinistic dominance. Of the burghs which moved Andrew Fairservice to admiration, Crail can show most of the items in his inventory. It has a routh of comely old houses, not large, stone-built, harled, pantiled or slated. The steepled tolbooth is more than a symbol of burghal authority. It bespeaks the skill and integrity of the masons and wrights who put it together, men who had certainly seen or heard tell of Dutch modes; it recalls in subtle ways the hardihood of generations of men who had business in great waters, fishers and merchants alike.

The Tolbooth, Crail

Little houses in burghs which never felt the breath of salt sea winds gained distinction from cross-fertilization on the coast. A Dutch gable is as natural a part of the street scene in Haddington as in Pittenweem or, say, Norwich on the slack waters of the river Wensum. The nature of materials available – sandstone, whinstone or intractable granite (as in Aberdeen, Kintore, Inverurie and other places in the north-east) – set limits on form and detail up the east coast, and yet again in the west. There Ayr, Irvine, Dumbarton, Renfrew, Rutherglen and Lanark, king's burghs of great antiquity, had Newton-on-Ayr and Prestwick (burghs of barony) in addition to Glasgow in close companionship – and competition. To them European notions penetrated more slowly, at any rate via trade.

Insistence on basic elements of town planning gave the burgh its shape. The place must be defensible to some degree. There had to be space for fairs or markets. In the hinterland a common street plan was a simple, elongated parallelogram. The axis was the 'hie street'. On either side the burgesses were allocated individual strips of land. The place for the house was on the frontage. On the perimeter, at the end of the 'lang riggs' or kale yards, each burgess had to build his section of the town wall. With some adjustment the pattern served for a port or for a burgh set beside a river, such as Haddington and Kelso, too. The broad span of the 'hie street' became the market place. With business thriving, there came yet another twist to the general concept. There was need for a tolbooth – centre of burghal government, town treasury, weights and measures office, and town jail in one building. So a tolbooth arose, usually in the centre of the market space. Nothing reprehensible there, but somehow merchant burgesses and craftsmen burgesses persuaded themselves that they had a God-given right to the centre line behind the tolbooth. Timber booths became permanent structures, and the timber was gradually replaced by stone. Kelso and Haddington acquired on the sites of the booths a double row of houses, possibly Scotland's first example of 'back to back' building. Mercifully, there was room at the other end of the 'hie street' for the krames, the simple stalls from which country folk, who paid market dues, sold their produce.

Haddington replaced its tolbooth with a town house (architect, William Adam) in 1748. Kelso followed suit in 1816. Economic advance set off by agricultural 'improvement' gave an unprecedented amplitude to life in these typical Lowland market towns. Today the 'borrowed' ground and the margins of the old 'hie street' are occupied for the most part by buildings of eighteenth- and early nineteenth-century date. Two-, three- and four-deckers, they conform neither to a regular roof-line nor to regular footings at pavement level. This is part of their charm. Individually and collectively they are worthy of, and receive, the protection of planning law. Even more heartening is the care and concern of individual owners.

Haddington was the first town after Norwich to accept a Civic Trust prescription for a 'face lift' for old houses and commercial premises, in High Street, Market Street and Court Street. Kelso, having been tempted by a prospectus for 're-development' on a commonplace rectilinear plan, resolved with a little prompting by the Trust to hold what it has in Horsemarket and Woodmarket.

The farmhouses and rural buildings of the same period are equally substantial, well proportioned and economical in the use of external decoration. Fitness for purpose, the chief characteristic, carried over into barns, stables, cattle courts, horse mills and the cottages in the villages.

But it is in the coastal burghs all the way north from Berwick to the Fisherbiggins in Thurso that the evolution of the little house can be traced most easily. As in the Low Countries the older the house, the steeper the pitch of the roof, up to 55 degrees. The walls are of rubble (undressed stone), covered almost invariably by harling to prevent penetration of dampness. The height may vary from one to three storeys, less often to four, and only in the Edinburgh tenements to the dizzy height of a skyscraper. In the gables the flues were carried up to stout, stone-built lums (*anglice*, chimneys). As lately as the end of the eighteenth century the wall-heads were topped with crow-steps, most often thereafter with straight skews. It was not uncommon for the main gable to face the street; one can see examples in Culross, Kirkcaldy, St Monans, Montrose, Dingwall and Cromarty. Later houses were built end to end on a continuous line, again seldom on precisely symmetrical footings, and forestairs and stair-towers made additional breaks in the street line.

St Monans

The aspect of the Fife ports from the sea that truly gives the heart a lift, in any weather, is sight of the old red roofs. Though pantiles came to Scotland relatively late, the S-shaped red tile saw, centuries before the switch from square sail to fore-and-aft rig, the setting out of many a trading venture for the Danish Sound and Biscay. There is a legend that substantial quantities of tiles came into east coast ports from Europe, either carried as part-cargo at low rates or shipped as ballast to be sold for what they would fetch on the quay. The fact is that pantiles were until lately the hap on uncounted buildings between the Thames and the Tay, in any district where clay had been cheap and thatch or slates dear or unobtainable. 'Improvement' in the countryside brought a prodigious proliferation. Kilns which fired drainage tiles for the fields could just as easily turn out roofing tiles by the thousand. (Pantiles are still counted by the thousand; and 1,000 approximating to the Scottish type will cover a superficial area of 65 square yards, sufficient for the roofs of two houses of fair size.) But the rate of mortality has also been prodigious. Only in Fife has the corollary to the rescue of numerous little houses been the perpetuation of the pantiled roof.

Appreciation of the burghs' inheritance of stone and lime has made slow but steady progress during the past fifty years. It is the more constant because the proponents of preservation drew a clear distinction between antiquarian or romantic interest (the adventitious beauty which age can give) and architectural merit, the potential of an individual building or a group and hard political reality.

In the 1930s housing authorities were making a first concerted assault on slums. Most of these were buildings which were inadequate by any standard when they were thrown up in the previous century to house workers who flocked to the coal and iron belt and the mushrooming industrial towns. But there were conspicuous exceptions. However, a disposition to condemn every old house as a bad house, or a poor one beyond redemption, appeared to be tolerated by central government. Apprehension was intensified in 1935 by the terms of a new Housing Act. The alarm bells were triggered in Edinburgh by the Cockburn Association. At the urging of the city's amenity societies the National Trust for Scotland set up an Old Edinburgh Committee. Within twelve months the fourth Marquess of Bute enabled the Trust to lift its sights by providing the funds to make a national survey. The commission was given to the late Ian Lindsay; and the survey identified in a hundred towns 1,149 traditional or vernacular buildings of which 136 were of outstanding importance.

Central government modified procedure. The 'Bute lists' and annotated maps were supplied to the Department of Health for Scotland in order that local authorities might be informed of each building which met Ian Lindsay's rigorous criteria. The Second World War put an end to the survey, but twelve years after the Trust initiative central government took over. Section 28 of the Town and Country Planning (Scotland) Act 1947, the vesting date for which was July 5th, 1948, required that an official list be prepared of all buildings of 'special architectural or historic interest'. The 'Bute lists' first gave substance to that compendium.

Though 'listing' gives no guarantee of permanent preservation – which can be achieved only by restoration or renewal for a modern use – much has been accomplished. The National Trust for Scotland demonstrated that little houses can be restored, re-equipped and given a new term of usefulness. This was done to such effect that local authorities were won over to the side of conservation, in some instances as active partners or as contributors of finance and professional assistance, in others as restorers of their own property. In Stirling the old streets around the 'tap o' the toon' show admirably what a town council could achieve. Edinburgh commissioned young architects to restore parts of the Royal Mile and, where restoration was impracticable, to design new buildings to match the old. These and other councils have set examples which the new regional and district authorities seem bound to follow.

Direct action by the Trust began with the entry into Culross in 1932. The Council purchased the Study and nine other properties in the vicinity of the mercat cross at a total cost of £168. (This included 'a sum for certain immediate necessary repairs'.) Expenditure of a further £175 purchased a footing in the Sandhaven in order to protect the environment of the Palace. Following the Second World War housing associations were formed, first for Culross and then in 1953, Coronation year, for the salvation of Dunkeld. In this way grant aid was obtained for the restoration and adaptation of traditional buildings, but there was a formidable limiting factor. These became houses for rent at the same level as local authority housing and capital was locked up for a term of sixty years.

Culross:
the mercat cross

In 1960 a stroke little short of genius, the creation of the Revolving Fund, opened the way for a rolling programme. The initial capital amounted to £20,000, consisting of a grant of £10,000 from the Pilgrim Trust and the grant of a similar sum from the General Fund of the National Trust for Scotland. With this backing it became possible to purchase, restore, adapt, equip and resell appropriate buildings, then to employ the cash on a fresh project. Very soon it became apparent that variation to meet individual cases and different local situations was feasible. Full advantage has been taken of the fact. At this date the value of work completed under the Little Houses Improvement Scheme is £3 million.

The Scheme is managed, as one of a number of assignments, by a Deputy Director. Two qualified surveyors, one in the east of Scotland, the other in the west, form with him the nucleus of an intelligence network and supply professional expertise. When a building is identified as being worthy of restoration a uniform scale of criteria and priorities is applied before purchase: (1) architectural and/or historic merit; (2) vacant possession; (3) market price; (4) probable cost of restoration; (5) saleability. Thereafter there are three possible courses of action. The building may be purchased from the Trust and restored by the purchaser, employing his own architect; the purchaser may invite the Trust to become his restoring agent; the Trust may undertake restoration at its own expense, because of the environmental importance of a building, and rely on recovering costs from the resale. In all instances the restoration scheme must be under the control or have the approval of the Trust, and the purchaser is required to guarantee the integrity of the building in perpetuity by entering into a Conservation Agreement.

From a Trust point of view the most satisfactory variant is the 'restoring purchaser'. The least satisfactory is restoration for resale. There are occasions when it is inescapable, but it may tie up capital for an inconvenient length of time.

Buildings of exceptional merit or of special significance in a group may qualify for a government grant on the recommendation of the Historic Buildings Council for Scotland, whose interest and support have encouraged the Trust and local authorities alike. Housing grants are normally available for the provision of internal facilities required to bring a house up to modern standards.

At the outset the Revolving Fund was soon refreshed and augmented by donations, legacies, interest-free loans from institutions and individuals, and a margin of profit on transactions. Prior to the reorganization of local government in 1975 the county councils of Fife and East Lothian granted generous financial help. Since that event regional authorities have given practical encouragement, especially welcome in a period of financial stringency. Fife Regional Council furnished interest-free loans of £10,000 for the Trust's general programme in Fife and £10,000 for work done in association with local conservation societies. Strathclyde Regional Council made £75,000 available and the Borders Regional Council £20,000 with which to finance work within their respective areas.

The results of Trust initiatives are most readily apparent on the coast of Fife, all the way east and north from Culross to the Tay estuary. It is there that growth and redevelopment of towns have dealt least harshly with the investment which prosperous citizens made in stone and lime through the sixteenth, seventeenth and eighteenth centuries. There also the former county council and town councils were prepared at an early date to enter into joint enterprises. Seeing what was achieved, the Commissioners for Crown Estates resolved to participate, first at Crail and later on a greater scale at Dysart.

In other areas single demonstrations of what was feasible had an enlivening effect on public attitudes to conservation. In North Berwick, The Lodge, a sturdy group of eighteenth-century buildings near the heart of the town, was saved by adaptation and conversion into eight flats. In Cromarty restoration of the nineteenth-century Miller House gave Hugh Miller's birthplace a seemly neighbour. Following the restora-

The Lodge, North Berwick

tion of Abertarff House in Inverness, the renewal of Nos 109–11 Church Street as a block of offices contributed further to the effort to conserve the stock of eighteenth-century architecture in that quarter. The Old Inn at Fowlis Wester in Perthshire, converted to a dwelling-house, repeated in a rural setting the object lesson of Dunkeld.

A preliminary venture in the Borders was strictly an extra-mural exercise. It achieved, in co-operation with St Andrew's Episcopal Church, the rehabilitation of Turret House, Kelso; the most prominent building in Abbey Court, it is an eighteenth-century house of two storeys with a projecting stair tower fit for a small castle. The next project added to the list of Little Houses a dwelling-house established in an eighteenth-century smithy at Bowden. Subsequent work in the county of Roxburgh gave new life to comely houses in St Boswells and to the Manor Inn at Lanton.

Similarly, in the west of Scotland the restoration of No. 92 Main Street in Dunlop became a precedent for projects in Dunure, Douglas and Eaglesham. The work of restoring Powrie Castle in Dundee was completed in 1980, and in the neighbouring county of Angus other 'restoring purchasers' took on the rehabilitation of the Thatched Cottage in Glamis and two houses and two flats in Broughty Ferry. Farther north, in the Buchan region of Aberdeenshire, a rescue operation on Nos 13–14 The Square, Stuartfield, has shown an aspect of the Trust somewhat different from its association with castles and great houses, but the object is broadly the same.

The Trust first primed the pump in the north-east with interest-free loans to local preservation societies. Notable results have been achieved in Banff. Similar financing – repaid in full, as in all instances – was employed in Tayport, on the north coast of Fife, to convert an early nineteenth-century coaching inn into two houses; in Ceres, in the north hinterland, to restore an eighteenth-century Masonic Lodge as a dwelling-house and to adapt the seventeenth-century Weigh House and adjacent cottages to accommodate the Fife Folk Museum. More recently an interest-free loan from the £10,000 supplied by Fife Regional Council for benefit of conservation bodies enabled the East Neuk Preservation Society to establish in No. 3 Station Road, St Monans, an office and a meeting room for themselves and a flat for sale.

News of what was being accomplished in Scotland filtered out by normal channels. In 1974 the Little Houses Improvement Scheme was brought formally to international notice. It was nominated by the British Government and accepted by the Council of Europe for listing as one of Britain's four pilot projects for European Architectural Heritage Year. One of the principal conclusions of a Council of Europe seminar in Edinburgh was: 'The principle of the Revolving Fund of the National Trust for Scotland for the restoration of Little Houses, as well as other schemes and working methods of the National and Civic Trusts of Great Britain, should be adopted in other countries where circumstances lend themselves.'

The initial effort to give the principle general application over Britain as a whole was made with the foundation of the Architectural Heritage Fund in 1976. In theory this was the Revolving Fund writ large. The object was to start with working capital of £1 million. To this end the Government undertook in 1975 to match private contributions pound for pound up to a limit of £500,000. The Civic Trust, in which administration is vested, had to start with finance still short of the million mark and a difficult remit. Whereas the Little Houses Improvement Scheme has succeeded by concentrating resources in the hands of a small group with the requisite skills to see any job through, the essence of Architectural Heritage Fund procedure is diffusion. It relies on local preservation trusts, given low-interest loans for terms of two years, to undertake projects of repair and resale. That more than a score of such trusts are making the venture in locations as dissimilar as King's Lynn, Preston and London, says much of confidence in the Civic Trust and acceptance of loan funding for financing conservation work, hitherto a novelty in England and Wales.

A point made by Sir John Stirling Maxwell in 1937 is as valid there as on this side of the border: the homely aspect of national life is recorded more fully in buildings than in books. Over the years the historians have done better by the Crown, the kirk and the baronage than by the commons.

Little Houses

10 miles south of St Andrews by A959, on A917

Three burghs 'yoked end on end' make up modern Anstruther. They were formerly Anstruther Wester, Anstruther Easter and Cellardyke, the seaport of the royal burgh of Kilrenny, and they had one *raison d'être*. And Harbourhead, East Green, in Anstruther is the logical place for the Scottish Sea Fisheries Museum.

No. 1 Harbourhead was the happiest possible choice for one of the Trust's first restoration projects in Cellardyke. This two-storey house shows a handsome eighteenth-century face to the world. A white finish on external walls lends emphasis to bold surrounds on door and window openings and to upstanding lums. The windows conform to the golden mean (six panes in the upper sash, six in the lower). A roof of red pantiles is exactly right for such a bield. Its neighbour No. 2 Harbourhead and No. 1 Dove Street (a late eighteenth-century house restored in 1967) are also Little Houses Improvement Scheme subjects worthy of attention.

Renewal in Anstruther began in 1965. An L-shaped eighteenth-century group on the Esplanade called the White House, a Category A 'listed' building, was restored privately to Trust specifications. The acquisition of St Ayle's Land in

*Anstruther:
the White House*

285

Shore Street, a group of houses and sheds varying in date from the sixteenth to the nineteenth century, was the first step towards the establishment of the Sea Fisheries Museum by remarkable local initiative. The Trust made a generous contribution towards the cost of rehabilitation. Also in the L.H.I.S. programme, Buckie House, with the house next door, restored as a dwelling-house and art gallery, are eighteenth-century buildings, in contrast to Johnston Lodge, converted into three flats, which was built in 1829, with a wing added in 1900.

Anstruther : Buckie House

Crail, Fife

10 miles south of St Andrews by A918, on A917

Crail was the testing ground for the Revolving Fund procedure in its original form – purchase, restore and sell in order to employ the capital as soon as possible on another restoration project. Nos. 5 and 6 Rumford, small two-storey houses of seventeenth- and eighteenth-century date, were restored as one house in 1961. No. 54 High Street (seventeenth century) was restored as two flats in 1963 and Nos. 16 High Street 2 Castle Street (North House, mid-eighteenth century) have received similar treatment.

Crail, a king's burgh from the fourteenth century

In Crail too the Trust achieved its first gratifying success as agent for a 'restoring' purchaser. The Commissioners for Crown Estates bought the Customs House, a stout three-decker under a steep-pitched roof, which dominates the harbour. Constructed in the late seventeenth century, dignified by crow-steps on the gables and a ship motif on the lintel over the main door, it had declined in status and was being used as a store. The object of converting the building into a dwelling-house was achieved in 1968 and the Commissioners turned their thoughts to a larger enterprise at Dysart.

*Crail: the Customs
House*

Culross: the Ark and Nunnery

Culross, Fife

12 miles west of Forth Road Bridge, off A985

The purpose of Trust involvement in the royal burgh of Culross is simply expressed – to secure the conservation and purposeful use of as many buildings as possible of this unique three-dimensional document. Culross is precisely that – a living exemplar of a sixteenth-century Scottish burgh, recipient of its royal charter in 1588, and one of that chain of harbour-towns that marked the renaissance of Scottish trade and industry in the reign of James VI. The basic industry here was the production of coal, and this was coupled with the attendant enterprise of boiling salt from sea water at Culross Pans. There was also, however, the manufacture of girdles for domestic baking while 'Tanner's House' and 'Snuff Cottage' up the long hill may indicate other smaller industries.

The lay-out of Culross and its burghal appointment are first-class illustrations in social history. The Mid Causey, the Little Causey and the Back Causey, set with rough cobbling but eased with flags for the pedestrians at their crowns, are typical of a sixteenth-century town plan, while the Tanhouse Brae runs away uphill, linking harbour and church and representing the original access from the landward districts. Again, the individual parts of a burgh are clearly to be seen – the town house upon the Sandhaven, the mercat cross in its small square and the kirk on the Parley Hill.

288

The town house is a building of 1626, rebuilt with a tower in 1783, and presented to the Trust in 1975; it is now the headquarters of the Trust's presence in the town. It comprises internally the 'Iron House' for the detention of miscreants on the ground floor, the council room with painted ceiling and the so-called 'debtors' room' on the first floor, and the 'high tolbooth' with facilities for witch-watching, in the garret. Outside stood the tron or weighing-post for the control of commodity sales. The other houses to the west of this, on the Sandhaven and beyond the Palace, are largely seventeenth century and include 'Bessie Bar's Hall'. Bessie Bar, politely Mrs Elizabeth Paterson, was a widow of enterprise who between 1577 and 1597 sold malt and developed a character strong enough to leave her name with the hall, a well and the precipitous footpath called 'Bessie Bar's Hagg'. An inspection of 1590 found her 'tenement of lands, houses and byggins thereof with the pertinents sufficient in the stanework thereof except ane little on the bak syd, and there 6s. 8d. money bestowit and warat thereupon will mak the samyn to be als sufficient as the rest'. More recent restoration has again ensured long life for Bessie Bar's Hall!

Overlooking the mercat cross, itself a twentieth-century re-creation, is the building called 'the Study' from the small, withdrawn room at the top of its tower. This is an L-plan

Culross: the Study from the Back Causeway

Culross: Tanhouse Brae

Culross: the Townhouse and the Sandhaven

Culross: the Townhouse and the Sandhaven

Culross: hope of God's providence

house of the late sixteenth century. Its rooms were once wholly panelled with oak dated 1633 and initialled IA:AP for John Adam and Alison Primrose. A new painted ceiling was provided experimentally in one room in 1968.

From the cross other seventeenth-century houses of interest, all privately occupied, can be seen. The house adjoining the Study has the over-lintel promising in Greek the hope of God's providence, while the buildings called 'the Ark' and 'the Nunnery' (1609) can be seen at the small street opposite. Nearby, facing the Dundonald Arms Hotel, is Bishop Leighton's house, occupied on visitations from Dunblane Cathedral when episcopacy was the established form of worship. Up the hill are the 'Butcher's House' (1664) showing a cleaver and yard upon its wall-front, 'Snuff Cottage' (1673) and 'Tanner's House'. This recital by no means exhausts the list of sixteenth- and seventeenth-century properties in Culross where the constant sense of discovery is one of the town's chief attractions.

At the top of the hill, adjoining part of the Cistercian monastery of 1217, stands the parish church, rebuilt in 1633 together with its manse. In the church is a spectacular monument in alabaster, raised by a dutiful son in 1642 in memory of Sir George Bruce, builder of the Palace. Parleyhill House beside the church is otherwise called the House with the Evil Eyes on account of its pair of *œil-de-boeuf* windows in the west curvilinear gable.

Since 1954 the National Trust for Scotland has owned twenty
houses in Cathedral Street and High Street, Dunkeld, which
now present not only a splendid example of 'Little House'
conservation but also a remarkably unaltered specimen of
small burgh building of the late seventeenth to early eighteenth
century. The town plan is, of course, much older. In its long
street connecting market-place with ecclesiastical foundation,
and in its traces of burghal lots running back behind the
houses, it has much in common with Culross. But the houses
themselves have to be dated to the decades following 1689
when the more primitive dwellings of an earlier Dunkeld were
burned down by the Jacobite forces in the aftermath of
Killiecrankie.

To our eyes the little houses that were erected on the earlier
sites are modest and unassuming. But in terms of the decade
around 1704 when Dunkeld received its status as royal burgh
they were modern, commodious and of the degree of pretension suited to the dignity of the merchants trading between
Lowland ports and Highland markets whom the burgh charter
was intended to encourage. They steal a trick by their quiet,
well-mannered uniformity, which is varied only by the rhythm
established by the open pends; but this uniformity results not

*Dunkeld: Cathedral
Street*

from an overall sophisticated plan but from innate obedience to the dictates of economy and a recognized convention based on practical needs.

The Trust's effort on the north side of Cathedral Street has been matched by a parallel improvement programme carried out by the former Perth County Council on the south side. If a niche is sought into which to fit this entire restoration in terms of the history of town building in Scotland, it could not better be regarded than as a half-way post between the vernacular of Culross and the polished elegance of Charlotte Square in Edinburgh.

Dysart, Fife

2 miles north of Kirkcaldy on A955

Sam Bough, a devil-may-care Cumbrian whom the Royal Scottish Academy elected to full membership but never converted to circumspect habits, painted Dysart harbour in 1854. In an animated seascape, craft of all sizes are running under sail. Of the mechanical shipping which killed off the small ports there is not a trace; and there is not much by way of architectural record. Fortunately, the tangible evidence of Dysart's vigorous life in former times is substantial: up the hill, in a tolbooth of 1576 and in old houses on wandering street lines;

Dysart: Pan'Ha and Girnal Wynd

just above the shoreline, in the tall tower of St Serf's Church and in Pan Ha' and Girnal Wynd.

No. 11 Pan Ha' was the Shoremaster's House, No. 10 the Pilot's House, No. 9 the Tide-Waiter's House, No. 8 the Covenant House and No. 7 the Girnal. All were built in the seventeenth and eighteenth centuries. The Bay Horse Inn, farther south, is dated to 1583, and is listed Category A; on its seaward wall it has a vast lum, supported by corbelling, which is as prestigious as any Dutch gable. All six buildings were restored as dwelling-houses and five new houses were built to fill a gap site between the Girnal and the Bay Horse Inn, the Trust acting as agents for the Commissioners for Crown Estates in a co-ordinated scheme in which Kirkcaldy Town Council participated. Her Majesty Queen Elizabeth the Queen Mother, the Patron of the Trust, performed the opening ceremony in 1969. The group has a felicitous northern terminal in The Anchorage in Shore Road. This sixteenth- to seventeenth-century house of three storeys, listed Category A, was restored as two flats in 1966 and earned a Civic Trust commendation.

Dysart: the Anchorage and Saut Girnal Wynd

Further collaboration between Kirkcaldy Town Council and the Trust has given new purpose to an important building in Fitzroy Street, the birthplace of the great explorer of Australia, John McDouall Stuart (1815–66). Within its walls (eighteenth century with a lintel dated 1575) there are two flats and a museum, the latter financed and operated by the local authority.

11 miles north of Kirkcaldy, 11½ miles west of Cupar on A912, 3 miles off A91 at Auchtermuchty and 38 miles from Edinburgh via M9

Falkland, Fife

In Falkland the legacy from Stuart times is evident at once, thanks to the diligence of the Crichton Stuarts since 1887, the year in which the third Marquess of Bute became Hereditary Constable, Captain and Keeper of the palace. Moncrief House was built in 1610 (according to the marriage lintel) for Nicol Moncrief, a member of James VI's bodyguard who became an eminent court official. It stands opposite the palace, a superlative example of renewal, done at the instance of the present Keeper, Major Michael Crichton Stuart. Its thatched roof, topping two storeys of cut stone, is the last of the type in the royal burgh. That Key House (1713) immediately to the west of the palace was also thatched may be inferred from the height of the crow-steps on the gables. Formerly the Palace Inn, it has been happed in Angus slabs and makes a modest neighbour to

Falkland : Key House

St Andrew's House. Both are harled, both two storeys high, but the latter is a courtier's house of the mid-seventeenth century, standing tall under a soaring roof of red pantiles. These two were also restored by Major Crichton Stuart. He made a gift of St Andrew's House to the Trust in 1950 and later presented Brunton House, another courtier's house of cut stone.

Brunton House, listed Category A, is one of two three-deckers in Brunton Street. It was the home of the Simsons of Brunton, Hereditary Falconers (a carved stone which exhibits their arms under the crest of a flying falcon is dated 1712). The house was modernized in 1970.

The High Street contains two excellent examples of the restoration of eighteenth-century buildings by the Trust, Saddler's House and Fountain House. To the west of these the Reading Room was saved by a flash of imagination and concern by the South of Scotland Electricity Board (it accommodates a sub-station). In the West Port the first Little Houses Improvement project in Falkland (1961) made an agreeable single-storey house from two weavers' cottages. This has an intriguing counterpart in the East Port; the Trust visitor centre, similar in outline on the street front, is, at a lower level within the palace precinct, a stately garden pavilion. In addition to the restoration of buildings (many more than are enumerated here), the Trust has contributed in two noticeable ways to the integrity of palace and town. The renewal of cobbled street surfaces, where appropriate, is done with infinite care by a 'flying squad' with long experience of such work. The construction of a large car park on a convenient and inconspicuous location reduces the temptation to litter an historic street scene with vehicles.

In 1970 the former Fife County Council designated Falkland a Conservation Area, the first in Scotland, an even-handed declaration of the importance of the palace and the little houses in the streets and wynds.

Falkland: the Royal Precinct

27 miles west of Edinburgh on A9

Linlithgow, Lothian

Nos. 44–48 High Street are probably the oldest surviving buildings in the main street of Linlithgow. Their dating to the late sixteenth or very early seventeenth century rests purely on stylistic grounds and is supported by their narrow, gable-on frontages, each defining the lateral extent of one burghal lot, and the open staircase leading to the upper floors of one house. Also interesting in point of date are the openings high in each

*Linlithgow: Nos. 44
and 48 High Street*

gable, which were originally perhaps identical with the pigeon-loft accesses which can be noted in the seventeenth-century houses in West Bow, Edinburgh.

When these houses were built, possibly in replacement of earlier timber constructions, Linlithgow was at its prime as a mercantile centre. Enjoying the monopolistic privileges of a royal burgh and trading outwards through its thirled port of Blackness, it was also developing its own industries, particularly that of shoe-making. Most of the High Street properties therefore were at one time or another merchants' houses. But the name associated with 44–48 High Street is that of the important local family of Hamilton, the Hamiltons of Pardovan, a small estate three miles to the east of the town. At the opposite end of Linlithgow, Hamilton of West Port erected a notable house of similar date, and it was a Hamilton (of Bothwellhaugh) who murdered the Regent Moray in Linlithgow's High Street in 1570.

Nos. 44–48 were restored by the National Trust for Scotland in 1958 and leased to private occupiers as dwelling-houses. They are not open to the public.

Uptown in Pittenweem, the reinstatement of Kellie Lodging
has brought back to the High Street as fine an architectural
flourish as houses of slightly less antiquity give to the harbour
front. The Lodging is the burgh's link with the landward side.
A family named Oliphant built it about 1590, at the same time
as they built their castle three miles inland, and had to sell in
1613 to Thomas Erskine, first Earl of Kellie. (Kellie Castle has
been in the care of the Trust since 1970.) The square stair-
tower of the Lodging, which thrusts across the pavement, is of
coursed rubble, corbelled out to make room for a small
chamber at a level of two and a half storeys, which is the height
of the main house.

Kellie Lodging, restored as one house in 1972, is listed
Category A, in common with No. 18 East Shore, the Gyles and
Gyles House, which, however, grew out of profits from the
seaward trade. That trade was of sufficient importance by 1542
to gain for Pittenweem the status of a royal burgh. It continued
to flourish for more than two centuries thereafter. Sloops and
brigs, competing with fishing boats for quay space, carried

*Pittenweem: Gyles
House and The Gyles*

outward cargoes of salt, malt and fish and brought inward from
Continental ports large quantities of Memel pine and more
modest ladings of wine, silks and suchlike commodities.

Gyles House is a seventeenth-century sea captain's house.
The building, restored as a private residence, was acquired by
the Trust and used for a summer as a show house for the Little
Houses Improvement Scheme; it was then sold. The composition of two-storey house and a single-storey storehouse abutting
on the seaward gable is only a little less idiosyncratic than that
of the Gyles (three storeys with an attic room in a frontal gable)
across the way. The Gyles too may have begun life as a town
house, lacking nothing of the panache of Kellie Lodging but
because of its later date (seventeenth to eighteenth century)
somewhat different in style. The building was restored in 1965
to provide one house and three flats.

None of these puts No. 18 East Shore out of countenance.
Smaller than the Gyles, larger than Gyles House, it has a

many-windowed front and a gable suggesting Dutch influence, which have been comely features on the other side of the harbour since the latter part of the seventeenth century. In the same area Nos. 3, 4–5 and 13–14 East Shore carry the traditional pattern into the nineteenth century; and Nos. 4–8 High Street fulfil the same purpose in close proximity to Kellie Lodging. The diversity of buildings capable of adaptation can be seen in Nos. 8–9 Cove Wynd and in the Meeting House in Abbey Wall Road where an eighteenth-century Relief Church has been converted into an admirable house.

9 miles west of Edinburgh off A90

South Queensferry, Lothian

It is quite possible to overlook the historical importance and present interest of South Queensferry against the more obvious charms of the Fife village-ports across the Forth. But the royal burgh of Queensferry shares with Culross, Anstruther and Crail a sixteenth- and seventeenth-century history as an important harbour, trading to the Low Countries and the Baltic, and with a respectable merchant community. The contemporary merchants' houses of the High Street terraces are evidence of affluence, while two houses that share the same generation stand out as buildings of greater size and status: these are Black Castle, between the East and Mid Terraces, and Plewlands at the west end of the burgh.

Plewlands was formerly the mansion of a smallholding immediately outside the burgh bounds. The date, 1641, and the initials of the builder and his wife, Samuel Wilson and

South Queensferry: the High Street

Anne Paton, appear on the lintel of the door along with the motto 'Spes Mea Christus' and an anchor which may indicate a sea-trading interest. Architecturally, the building is curious in that, while it is ostensibly a copy-book L-plan with contained stair-tower, this stair is not placed neatly in the angle of the block but almost half-way along the side of the north wing. One could suspect that Plewlands is in fact of two dates – the south wing being tacked on as a later addition.

In the eighteenth century the property belonged to the Hopes of Hopetoun and in the nineteenth to the Hamilton-Dundas family of Duddingston House one mile south. Later, however, the house was subdivided, and in 1889 Mrs Tuck of 'Plewlands laundry' can be found respectfully soliciting 'public patronage of her home-business of washing shirts and smalls and ironing dickies and cuffs'. The Trust was given Plewlands in 1953 by Miss Irene Ferguson and has restored the interiors to provide private housing. The building is not open to visitors.

St Monans, Fife

On A917 between Pittenweem and Elie

In St Monans, a fishing port from the fourteenth century and a burgh of barony which remained outside the conventional system of local government until 1933, the ultimate rise, decline and fall of the main industry followed the same path as in harbours up the coast. A fleet consisting of a hundred sail-boats in 1900 was supplanted by steam drifters by 1914. Many of the latter had been sold for scrap before the outbreak of the Second World War in consequence of the loss of overseas

St Monans: West
Shore

St Monans: Nos.
4–5 West Shore

markets and failure of the herring fishery. Post-war recovery was slow, painful and by no means consistent. The town shows the scars, but the community has set out to conserve at least part of their patrimony in partnership with the National Trust for Scotland.

The Trust started on the rehabilitation of West Shore with the restoration and sale of No. 4, an eighteenth-century house, and the conversion of Nos. 5–7 into two flats and a shop. As agents for the town council, the Trust then produced two more flats and a shop from Nos. 8–10 and fashioned, from nineteenth-century buildings in Narrow Wynd, two houses for council tenants. By other applications of the Scheme No. 1 West Shore, Nos. 4–5 and No. 6 Mid Shore, No. 5 The Cribbs, Nos. 1–3 Forth Street and Nos. 28–30 Station Road have all been restored, as one house in each instance.

A 'restoring purchaser' resolved to mark the Trust's jubilee year by opening No. 15 East Shore temporarily to visitors.

IX GOOD INTENT, GOOD OFFICES

by Robin Prentice

Involvement in external affairs is of the natural order of things for the National Trust for Scotland. The purpose of *promoting* 'the permanent preservation for the benefit of the nation' of land, buildings, articles and objects of historic or national interest is accepted as the imperative in the constitution. This may entail arguing a case at a public hearing or sustaining a confidential, low-key dialogue in order to advance a policy or clear the way for effective action by other agencies. One Trust initiative led to the establishment of the Countryside Commission for Scotland. Another set the Burrell Collection on the road towards an acceptable site in the Pollok estate in Glasgow.

The Burrell Collection is the abundant embodiment of the taste and aspirations of a Glasgow man, Sir William Burrell (1861–1958), shipowner and connoisseur. At his birth, Glasgow, confident of perennial status as Second City of the Empire and ruled by men of substance, was beginning to push municipal enterprise towards a point at which the label of 'gas and water socialism', had anyone thought of it, would have been applicable but inadequate. (The consequences as they relate to art were permanent; in Edinburgh the great collections in corporate ownership are in national galleries and museums, those in Glasgow are Glasgow's property.) The Glasgow of the 1860s was also a city of innovation and opportunity. It was nurturing a brood of tycoons and painters who were to make a more than ordinary impact; and there arrived in the person of a new laird of Pollok, Sir William Stirling Maxwell, Bt. (1818–78), a connoisseur, collector and virtuoso of international repute. It was he, the founder of the Stirling Maxwell Collection in Pollok House, who brought to the notice of the rest of Europe the quality, character and history of Spanish art; his study of Velasquez, one of many scholarly publications, was translated almost immediately into German and French.

Le Meunier, son fils et l'âne *by Daumier* – *Burrell Collection*

The tycoons were consistent only in their pursuit of fortune. (Sir Thomas Lipton put much of the money which he made from groceries into yachts, including a succession of *Shamrocks* to contend for the America's Cup, and consorted with royalty. James Buchanan, Baron Woolavington, moved wealth earned from Scotch whisky into philanthropy and horse racing – he was a member of the Jockey Club, and the owner of two winners of the Derby and two of the St Leger.) William Burrell, twelve years younger than Buchanan, eleven

Coloured limestone Madonna and Child, French, fourteenth century – Burrell Collection

years younger than Lipton, entered his father's office at the age of fifteen. He throve in business, and made discreetly the first discriminating purchases on which he based his superlative collection. By the time he was thirty the 'Glasgow School' (more precisely, a loose federation of George Henry, Edward Hornel, Joseph Crawhall, James Guthrie, E. A. Walton and other adventurous, anti-establishment artists) was the talk of the town, and of other towns besides – London and Munich in particular. Burrell's welcome to the 'new men' was not, however, restricted to the Scots contingent. It stimulated a spasmodic local interest in Whistler. He himself bought 'The Fur Jacket' in 1898 (for £1,000). Of the pictures bought for the public good, the best went into the Hunterian Museum, but not 'La Princesse du Pays de la Porcelaine'. Burrell bought that too. He went on buying until Hutton Castle, his home in Berwickshire, could not contain his acquisitions, a vast accumulation in which paintings of widely varying dates and provenance were mingled with tapestries, carvings and a fabulous array of Chinese pottery and porcelain.

In 1944 Sir William presented his collection to Glasgow Corporation (omitting scarcely anything but a group of paintings which he gave later to the borough of Berwick-on-Tweed). He also made provision for a gallery to house it, but he made it a condition that the gallery be built on one of two sites which he nominated on the perimeter of the city (he had little faith in the mechanisms available during his lifetime for control of air pollution, humidity and temperature). It turned out that building was impracticable on either site. The problem of what to do stood unresolved at his death in 1958. In the face of incontrovertible physical facts and Sir William's plain statement of wish, his trustees and the corporation could not agree on an alternative course of action. It took nine years, intervention by the Trust and an act of unexampled generosity by the granddaughter of that other connoisseur and collector, Sir William Stirling Maxwell, to reconcile the differing points of view and make Pollok the place for Burrell.

Pollok has been in the possession of the Maxwell family for seven centuries. Sir William Stirling Maxwell, ninth baronet of Pollok, was succeeded by his elder son, John. Sir John Stirling Maxwell (1866–1956) inherited his father's public spirit and his flair and judgment in matters of art, became an authority on architecture and sylviculture and had a total regard for people and environment. Agreement to establish the National Trust for Scotland was reached at an informal meeting in Pollok House. Sir John was one of the first Vice-Presidents and subsequently became President (1943–56). In respect of Pollok estate he became in 1939 'the First Party' in the Trust's first Conservation Agreement ('protective coven-ant' in English terms, 'scenic easement' in the American), being 'desirous that the said lands should remain forever as open spaces or woodlands for the enhancement of the beauty of the neighbourhood and so far as possible for the benefit of the citizens of Glasgow'. (The 'said lands' extend to 1,118 acres; and from 1911 the citizens of Glasgow had had the freedom of 121 acres in the Pollok Grounds, an early and superb example of Sir John's accomplishment in landscape planting and design.) The Conservation Agreement was made with the sanction and approval of Glasgow Corporation; one of the provisions gave the city a right of pre-emption if it were ever intended to dispose of any part of the estate.

The Trust's line of communication with the city chambers sufficed in the end to resolve the difficulties of the corporation and the Burrell trustees. A proposition that Pollok should be accepted and endowed as a Trust property touched Glasgow's interest to an extent which allowed of practical and strictly unofficial discussion of contingent possibilities. This was the preliminary to one brief meeting in a Glasgow hotel. There the late Sir Peter Meldrum, Lord Provost of the city, proposed to the Earl of Wemyss that the Burrell Collection should be housed in the grounds of Pollok and that the Trust should use its good offices to achieve that object.

Mrs Anne Maxwell Macdonald, Sir John Stirling Maxwell's daughter and successor at Pollok, was in no doubt of what her father would have wished. In 1967 she and her family presen-ted to Glasgow Corporation 361 acres of land in the north-east quadrant of the estate together with Pollok House, the Stirling Maxwell Collection, the library, the gardens and subsidiary buildings. The presence together of the Burrell and Stirling Maxwell Collections in such a setting must give Glasgow a singular distinction among the art centres of the world. The latter is representative of European art from the Renaissance up to William Blake and has possibly the finest assemblage of Spanish paintings in Britain, including works by El Greco, Goya and Murillo.

The Trust provided one member of the panel which adjudi-cated on architectural design for the gallery; a major part of the Trust's obligation to ensure the integrity of the whole estate is discharged through a Pollok Advisory Committee on which the Maxwell Macdonald family, the Glasgow District Council and the Burrell trustees are represented.

Sir Frank Fraser Darling put into the Reith lectures of 1969 a passage which was as much a challenge as a vote of confidence: 'I would say that the Scottish Trust now leads the world in the wholeness of its approach to environmental management.' No one knew better than he what the making and monitoring of conservation policy demands. It is about questing, about journeying, not arriving; conclusions can seldom be final. The Trust's commitment relative to lands is to promote 'the preservation (so far as practicable) of their natural aspect and features and animal and plant life'. There is no standard procedure, no fail-safe formula by which that purpose can be fulfilled within the compass of Trust properties or on the national scene. Scotland is fortunate in that one Minister, the Secretary of State for Scotland, has overall responsibility for regulating conservation and provision for recreation. The official agency, the Countryside Commission for Scotland, from which he can ask advice also has power to offer advice on its own initiative. But pressure on hill land, farmland, river systems, lochs and coastline is caused only in part by need for more recreational space. The word 'oil' began to have an ominous connotation by the beginning of the 1970s, and proposals for 'provision for recreation' may mean a roadside picnic place or a holiday complex in the style of Aviemore, the ski resort in the Cairngorms. The philosophy of the Trust, underpinned by experience 'on the ground' and the results of diligent reconnaissance and observation, makes slow and steady growth.

Governmental apparatus intended to protect places of natural beauty differs from country to country. None has produced an equation which satisfies both conservation and commercial interests. America began in 1872 by designating the Yellowstone region in Wyoming, Idaho and Montana as a national park, the first in the world; today the area within national park boundaries (all government lands) is larger than Scotland's total land surface. The National Park Service was created within the Department of the Interior in 1916 to be the administrative agency. It developed a persona and evolved techniques and guidelines which had (and continue to have) a profound influence. In the circumstances of the 1930s a general application of the park principle had attractions for the Trust; the Glencoe and Dalness property was in all but name a national park. The need for earnest appraisal of the concept came early in the post-war years. A committee appointed by Government recommended that five areas out of a score which it had examined be designated as national parks and acquired by the state. Distrust of arbitrary classification of landscape hardened to a conviction that nothing would suffice for Scotland but a policy which sought to obtain scrupulous care for all parts of the countryside, acknowledged the existence of a complex mosaic of land-use and land-ownership, and was

backed by adequate funds and personnel. The Secretary of
State took the same view but only to the extent of deciding
that the provisions in the 1949 National Parks and Access to
the Countryside Act by which national parks were created in
England and Wales should not be applied in Scotland.

Using his powers under the Town and Country Planning
(Scotland) Act, 1947, the Minister declared the proposed
national park areas (Loch Lomond–Trossachs, Glen Affric–
Glen Cannich–Strathfarrar, Ben Nevis–Glencoe–Black Mount,
the Cairngorms, Loch Torridon–Loch Maree–Little Loch
Broom) to be Special Park Direction Areas and required local
planning authorities to refer to him all applications for planning
permission for development. A presumption that the nascent
planning authorities, of which there were approximately sixty,
could take a broad view on issues affecting conservation was
scarcely tenable in the absence of any statutory method of
consultation and co-ordination across their boundaries. As
chairman of the Trust's Council and Executive committee Lord
Wemyss represented to Ministers that only a specialist agency
comparable with the Historic Buildings Council for Scotland,
set up and financed by central government, could be an effective instrument in this situation or in the foreseeable future.
The proposition was not accepted. In 1960 the Trust found
itself on a collision course with one of the most vigorous and
reputable of government-financed development bodies, the
North of Scotland Hydro-Electric Board.

The board sought sanction for a hydro-electric scheme in

The Nevis gorge

Glen Nevis, Inverness-shire. This deep, diversified and magnificent trench which divides the Nevis and Mamore ranges is rich in natural wonders. The greatest of these is the Nevis gorge. In a rocky cleft, so irregular and boulder-strewn that the river Nevis is often lost to view, the water thunders and foams, descending 400 feet in the space of a mile. Time has brightened and ameliorated the precipitous banks by a splendid tangled growth of indigenous trees – rowan, birch, oak and old Scots pines. W. H. (Bill) Murray, mountaineer, explorer and the Trust's adviser on mountainous country properties, declared its distinctive character to be Himalayan, without a counterpart in this country. The board was diverted ultimately. In the interim the Trust commissioned Bill Murray to make his own assessment of the Highland mainland. His report (*Highland Landscape*, N. T. S., 1962) revealed the rate and scale of impairment. The fifty-two regions which he chose to investigate would, in his view, have been automatic choices in point of outstanding beauty ten to fifteen years previously. Out of that number sixteen had been disfigured in themselves or in their approaches and ten were under threat. In the twenty-one regions chosen finally as outstanding only six were totally unspoiled, of which five (Knoydart, Kintail, Applecross, Torridon, Ben Damph, and Coulin Forests) were in the West Highlands and one (Balmoral Forest) in Aberdeenshire.

Other bodies were moving simultaneously on the problem. The first circular which the newly formed Scottish Development Department issued to planning authorities (S.D.D.2/62) was in effect a directive to delineate in the statutory development plans for their territories areas of high landscape value and to proceed on the principle that no avoidable intrusion should be permitted on such land. In 1964, following the Duke

Balmoral Castle, Balmoral Forest and Lochnagar

of Edinburgh's first conference on the theme of 'The Country-side in 1970' (and formal and successful objection at a public local inquiry to a motel project on the eastern march of Glencoe), the Trust convened a countryside conference in Inverness.

This failed to produce a consensus what further action was required. A study group set up, under the chairman-ship of Professor Sir Robert Grieve, to report on countryside planning and development in Scotland in preparation for the Duke's second conference in 1965, had a straight answer. Government accepted the principal recommendation. The Countryside Commission for Scotland was constituted in 1968 to fulfil the purposes of the Countryside (Scotland) Act 1967.

The hills of Applecross beyond Loch Kishorn

It has the duty of ensuring 'the provision, development and improvement of facilities for the enjoyment of the Scottish countryside' and 'the conservation and enhancement of the natural beauty thereof'. The Commission classifies 98 per cent of Scotland as 'countryside'. In addition to the Scottish Development Department there are four cognate bodies with which it can and does consult and co-operate, formally or informally – the Forestry Commission, the Nature Conserv-ancy Council, the Scottish Tourist Board and the Trust. For all of these, constant 'intercom' is common practice. If on occasion agreement amounts to a friendly agreement to differ, that does not diminish the value of the dialogue.

The same spirit informs and animates the Trust's relation-ship with conservation agencies furth of Scotland, and furth of Great Britain and Europe. The circle is broadening in Canada in liaison with the Department of Northern Territories and Indian Affairs (the administrative arm for national parks and historic sites) and Heritage Canada. A more regular and systematic 'exchange' programme instituted in association with the Scottish Heritage (U.S.A.) Inc. provides for a two-way flow of personnel, information, experience and ideas between Scotland and the United States. The Heritage, a non-profit foundation approved by the U.S. Internal Revenue Service, was established in New York State in 1964. Its support enables the Trust to study in depth the mores and methods of the National Park Service in Washington, at its training centres and in the field, and the Service maintains constant communi-cation with Scotland. A reciprocal arrangement for study tours by members of staff of the Adirondack Park and of the Trust was tested initially in 1974 at the instance of the Heritage and with the approval of the New York State Department of Environmental Conservation and the Adirondack Park Agency. The task of the Agency and the park staff in an ex-panse of six million acres, replete with natural forest, mount-

Old Faithful geyser, Yellowstone National Park, U.S.A.

ains, lakes and rivers, has special relevance for Scotland. There are areas in which recreational use is as intensive in winter as in summer. Even more to the point, 62 per cent of its surface is private land, and the Agency operates on the premise that private and public holdings are indispensable to the viability and vitality of the park.

The power of the National Trust for Scotland to enter into agreements restricting the use of land was granted by Parliament in 1938 and first exercised at Pollok in the following year. Growth of statute law has not reduced its value as a safeguard in management of the environment. The principle is simple, the terms flexible. In brief, an owner does not divest himself of ownership but the effect of the agreement is that no change of use will be permitted by him, his heirs or successors without prior approval of the Trust. It is essential to every agreement that the Trust considers the area to be worthy of conservation in the national interest.

The second Conservation Agreement, which was contracted in 1943 on the invitation of a landowner in Kirkcudbrightshire, put under protection a great length of shoreline in Fleet Bay; since 1944 the third agreement has applied to the West Links of North Berwick on the Firth of Forth. These precedents have great significance. The Scottish coastline omitting the islands, of which there are 787, is longer than that of France and subject to the same pressures as the shores of England and Wales. Harsh economic reality forbids any attempt to emulate the National Trust by mounting an 'Enterprise Neptune' to acquire coastline 'for the benefit of the nation'. The logic in these circumstances is for the Scottish Trust to follow its established practice – that is, to move in concert with local planning authorities and such arms of central government as the Countryside Commission for Scotland and the Nature Conservancy Council, and to reinforce by Conservation Agreements the effort of individual councils. The latter had, prior to the reform of local government, a growing armoury of powers and access to finance; a substantial number embarked on sensible and imaginative programmes. The regional and district councils constituted in 1975 have the capability to oversee much larger areas and to co-ordinate action. The record from 1958, when an agreement in respect of another length of shore in Fleet Bay was made with another proprietor, accords with the Trust's resolve to make conservation of coastline a first priority.

In Ayrshire three agreements secure the five miles of seashore from the Heads of Ayr to the Croy burn, north of

Culzean Castle; a guarantee against, *inter alia*, any intrusion on *Ailsa Craig*
the expansive view from the coast road (A719) across the
Clyde estuary to Holy Island, Arran, Ailsa Craig and the long
arm of the Kintyre peninsula. Beyond the Clyde the pattern is
irregular but indicative of a disposition by landowners to put
preservation of the natural scene above the prospect of profit
from 'development' – one mile in a critical sector north of
Oban, half a mile on the east coast on Skye, two miles on Loch
Shieldaig to the south of Gairloch, thirty-four miles on the
shores of Loch Broom and Little Loch Broom. The first
agreements in Sutherland, relating to one estate, safeguard
five miles of spectacular cliff scenery, sandy beaches and an
adjacent island on the north coast at Durness; subsequent
agreements have added ten miles around Tongue and eight in
the vicinity of Bettyhill. On the east coast one of the last acts of
the town council of the royal burgh of Elie and Earlsferry was
to enter into an agreement in respect of Elie Ness and Chapelgreen; a similar agreement with the royal burgh of North
Berwick extends over the East Links, the harbour and Glen (a
total of two miles of coastline) in addition to North Berwick
Law.

The Law, a conical volcanic 'plug' 613 feet high, is by no
means the only hill in the register. A Conservation Agreement
over Caerketton and Allermuir, the most easterly summits of
the Pentland range, was obtained by purchase in 1961 in order
to keep inviolate the skyline on Edinburgh's southern boundary. Agreements over land on the perimeter of inalienable
properties (Craigievar, Grey Mare's Tail and Leith Hall) are an
insurance against unacceptable building or change of use.
Others assure the integrity of ground adjoining a celebrated
viewpoint on one of the approaches to Loch Lomond from the

North Berwick: the Law, the town and the coastal strip

south, the indispensable half acre behind the north block of Charlotte Square, Edinburgh, and the former Cloch lighthouse, the light-keepers' houses and their curtilage in the island of Little Cumbrae in the Clyde.

A poll of members on the value of extramural activities of the Trust would probably put cruises, expeditions and meets in top places – possibly rightly. These are ways of pursuing serious purposes without solemnity, cheerful exercises with the object of stretching minds as well as muscles; and cruising has been the means of forming a fraternity, international in scope, whose concern with conservation through the Trust is practical and constant.

It is not altogether irrelevant that the cruises afford one visual experience which coastwise shipping lines have ceased to supply, the ever-changing aspect of Great Britain from the sea. They were started for other reasons. The gift of Inverewe Gardens in 1952 put the Trust in possession of a property different in content and character from the five gardens which it held previously – Crathes, Culzean, Falkland Palace, Leith Hall and Pitmedden. Inverewe's affinities were with places at greater distances which also derived year-round from the influence of the Atlantic Drift the boon of moderate temperatures. An urge to explore in the Trust interest was sharpened by the wish of garden owners to see for themselves those other gardens in the favoured Atlantic bracket. The question of how to set about it presented no difficulty to Mr Michael Noble, then nine years away from his appointment as Secretary of State for Scotland and twenty-two from elevation to the peerage as Baron Glenkinglas of Cairndow. He had the thought that by chartering a ship it would be possible to take a reasonably large group on a round of six or seven, even eight or nine, gardens in the space of a week at less expense than by any other mode of travel. So the spring Gardens Cruise was born; the first put to sea in 1953.

One venture led naturally to another. What was needed for the Gardens Cruise was a ship of a size to get into small harbours, a mettlesome yet temperate master and boat work good enough to get passengers expeditiously on and off a beach where no pier or landing-stage existed. Adequate cruising speed was a 'must'. The first objective might be in Brittany or the Channel Islands and the last in the Hebrides, with diversions en route into Cornwall, Wales, Eire and Northern Ireland. A ship which met this specification would be capable of putting into St Kilda and Fair Isle. The Islands Cruise has also become an annual enterprise in May, preceding or following the Gardens Cruise; it made a cast invariably for St Kilda and at intervals for such dissimilar examples of the Atlantic rocks as the Monach Isles, the Aran Isles, Faroe and the outliers of Orkney, Shetland and Norway.

With the 1970s there came increasing difficulty in finding for charter a small ship of the right specification. Fortunately, the Trust's 'big ship' cruises bridge a gap which one hopes *A Trust cruise off* will be only temporary. These are primarily low-budget *Fair Isle*

exercises. They have the object of giving the largest feasible numbers a sight of faraway places and many aspects of Trust work. Enthusiasm has never flagged since the school ship *Dunera* first occupied the deep in 1961 with adults in dormitories – 500 in a passenger list of 700. (The fare for that 'Bargain Sail' was £12 10s., less than one old penny per mile.) 'Big ship' cruising treats every relevant theme with the *élan* and authority which the Gardens and Islands Cruises made traditional. The roster of voluntary lecturers, commentators and guides for shore excursions is distinguished and extensive. 'Know your country', the slogan coined by Bill Murray on the first voyage in *Dunera*, is given a broad interpretation – for larger numbers of passengers – in her successor, the *Uganda*. The Scots are not the only northern people to seek thrifty methods of conserving lands and buildings or to begin to look more closely at ancestral roots and relationships.

These are purposes which have been served to an extraordinary degree. It was on an early Gardens Cruise that the late Ward Melville, founder of Scottish Heritage (U.S.A.) Inc., became acquainted with the Trust and identified with it for life. Cruising sparked the thought, then demonstrated the practicability of 'twinning' two historic ports, Culross on the Forth and Veere in Zealand in the Netherlands. Veere was from 1541 the Scottish Staple or free trade area in Europe, with a conservator of Scottish privileges serving as consul or commercial agent under the superintendence of the Convention of Royal Burghs.

Cruises, in common with field work in St Kilda, Fair Isle or the mountainous country properties, afford spectacular backdrops for voluntary effort. ('Operation Clean-up' in Glencoe, initiated by the late Colonel Jimmy Stewart, has been an annual event for many years.) In more domestic environments supportive effort is a self-imposed, year-round task for individual members, for specialist groups (of which one has been attached to Georgian House in Edinburgh since the day it opened), and for task forces recruited within the Members' Centres. Among the centres Aberdeen and District and Edinburgh claim seniority by virtue of date of registration. Others, in alphabetical order and with acknowledgment of sterling work for conservation through the Trust, operate in Angus, Ayr, Banff and Moray, Borders, Dumfriesshire, Fife, Galloway, Highlands, Inverclyde, Kincardine and Deeside, London, North East Aberdeenshire, Stirling and Strathclyde.

And for them, as for the Trust itself, involvement in external affairs is of the natural order of things. The business of promoting the permanent preservation of the heritage has many facets.

Glossary

architrave: moulding round door or window; in classical architecture, part of entablature resting on column or pier

ashlar: stone walling, with evenly dressed surface

baluster: small pillar

barmkin: defensive enclosure, usually attached to tower

battlement: parapet with alternating indentations, or embrasures, and raised portions

bield: shelter, protection

bothy: permanent or temporary quarters for workmen

Broch: circular fortress tower, Iron Age. In Broch of Mousa, Shetland, double drystone walls are 20 ft thick and 43 ft high and contain internal stairways. Galleries on inner face overlook courtyard 22 ft in diameter

colonnade: row or range of columns

corbel: projecting stone block supporting beam or stonework

cornice: any projecting ornamental moulding on top of building or wall of room; also top, projecting, part of entablature in classical architecture

crow-steps: steps on coping of gable, common in the Netherlands, Flanders and Germany and 16th- and 17th-century Scotland, less so thereafter

cruck: in crude building, curved timber supporting roof

doocot: Scottish form of English 'dovecot'

dormer: window in roof of house

drip moulding: projecting mould on face of wall above doorway, arch or window to throw off rain; also called hoodmould or label

Dutch gable: gable with curvilinear outline

entasis: slight swelling of shaft of column

fenestration: arrangement of windows on building

finial: formal ornament on top of pinnacle, gable or spire

gable: triangular top part of wall supporting pitched roof

gablet: small gable

Gothic Revival: style based on growth of archaeological knowledge of medieval architecture, which followed 18th-century Gothick

Gothick: conscious choice of what was thought to be medieval Gothic style; developed and became fashionable after 1750 and continued into early 19th century

hap: to cover up, to shelter; also a cover, shelter or shield

harling: gravel and mortar mixture applied to outside walls against damp; in Scotland, used on uncoursed rubble walls

jamb: wing of building; also side of door or window

laigh biggins: service buildings (e.g. bake-house, stabling) in barmkin or walled courtyard of castle or laird's house; usually one storey, sometimes lean-to construction

lintel: upper part of door frame

lum: chimney, chimney-stack or smoke-vent

machicolation: gallery or parapet built on outside of castle towers or walls, with openings in floor to enable defenders to drop missiles on attackers

neo-classicism: post-1750 style based on study of Greek and Roman buildings as opposed to Palladianism (q.v.)

obelisk: quadrangular pyramid

ogee: moulding S-shaped in section; an S-shaped curve

ogival: formed in double curve, one concave, one convex

Palladianism: school of architectural design based on publications and buildings of 16th-century Italian architect Andrea Palladio; introduced in England by Inigo Jones early in 17th century, revived in early 18th century

pantile: curved, S-shaped roofing tile

pediment: in classical architecture, low-pitched gable above portico, formed by running top of entablature along sides of gable; also, similar feature above doors and windows. Usually triangular, it may be curved

pend: covered passage

pilaster: square column engaged in wall and projecting only a fourth or fifth part of its thickness

rone: gutter or pipe at eaves of roof to carry off rainwater

routh: abundance, plenty, profusion

rubble: walling of roughly dressed or unhewn stones; coursed rubble, roughly hewn stones in horizontal rows or courses; random rubble, walls of unhewn stones straight from quarry or land, not laid in regular courses

rusticated: masonry cut in large blocks on which face of stone is left rough, with smoothed margins at joints

screens: partition separating hall of medieval house from service space, pantry and kitchen

skew: coping of gable

skew-put: lowest stone of coping of gable

strapwork: decoration originating in Netherlands *c.* 1540, interlaced bands like fretwork or cut leather; usually in plaster or stone on ceilings, screens or parapets

string-course: continuous horizontal line of projecting mouldings on surface of wall

swey: horizontal iron bar on vertical pivot at fireside to hang chains, pot-hooks, and pots and swing over fire

National Trust for Scotland Properties not Described in the Text

Balmerino Abbey, Fife 5 miles west of Newport, off A914. Ruined remnant of Cistercian monastery founded in 1226, burned by English troops in 1547 and suppressed at the Reformation. Not open to visitors.

Blackhill, Stonebyres, Strathclyde 3 miles west of Lanark, off A72. Viewpoint overlooking a lush middle sector of the Clyde Valley.

Bruce's Stone, Dumfries and Galloway 6 miles west of New Galloway on A712. Granite boulder on Moss Raploch, scene of Robert the Bruce's victory over the English after his return to the Scottish mainland in 1307, the first of many in his seven-year advance to Bannockburn.

Caiy Stone, Edinburgh In Oxgangs Road. Monolith nine feet high; its history is not known.

Cammo, Cramond, Edinburgh Off Cammo Road. Estate of approximately 100 acres granted by feu charter to Edinburgh District Council for use as a 'wilderness park'.

Castle Campbell, Dollar, Central Off A91. The castle dates from the late fifteenth century; it is under the guardianship of the Scottish Development Department (Ancient Monuments). See also Dollar Glen.

Clava Stones, Culloden, Highland 6 miles east of Inverness, off B9006. Stone circles from 32 to 420 feet in circumference, dating from about 1,600 B.C. Under the guardianship of the Scottish Development Department (Ancient Monuments).

Crookston Castle, Glasgow Off Paisley Road West. A fourteenth-century fortalice with later additions. Mary Queen of Scots and Darnley spent some days here after their marriage in 1565. Under the guardianship of the Scottish Development Department (Ancient Monuments).

Cunninghame Graham Memorial, Central Originally at Castlehill, Dumbarton, moved (1981) to Gartmore, Stirlingshire, Central. Erected in 1937 in memory of R. B. Cunninghame Graham of Gartmore, 'Don Roberto', eminent author, traveller and (briefly) conspicuous Member of Parliament in company with Keir Hardie.

Dollar Glen, Central By Dollar on A91. Sixty acres of wooded glen with paths and bridges, adjoining Castle Campbell (see reference above).

Glebe, Glenluce Abbey, Dumfries and Galloway 11 miles east of Stranraer, off A75. Small section of grassland adjoining Cistercian abbey, which was founded in 1191. Under the guardianship of the Scottish Development Department (Ancient Monuments).

Greenbank, Clarkston, Glasgow In High Flender Road. Sturdy example of eighteenth-century architecture, deriving its character from elements of earlier styles. One-sixth of its fifteen acres consists of a series of small gardens displaying flowers, shrubs, vegetables and fruit, fully equipped and staffed as a garden advice centre. The house is not normally open to the public.

Parklea Farm, Strathclyde 1 mile east of Port Glasgow. Sixty-eight acres on a narrow strip of level land between the south bank of the Clyde and the raised beach. Purchased from a bequest by a citizen of Port Glasgow. Leased at nominal rent to local authority for playing-fields and recreation ground.

Priorwood Gardens, Melrose, Borders Beside Melrose Abbey on B6360. An early nineteenth-century house, now the Trust visitor centre and shop for the Border area. The eighteen-foot high garden wall is enriched by four wrought-iron panels designed by Sir Edwin Lutyens.

Provan Hall, Glasgow In Auchinlea Road, E.4. Fifteenth-century mansion house, probably the most perfect example in Scotland.

Suntrap Gardening Advice Centre, Gogarbank, Lothian 5 miles west of Edinburgh off A8. Demonstration areas, glasshouses and lecture hall for benefit of owners of small gardens. Site (two acres) and gardener's house presented in 1966 by the late Mr George Boyd Anderson, M.B.E., M.C.

Threave Castle, Dumfries and Galloway 1 mile west of Castle Douglas, off A75/A713. Fourteenth-century stronghold of the Douglases on Threave island in the river Dee. Under the guardianship of the Scottish Development Department (Ancient Monuments).

Acknowledgments

The National Trust for Scotland has through its properties a presence in every region from the English border to Shetland and from Grampian to St Kilda, the uttermost western limit of the Hebrides. The purpose for which the Trust was founded, to promote conservation of the whole environment in Scotland, is pursued in concert with governmental and independent agencies in the United Kingdom and overseas. This, therefore, is a Guide to an organization whose range of activities is remarkable, especially so in relation to its size. The task of the editor in preparing it would have been much more formidable but for the participation of very many people with a deeper understanding of the nature of the Trust and of the country and the nation within which the Trust operates. (In this context 'nation' comprehends, of course, large numbers of expatriate Scots.) He is indebted to every one of these for their testimony and guidance.

The editor is also grateful to Sally Jordan and George Naftel for painstaking research on extramural as well as domestic subjects, to Judy Aitken for similar support and impeccable secretarial assistance and to Philip Sked whose phlegm and technical expertise were indispensable elements at every stage of the project, from first to last.

For information and counsel which that circle could not supply thanks are due to Mr J. D. Boles, Director-General of the National Trust, and to Mr Gordon Abbott, Jr., Director of the Trustees of Reservations in Massachusetts.

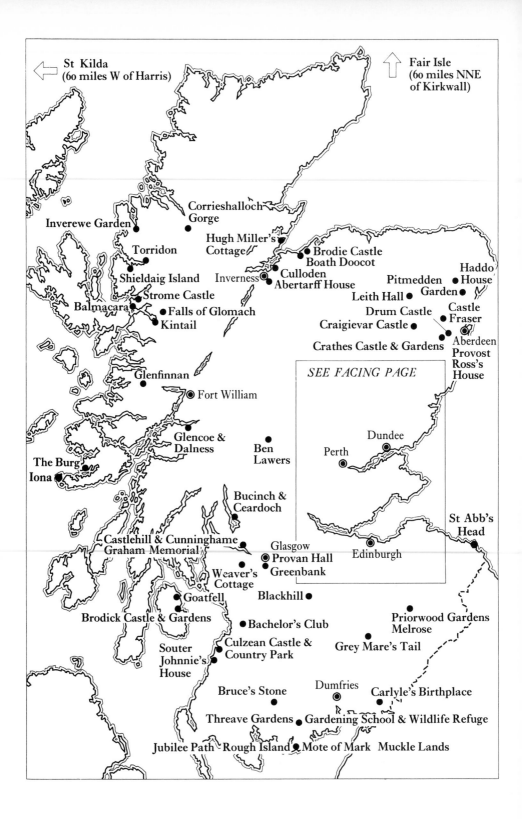

St Kilda
(60 miles W of Harris)

Fair Isle
(60 miles NNE
of Kirkwall)

Corrieshalloch
Gorge
Inverewe Garden
Hugh Miller's
Cottage
Torridon
Brodie Castle
Boath Doocot
Shieldaig Island
Inverness
Culloden
Abertarff House
Haddo
Pitmedden
House
Leith Hall
Garden
Strome Castle
Balmacara
Falls of Glomach
Drum Castle
Castle
Kintail
Craigievar Castle
Fraser
Crathes Castle & Gardens
Aberdeen
Provost
Ross's
House
Glenfinnan

SEE FACING PAGE

Fort William

Dundee
Glencoe &
Dalness
Ben
Lawers
Perth
The Burg
Iona
Bucinch &
Ceardoch
St Abb's
Head
Castlehill & Cunninghame
Graham Memorial
Glasgow
Provan Hall
Edinburgh
Weaver's
Greenbank
Cottage
Goatfell
Blackhill
Priorwood Gardens
Brodick Castle & Gardens
Bachelor's Club
Melrose
Souter
Johnnie's
House
Culzean Castle &
Country Park
Grey Mare's Tail
Bruce's Stone
Dumfries
Carlyle's Birthplace
Threave Gardens
Gardening School & Wildlife Refuge
Jubilee Path Rough Island Mote of Mark Muckle Lands

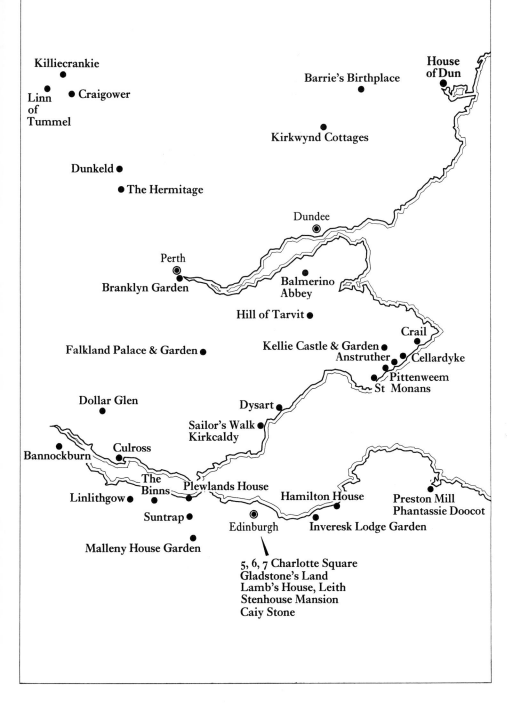

Killiecrankie

Linn
of
Tummel

Craigower

Barrie's Birthplace

House
of Dun

Kirkwynd Cottages

Dunkeld

The Hermitage

Dundee

Perth

Branklyn Garden

Balmerino
Abbey

Hill of Tarvit

Crail

Falkland Palace & Garden

Kellie Castle & Garden

Anstruther

Cellardyke

Pittenweem

St Monans

Dollar Glen

Dysart

Sailor's Walk
Kirkcaldy

Bannockburn

Culross

The
Binns

Plewlands House

Hamilton House

Preston Mill
Phantassie Doocot

Linlithgow

Suntrap

Edinburgh

Inveresk Lodge Garden

Malleny House Garden

5, 6, 7 Charlotte Square
Gladstone's Land
Lamb's House, Leith
Stenhouse Mansion
Caiy Stone

Picture Credits

The letters (a) and (b) after a page-number represent, respectively, illustrations at the top and bottom of a page.

The National Trust for Scotland and the publishers are grateful to those agencies, institutions and photographers holding copyright who gave permission to reproduce items in their collections – Aerofilms and Aero Pictorial Ltd: 260, 314; Aquila Photographics: 227; British Tourist Authority: 30; British Travel and Holidays Association: 261; British Travel Association: 57, 67, 152; *Country Life*: 36, 90 (b), 135, 138; Crown Copyright, reproduced by permission of the Department of the Environment: 86, 109, 110, 175; Glasgow Art Gallery and Museum: 305, 306; Highlands and Islands Development Board: 9, 311; Olive Kitson: 18, 208; C. K. Mylne: 11, 137, 206, 219, 248, 298 (a); Jim Nicholson: 187 (b), 195; Robert L. Nicholson: 246; *Scotsman*: 44, 207; W. S. Scott: 257 (b); Scottish Tourist Board: 15, 222; John Topham Ltd: 228; Tom Weir: 309; Wheeler & Sproson: 120.

All other photographs are from the National Trust for Scotland Library. The photographers are – Robert M. Adam: 193; Geo. B. Alden: 277; Morris Allan: 21; Stewart Burness: 189, 209; J. Campbell Harper Ltd: 73; Alex C. Cooper: 255; Stewart Guthrie: 64, 65; P. K. McLaren: 257 (a); Doris Nicholson: 200; Robert L. Nicholson: 251, 254, 263, 268, 269; Photocraft: 264; Tom Scott: 26, 72, 89, 90 (a), 111, 146, 165, 166, 292; Scottish Studios and Engravers Ltd: 202; Henk Snoek: 196, 197; Studio Morgan: 119; W. J. Webster, Dingwall: 170, 185, 259.

Index